Praise for *Fly Safe*

"Cody has an uncanny way of giving us a vulnerable look behind the curtain of a commander in theater and the woman who loves him back on post. Her intimate details of 'deployed love' are honest and heartfelt . . . with a level of candor I've never before seen."

—**Heidi Collins**, former CNN news anchor
and proud wife of USAF fighter/attack pilot
Capt. Matt Collins

"With unparalleled grace and humility, Vicki Cody pours her soul out on the page for all to experience. In bearing her soul, she captures our hearts. *Fly Safe* is a must read for all Americans."

—**Jimmy Blackmon**, author of
Pale Horse and *Cowboys Over Iraq*

Fly Safe

Fly Safe

*Letters from the Gulf War
and Reflections from Back Home*

Best wishes!

Vicki Cody

Vicki Cody

SHE WRITES PRESS

Published 2021
Printed in the United States of America
Print ISBN: 978-1-64742-144-1
E-ISBN: 978-1-64742-145-8
Library of Congress Control Number: 2021906587

For information, address:
She Writes Press
1569 Solano Ave #546
Berkeley, CA 94707

She Writes Press is a division of SparkPoint Studio, LLC.

To Dick, Clint, and Tyler—my inspiration.

To the members of 1-101st Aviation Regiment, Expect No Mercy, during Desert Storm—heroes, each and every one of you.

To the Army spouses and kids who wait for letters and phone calls and live with the stress and the worry—you are every bit as courageous as those in uniform.

Preface

For years, the decorative hatbox sat in a closet or under the bed, at times all but forgotten. It is overflowing with memorabilia from a very significant time in my life. There are the journals I kept, the yellow ribbons that we tied around a tree in the front yard to signify that someone in our family was deployed, and the engraved metal wristbands that my sons and I wore in honor of their father, my husband, bearing the inscription "LTC Dick Cody—Apache Pilot—Operation Desert Storm."

Also in the box, and most important, are the letters my husband wrote to me while he was deployed. Tied in bundles with red, white, and blue ribbon, they survived the next thirty years and another nine moves. When Dick retired from the Army and we settled into our forever home, I found the perfect place for my hatbox, in the sitting room off our bedroom. Every time I clean, I have to vacuum around it, so it's not as if I don't know of its existence, but I rarely take the time to look at the contents.

In 2016, while writing my first memoir, *Army Wife*, I sorted through some of the letters for reference and dates but didn't have the time then to really look at everything. I mentioned the letters in my memoir, but because that story encompassed more than thirty years of Army life and covered so much material, I couldn't spend as much time on that era as I wanted to. I always felt there was more to say about that particular year, 1990–'91—such an important time in our lives.

Now that my memoir is published and out in the world, I have more time on my hands. I recently stumbled upon the box while vacuuming, and something made me stop what I was doing and go through its contents. Hours passed while I read letters. Like a good song that transports you to another place and time, so too did the letters from my husband. Even after forty-five years of marriage, looking at his handwriting, rubbing and sniffing the paper, and reading his expressions of love and pride for me made my heart beat just a little faster, and I couldn't help but smile.

But it is not just his love that I feel from the letters; they also fill in a nine-month gap in our marriage and serve as a window into his life then, as well as into world events as they were unfolding: the stifling summer heat in the desert of Saudi Arabia, the soldiers' abysmal living conditions, the stress and responsibility of command, and eventually the moral dilemma of picking the flight crews that would go into battle alongside him. All of that was set against a backdrop of impending war.

The year 1990 would prove to be monumental for me in terms of growth and self-discovery as a wife and as a mother. My husband would make military history that would chart the course of the rest of his Army career. At the same time, it was a coming of age for our two young sons, putting dreams in their heads of one day following in their dad's footsteps.

Dick and I were fifteen years into our marriage at that point, and he was about halfway through what would turn out to be a thirty-six-year Army career. As a career officer and helicopter pilot, Dick lived on an exciting edge, doing exactly what he had dreamed of doing since he was a young boy. He had been part of deployments, missions, training exercises, and operations that had taken him all over the world, for varying lengths of time. We had even postponed our wedding because of a deployment, so I was no stranger to the realities and challenges of Army life. But when he left, quite unexpectedly, in August 1990 for Saudi Arabia, I could feel in my gut that that deployment was different. Dick was a lieutenant colonel (LTC) and the commander of an elite attack helicopter battalion in the storied 101st Airborne Division, and the events leading up to his departure made me pretty sure that he was heading into combat. While he was living *his* dream, I prepared myself for what I could only guess would be a very challenging and stressful time. Before he left, I began writing in a journal, and when his letters finally began to arrive, I kept every single one—all ninety-four of them.

It was a historic time for the United States and certainly for our military. It was the first time the Army deployed its all-volunteer force to fight what would later become that generation's protracted war on terrorism. It was the first time I had heard of a dictator named Saddam Hussein. It was also a time of patriotism in our country.

With all that serving as the backdrop, let me take you back to a time when we still corresponded by mail, few of us had personal computers, and there was no internet, no email, no iPhone, no texting, no tweeting, and no Facebook. I didn't even have an answering machine yet! When my husband deployed, it was weeks before they even had phone service. When they did get phones, he and his soldiers waited in long lines at phone banks to call home. Phone calls were expensive and few and far between.

It was a time when our written letters to each other were our only communication, our only connection. Knowing the risks and dangers in what he was doing, and unable to tell him in person, I ended every letter with the words I had been saying to him since his very first flight: "Fly safe."

1

April 1990

The call came when I least expected it. I had just walked in the door of our quarters at Fort Campbell, Kentucky. My mom was with me, visiting for a week while my husband was on a four-month training exercise at Fort Hunter Liggett, in the California desert. We were busy unloading packages and talking excitedly about the yarn we had found for our knitting projects, when my neighbor suddenly appeared at the open front door. She had a frantic look in her eyes and her voice shook as she told me that Colonel (COL) Loftin, Dick's brigade commander, had been trying to get in touch with me.

My radar was up immediately, and, as I started to ask her what had happened, my phone rang. I ran back into the kitchen and picked up the wall phone, sensing that it was not good news. The old, familiar feeling came rushing back—that sick sense of dread that made me want to run the other way—but at the same time, I had to know. Dick and I had experienced more than our share of tragedies and accidents, many of them right there at Fort Campbell. You would think I would be used to that feeling, but I wasn't.

"Vicki, it's Dave Loftin. There's been an accident. I need you to come out to my office at the airfield."

Dick had worked for Dave Loftin twice, and we were very close. I was on a first-name basis with him. "Dave, what happened?"

"I'll tell you when you get here."

"My mom is coming with me. We'll leave right now."

I thought I was okay, but my mouth was so dry, I could barely swallow, and my hands were on the steering wheel in a death grip. Sensing that I was struggling, my mother said, "Vicki, why don't you pull over? Do you want me to drive?"

I pulled off onto the shoulder, put the car in park, and turned to her. "I'm okay, Mom. I just need a minute. I can do this." I was fighting back tears but didn't want to get hysterical just yet. I needed to get myself under control because the sooner I could get us to the airfield, the sooner I would know what had happened. I just kept telling myself, *It's going to be okay. Maybe it was just a minor accident, maybe a hard landing.* The rational part of my brain knew that if it was Dick who was injured, someone would have come to my house to tell me. But the irrational part of me was thinking, *This is it, Vicki. This time, it's your husband.*

Why did I think it was Dick? I suppose that, after years of going to memorial services, burying close friends, sitting with grieving young widows, and living with a husband who defied the odds every time he took off in his helicopter, in a moment of weakness I thought maybe our luck had run out.

"Mom, I should've asked Dave if it was Dick. Why didn't I just ask those words? He was so official and didn't seem to want to say anything, and I just wanted to get off the phone."

"I can't imagine he would make you drive out to the headquarters to hear news about your husband."

"You're right. It's just that I've never been this scared."

We continued on our way, and I pulled into the parking lot of the aviation brigade headquarters. As I was getting out of the car, I saw Father DeGregario, our battalion chaplain, coming toward me. I thought I was going to be sick. I ran to Father D., and as we hugged, I asked, "Is it Dick?"

"No, Vicki, it's not Dick. But there's been an accident. COL Loftin is waiting for you."

For a brief moment, I felt tremendous relief, but then guilt. I knew something had happened to someone else's loved one.

Dave was on the phone when we entered his office. Mom sat down as he motioned me over to his desk. With his hand over the receiver, he mouthed that he was on the phone with Dick. He then pointed to a pad of paper with four names on it. Another moment of relief as I saw the word "injured," not "deceased," by the names. But I knew all of them, and two of the four were married. I looked at my mom. She looked lost, and I felt terrible for putting her through this. Throughout the years, I had called my parents and Dick's every time there was a mishap, an accident, or even a close call. I always started those calls with, "Dick is okay, but there's been an accident." On some level, they felt our pain and were always sympathetic, but there was no way they could understand the harsh realities of Army life; no one can, unless they're in the moment, watching events unfold. My mom was getting a full dose of reality now. That day in Colonel Loftin's office was the real deal.

When Dave got off the phone, he explained that two of Dick's Apache helicopters had collided in midair. I knew what that meant, as very few pilots survive a midair collision, but miraculously, that time, three of the four pilots had walked away with non-life-threatening injuries. One pilot was critically injured and had been airlifted to the nearest trauma center, in San Luis Obispo.

"Vicki, CW2 [Chief Warrant Officer 2] Chuck Noble is in really bad shape—head trauma and burns. Dick is with him and will give us updates as soon as he can. I need to stay here and make arrangements. Dick and I would like you to go with the chaplain and the XO [executive officer] to notify Chuck's wife. Do you think you can do that?"

"Absolutely."

"Here's the thing, Vicki: The initial notification will be about the accident and Chuck's serious injuries." He hesitated for a second and then continued, "But if things change, it might be a death notification."

I felt the muscles in my stomach tighten at the implication and replied, "Okay, I can do this. I know Kelli pretty well, and they have twin boys who are about eight months old, so I need to be there for her. I want to help any way I can."

My mother and I were silent in the car as I drove us back home, each of us trying to grasp what had just happened, while I focused on what I needed to do before heading back out. My sons would be home from school, and they had soccer games, and I was thinking about the roast beef that I needed to get in the oven for dinner and a million other things that no longer mattered but served as a distraction from what I was facing: watching a wife receive terrible news that would most likely change her life.

We pulled into my driveway, and my mom looked at me and said, "Vicki, I don't know how you live like this."

"Sometimes I wonder that myself."

I called my best friend, Gail, and asked her to pick up my mom and the boys and take them to soccer, and then I put the roast in the oven. I couldn't call any of the other wives yet, since the notification had not been made. But I was terrified that someone would hear something and call me before I left.

On the way to Kelli's house, the XO briefed me on the procedure while the chaplain and I listened in silence. I felt like my heart was beating out of my chest. I had been through this before, but each time was unique, and I just never knew what to expect.

When we pulled up, I saw Kelli in the driveway, putting the trash out. She looked at us, and as soon as we got out of the car, I saw the fear register on her face and in her eyes. I didn't want to wait for the official statement because by then she would fear the worst, so I immediately went up to her, hugged her, and said, "Chuck is alive, but he's been in an accident." She deserved to know that he was alive; everything else could be sorted out when we got inside.

Luckily, her babies were napping, so the XO was able to read his statement and give her as much information as he had. Dick called and talked to Kelli, and as I watched her on the phone, I could see the veins in her neck pulsating. I felt like I was having an out-of-body experience. If I was feeling that way, I could only imagine what was going through her mind. She was so quiet, hardly acknowledging what Dick was telling her, and I realized that she was probably in shock. I knew that Dick was telling her that her husband was in critical condition and that she needed to come to California as soon as possible. The XO had already explained to me that the Army would pay to fly her, her babies, and her mom. Kelli then handed me the phone.

"Vicki, try not to react. I'll spare you all the details for now, but Chuck is in bad shape. Time is of the essence. We need to get her out here as soon as possible."

"Okay, I understand." I walked into the other room. "I think she's in shock, Dick. She's just sitting there, not moving."

I hung up the phone and went into planning mode. For a trip of that magnitude, which would last indefinitely, we had much to consider and prepare for.

When the last of the arrangements and phone calls were made, and Kelli's close friend had arrived and her mom was on her way, the chaplain and I left. Part of me didn't want to go, but another part of me felt like it was time to. I didn't want to be in the way, and there was only so much I could do.

When I got home, it was dark and my mom and the boys were just finishing dinner. I was exhausted but so glad to have Clint, Tyler, and my mother waiting for me, and so glad I didn't have to be alone. The emotional day I'd had reminded me yet again just how different my life was from that of my husband's and my siblings and our civilian friends.

I talked to the boys about the accident. They had been through this before, and at their ages—Clint had just turned thirteen, and Tyler was almost eleven—it was somewhat easier, as they were old enough to comprehend and process what I told them. When they were younger, I would try to explain an accident or why someone they knew had lost their dad in a crash, always walking that fine line between just how much to share and how much they could understand. So it was somewhat of a relief to be able to talk to them in a more mature way, although I was still careful with them. I knew what they were thinking: *It could have been our dad.* They had learned a lot already in their short young lives and had adapted gradually, but many times I worried that the realities of Army life were just too much for them. I worked hard to ensure that they could enjoy their childhood and not grow up too fast.

I went to bed that night praying for Chuck and Kelli and their babies. As in previous times, I questioned the life that Dick and I had chosen, wondering if we would all be okay. I always felt like we were the luckiest couple in the world, with two wonderful sons and supportive and loving parents, siblings, and extended family. We were healthy, and, while not rich, we didn't want for much. We lived a very decent Army life, making wonderful friends and memories each place we lived. And yet on that particular night when I went to bed and thanked God for my blessings, the weight of so many tragedies and the stress of my husband's career were piling up on me. The burden felt heavier than the blessings. Each incident, crash, or mishap chipped away at my normally upbeat and positive attitude. The cumulative effect was wearing away my resolve.

As I finally fell asleep, I thought, *I know that nothing in life is guaranteed to any of us. I know that life can be taken from us or change in an instant. At any given moment, we are each just a heartbeat away from death.*

2

Two months later, the boys and I stood in one of the cavernous hangars at Campbell Army Airfield, waiting for the sound of helicopters. Dick was in the last flight of Apaches returning from California. The long cross-country flight to Kentucky, along with the usual maintenance issues and weather, made it difficult to synchronize all twenty-four Apaches' arrival. Two flights of eight had landed the day before. Wives were chatting and kids running around; the excitement in the air was palpable. Four months may not seem like a long time, but so much had happened. All we could think about was seeing those helicopters land. We just wanted our soldiers home safe.

As an Army wife, I had witnessed more than my share of the impact of helicopter crashes, training accidents, mishaps, and the day-to-day stress of what my husband did for a living. When something happened while the unit was far away, it was even harder on the families back home; we had to cope and deal with it on our own. I worried about the wives who were new to the game and hadn't yet experienced the downside of Army life.

Finally, the helicopters were approaching. We could hear them before we could see them. Soon all would be right again. The fear and stress would recede into the recesses of my mind, and it would be as if my husband had never been gone.

Dick was the commanding officer of the 1-101st Aviation Regiment, nicknamed Expect No Mercy, in the 101st Aviation Brigade, in the great 101st Airborne Division, at Fort Campbell, Kentucky. He had taken command of the unit the year before, in the summer of 1989. He was living his dream of commanding an attack helicopter battalion, also called a regiment, and the fact that it was an Apache unit was just the icing on the cake. The Apache helicopter, which had replaced the Vietnam-era Cobra gunship, had come out of production in the mid-1980s and was still in the process of being fielded into all the aviation brigades, Army-wide. Dick's was the first and only Apache unit in the 101st Airborne Division at that time. That created a certain amount of pressure, above and beyond the typical responsibilities of commanding a unit, since the Apache was new and as yet untested in combat. The aircraft was hugely expensive, featuring state-of-the-art technology, avionics, sight systems, and, of course, firepower. As with any new military aircraft, there was the usual speculation and scrutiny about how well it would perform and if it was worth the cost. But Dick was "Commander Cody," test pilot extraordinaire of multiple aircraft, with a great reputation and respected throughout the Army, so if anyone could handle the pressure and spotlight, it was he.

The 1-101st was a typical attack helicopter battalion, and while it consisted of twenty-four Apaches, it also had two other types of aircraft, each with a different mission or purpose: thirteen OH-58 Scout helicopters for observation, and three Blackhawks for command/control and troop carrying.

Dick's right hand, or right arm, as they called it in the Army, was Command Sergeant Major (CSM) Roger Ehrke, the top noncommissioned officer (NCO) in the battalion and the leader of the enlisted soldiers and NCOs. The battalion had five companies: headquarters and service company (HSC), and A, B, C, and D companies, each commanded by a captain (CPT), with a first sergeant (1SG) as the captain's right arm. Lieutenants (LT's)led two platoons in each company, and the battalion consisted of approximately 350 personnel: soldiers, NCOs, warrant officers, and commissioned officers. Besides the pilots, there were crew chiefs, officers, and soldiers performing myriad duties in every aspect of aviation: communications, avionics, armament, and aircraft maintenance. Truck drivers, mechanics, medics, and food-service personnel rounded out the mix.

The pilots' experience levels ran the gamut from Vietnam veteran Chief Warrant Officer 4 (CW4) Lou "Chip" Hall and my husband, who had each logged more than four thousand hours, to some brand-new lieutenants and warrant officers less than a year out of flight school and everything in between.

Battalion command is one of the greatest joys for an officer, something that my husband had dreamed of and strove for since he was commissioned at West Point in 1972. While it is a most coveted leadership position, it also comes with huge responsibilities, but, like Dick, I believed it was an honor and a privilege to have the opportunity to make an impact on soldiers and their families. Dick had two years to lead them, and with my help, he would coach, mentor, and care for them while preparing them for their journey in the Army, much as we would our own children. Dick had spent the previous year building a cohesive team by providing the best leadership he could. He spent most of his time in the hangar, rather than in his office, and he worked right alongside his men. Whether he was flying with every pilot, of which there were about eighty, turning wrenches in the hangar with his crew chiefs, or playing team sports with them, he was hands-on in every respect. Except for the accident at Fort Hunter Liggett, the unit had performed beautifully and shared a camaraderie that other units envied.

As the commander's wife, I had worked tirelessly to build a team of spouses and families who would support each other and could sustain the rigors of Army life and the inevitable separations. There were almost as many family members as soldiers in the unit—approximately three hundred. My goal was to keep the group connected and informed and create a family atmosphere. I did it because I believed that was what a commander's wife should do, I did it because I was as invested in Army life as Dick was, and, most of all, I did it because I wanted to be part of a very special and unique team. I liked being Dick's teammate and had never felt so much a part of his career as I did at that time.

A flurry of activity ensued as the helicopters taxied toward the hangar, blowing everything in their path and creating a deafening noise. And then the pilots emerged from their cockpits.

There he is! He's walking toward us right now. Clint and Tyler ran ahead, jumping up and down, thrilled to see their dad home safe and sound, and when I caught up, I threw my arms around my husband. In those first moments, we felt nothing but joy.

Each time I welcomed Dick home, I sensed that we were destined for this life, and as hard as it was sometimes, there was nowhere else I wanted to be than with Dick Cody. We had been soul mates from the very beginning of our relationship. We grew up in Vermont, but it was a chance meeting that brought us together in the summer of 1969, when I was just sixteen years old and Dick was a nineteen-year-old West Point cadet. After six years of dating, we married in 1975 and began our journey together as an Army couple. In fifteen years of marriage, we had experienced all of the typical joys, trials, and tribulations of life. But because of the Army, we had also endured separations, loss of friends, and stress. I felt like we had grown up fast and seen more of life than many couples our age. With that came a maturity on both of our parts, especially for me. I had learned to shoulder much of the responsibility of raising our two sons and maintaining our household by myself for weeks and months at a time. That made me feel capable and empowered each time Dick went away and I was on my own, but it came with a price.

I knew that in the coming weeks I could help Dick process and get through what had happened in California. But in that moment, the only thing that mattered was that my husband was home safe and we were a family again. All was well in the universe.

3

The unit had block leave for the rest of June, meaning everyone could take leave at the same time. We took the boys to Florida for ten days of togetherness: sun, surf, and no agenda—exactly what we all needed. Dick seemed to be transitioning back to family life, but his fellow pilot Chuck was never far from his thoughts. He talked to Chuck's wife daily, sometimes more than once. He got progress reports from the doctors and nurses from the ICU team, but I could sense that it was never enough. He wanted to physically be there when and if Chuck came out of his coma. I prompted the dialogue and asked questions coaxing him to open up and share his feelings. His reluctance to do so was foreign to me, as I had no trouble on that front; in fact, I was always looking to unload any baggage that was weighing me down.

It took those weeks in Florida for Dick to decompress and begin to express how he felt about Chuck's accident. As in previous times when we had been through similar events, I knew that once he could talk to me about it, we could sort it out together.

"Dick," I prompted, "I know your mind is still in California with Chuck. You're doing everything you can to support Kelli, but there's no way you can be there right now. She knows how much you care."

"But I feel like it's not enough," he said. "And it's hard to get the images out of my head. Chuck almost died, Vicki. On the medevac flight, he went into cardiac arrest, and I watched them bring him back. I thought we were going to lose him. Actually, when I got to the crash site, I was sure I had lost all four pilots. I was on my knees, staring at the smoke and twisted wreckage, when I heard voices calling out to me. Through the smoke, I saw three of my guys walking toward me. I couldn't believe my eyes. They motioned me over to where they had laid Chuck down after they got him out of the mangled cockpit. He was in bad shape. I didn't know how he could survive."

"I knew it was bad, Dick. I can't imagine seeing all that. But Chuck *is* alive, and maybe he'll be okay." I thought that because no one was killed, it would be easier to deal with, but in reality, a crash is a crash and the difference between life and death is just a split second.

"In those moments when I didn't think they had made it out," Dick said, "all I could think about was all the other crash sites I've been to, all the friends and fellow pilots I've lost, and all the wives I've had to face. I couldn't do that again." It was exactly what I had been thinking that day.

Gradually, Dick began to seem more like his usual, upbeat self. He played a lot of tennis with the boys, which was good for all of them. We had beautiful days on the beach. But mostly what brought us back together was just being able to relax for a short time, with nothing on the horizon. By the end of the vacation, I felt like Dick was doing well.

We returned to Fort Campbell rested and rejuvenated. The boys went off to 4-H overnight camp for a week with some of their buddies. It was a first for them, and the first time Dick and I had had the house all to ourselves. Dick had work to do after being gone for four months, but he had an easy schedule and we made the most of it.

Dick's battalion had quick reaction force (QRF) for the month of July, but that was nothing new. As part of the 18th Airborne Corps, a rapid deployment force, the 101st Airborne Division had to maintain a QRF, a brigade-size task force, consisting of infantry, artillery, aviation, and all the other supporting elements, that could be packed and loaded and ready to deploy within hours. QRF was part of our regular vocabulary at Fort Campbell. As the only Apache helicopter battalion, Dick's battalion spent a lot of time on QRF, but always for just thirty days at a time. QRF meant you could not go anywhere outside a thirty-mile radius from Fort Campbell, in case you got called up.

The boys returned from camp, and my sister, Chris, and her daughter, Ashley, came down for their annual summer visit. My sister and I had a close bond, even though our lives were very different. She had remained in our hometown of Burlington, Vermont, and had moved only once, from one house to another, just a few blocks away. I sometimes envied her predictable life; she was able to keep all the same friends and lived close to our brother and our parents. She, in turn, enjoyed visiting me at our various duty stations and getting to see other parts of the country. We counted on and looked forward to her summer visits.

So, with the distraction of houseguests and kids, I wasn't paying attention to anything on the news. My curiosity was piqued one evening when Dick casually said, "Hey, Vick, something interesting happened today. The division commander, General Peay, told me our battalion will remain on QRF indefinitely, past the usual thirty days."

"Hmm . . . I wonder why. You guys just got back from four months of training, we barely had ten days of leave, and you've been on QRF since we returned from Florida. It doesn't seem fair."

"Whoever said Army life was fair, Vick?"

QRF was a pain the neck, if you ask me. We spent our lives planning around training cycles, QRF, emergency deployment readiness exercises (EDREs), field exercises, etc. I felt like we were just getting back to normal, and then the Army was calling the shots again.

One hot summer day, we took Chris and the kids to a wave pool in Nashville. Along with our beach towels, cooler, and snacks, Dick carried the 1990s version of a mobile phone, which was literally the size of a brick. He called in to his headquarters periodically to make sure he had good communication (coms). He had a pouty and distracted look on his face the entire time we were there. I tried to ignore him so he wouldn't infringe on our fun.

It still caught me off guard a few days later, on August 2, when Dick got word that Iraq had invaded Kuwait and a dictator named Saddam Hussein had taken control of the oil fields. It was Dick's fortieth birthday, and I had a big surprise party planned, but all of that was secondary to what was going on in the world. The events of that day set a course for Dick and his unit that none of us saw coming. Well, my husband probably did, because he got up each day, put on his flight suit, and went to his headquarters or the hangar, thinking his unit might be called up. But that was just Dick Cody.

When Chris and Ashley left to go back to Vermont, I was alone with my thoughts and Dick's constant comings and goings to the emergency operations center (EOC). I had an overwhelming sense, almost a dread, that things were escalating and that Dick's unit would be deploying. Based on what he was telling me and the fact that he was still on QRF, I knew that if any part of the 101st Airborne Division deployed, Dick and his unit would go as well.

As Dick began his own preparations, the rest of the division was still awaiting the official alert notice. Because he was on QRF and the only Apache battalion, Dick was getting orders from higher up at 18th Airborne Corps, located at Fort Bragg, North Carolina.

"Vicki, I think some people here think I'm premature to be packing up, but I know what I'm hearing, and it's coming directly from 18th Airborne Corps. I don't want to get caught with my pants down when the alert order comes down for us to move out. We're barely recovered from the intense training and the long flight back from California. I have so much to do to prep my aircraft for an overseas flight."

"I hadn't stopped to think about all that. I guess with all of your aircraft, you have to do more than the typical unit to get ready. But do you honestly think you're going to deploy?"

"It's not if, but when."

And then on August 8, we heard on the news that an "elite" attack helicopter battalion from the 101st Airborne Division would deploy to Saudi Arabia. No more pretending, no more avoiding. I decided it was time to start a journal. If Dick was leaving, I was going to need someone to talk to—somewhere I could record my thoughts and emotions. That would be my outlet during the uncertain times ahead.

We quickly pulled together a family support group (FSG) meeting for the families in the unit. We met at the chapel, and more than two hundred people attended. Father D. spoke first, then I did, then Dick. It was eerily quiet; everyone's fear and apprehension were palpable. I had been so much a part of Dick's career, every step of the way, that I thought I had a handle on things, and it took a lot to rattle me. But that night, sitting up front with Dick and our chaplain, I was anything but confident. I was just a scared Army wife and the mother of two young sons, wondering how in the world I was going to handle what was ahead. But as I saw all those worried faces looking to Dick and to me for leadership, guidance, and support, I realized, *I'm in this as much as he is. I don't want Dick to shoulder the entire weight of this responsibility. I want to—I need to—do my part, because if not me, then who?*

Dick made a vow to everyone at that meeting. He told the crowd, "I promise I will bring everyone home safe." Even as I wondered, *How in the world will he do that?* I saw how the soldiers and families looked at him. I saw their worried looks begin to dissipate, and by the time Dick had finished speaking, the atmosphere in the chapel had changed. People were talking to each other and volunteering to help.

Afterward, Dick told me I said all the right things and told me how proud of me he was. He said I almost brought him to tears. I said the exact same thing to him. Dick had been in command for a year already, and, amid the recent training deployment to California, we had built a cohesive and close-knit team within the unit. We felt good about how many of the soldiers and family members we knew, I had great company commanders' wives and first sergeants' wives who took on their duties and responsibilities willingly. They were a huge help to me. There was always a turnover of personnel every summer, so it was important to have accountability from everyone, especially when the unit was deployed. Dick and I had learned those lessons early on. As we left the chapel that night, it was like we were all thinking, *We are a team, and we will get through this together!*

Another bright spot during that time was that Chuck's condition improved and he was brought out of his medically induced coma. Dick even got to talk to him a couple of times. It was perfect timing, as I couldn't imagine Dick and the unit deploying without knowing the fate of their fellow pilot.

4

Because I had known Dick since he was a cadet at West Point, I had complete faith and trust in his abilities. I had witnessed his gift of leadership and the confidence he instilled in everyone around him. He had a magical quality that inspired people and made them feel safe all at the same time. Over the years, his spirit had rubbed off on me and made me feel like I could accomplish anything.

Dick and I had never been closer, and now, with a possible deployment on the horizon, we banded together even more. We had always felt like it was us against the world. I guess Army life does that to you—it either makes you stronger as a couple or tears you apart. Living so far from family our entire marriage, we had always counted on each other. Our families back home were wonderful and loving supporters, but no one else truly understood the life we lived and the challenges we faced. All of that made Dick and me as close as a couple could be. We appreciated each other and our two sons and didn't take for granted our many blessings.

Besides Dick, I relied on my fellow Army wives for support and understanding. But my best and closest friend, Gail Greco, was still on vacation out West and wouldn't be back until right before school started. Dick and Gail's husband, Tom, had been West Point classmates and had known each other since they were eighteen years old. We had been stationed together three times, once at Fort Leavenworth and twice at Fort Campbell. Tom was commanding an infantry battalion, the 3-187th Rakkasans. Our kids were growing up together, and our relationship with the Grecos transcended friendship; we were family. The best part was that we were sharing the rigors, the stress, and the joys of command together.

With so much uncertainty about a possible deployment, I missed my friend more than ever. I was forced to process and try to make sense of things on my own. Dick was so busy, I hated to bother him with a battery of questions, so I tried to keep them to a minimum. When we watched the big TV announcement that the *entire* 101st Airborne Division was on alert, life at Fort Campbell got even more hectic. The TV vans and news crews converged on Fort Campbell en masse. Then the transport trucks and big rigs showed up, almost overnight. Hundreds of them came onto the post and parked in all the lots, waiting to get orders to help transport the division to the port of Jacksonville. I had never witnessed the movement of an entire division. It had not been done since the early days of the Vietnam War, so it was quite something to watch the process of moving approximately fifteen thousand soldiers and every bit of equipment needed to sustain a lengthy deployment. That was when I knew it was serious and that it wasn't just the QRF that was going somewhere. As Dick told me, "You don't move an entire city halfway around the world for the fun of it."

The post that had been our home off and on for so many years suddenly had a different feel to it. It was kind of eerie. Nothing seemed normal in those days after the alert announcement. I continued to make all the preparations for the start of our sons' school year. We all tried to act like nothing was out of the ordinary, but things were far from normal, and I know my children felt it, too. When Dick and

I talked to them in more detail about what was happening, Dick said we should prepare for a six-to-twelve-month deployment, which was a shock to the boys and me. Initially Clint and Tyler were upset and firing questions at Dick, and then we all calmed down and Dick and I mapped out the coming year. Everything would be the same, just without Dad. It was no different than other times he'd been deployed; it would just be for a little longer. Our boys were at good ages; they understood the significance of what their father was going to be doing. They had spent their young lives on Army posts, surrounded by Dick's soldiers. It was a way of life that they understood and respected. But it was still a scary time for all of us.

During that time, we experienced some lighthearted moments that offset the stress. One afternoon, I looked out our kitchen window to see Tom Greco and Dick in our front yard in their full mission oriented protective posture gear—clothing and masks used during chemical attacks. They looked like creatures from another planet.

"What are you guys doing?" I asked.

In muffled voices, they replied, "We're just trying out our chemical gear. It's so hot here, we wanted to get an idea what it will be like wearing this in the desert."

"You guys look so silly!" I said. And then we all just burst out laughing. Maybe because times had been so stressful, the sight of them wandering around in our yard made me feel like a valve had burst and released the tension. It felt so good to laugh.

One evening, our brigade chaplain, Sonny Moore, stopped by. Sonny was a Baptist preacher who had felt the "calling" and joined the Army late in life. He was older than my husband and a major in the chaplain corps. We were close friends with him, his wife, and their children. His son was Clint and Tyler's friend, and the older of his two daughters was engaged to one of Dick's pilots, Lieutenant (LT) Steve Mathias. We had all watched Steve and Pam's relationship blossom into engagement. They were to be married in two weeks, and

Sonny, of course, was performing the ceremony. But I could tell by the serious look on his face that something was up.

"Vicki, I need to see the boss."

I led Sonny into our kitchen, where Dick was just finishing his dinner. I pretended to be doing the dishes so I could eavesdrop— something I'm not proud of, but the situation called for it.

He and Dick sat at the kitchen table, and Dick asked, "What's on your mind, Sonny?"

"Sir, I need to ask you something, and I need you to be honest with me."

"You know I will, Sonny."

"You know we've got the wedding this month; I'm marrying Steve and Pam in two weeks. But I also know that you'll be on the first flight out of here. I want to go with you; I need to be with our soldiers. I already talked to Colonel Garrett, and he agreed."

"Okay, Sonny, that's great! I will need you when we land in Saudi Arabia."

"But, sir, what I need to know is, will Steve still be here in two weeks, and will I be here to marry them?"

Dick hesitated for a brief moment and then said, "Sonny, if I were you, I would marry them this weekend."

"Roger that, sir! That's all I wanted to know." And then he left.

I looked at Dick. I knew then that we were getting close to show time.

The following Saturday, we all gathered at the chapel and celebrated Steve and Pam's wedding. Most of the men in attendance were in their desert camouflage uniforms, and Dick couldn't stay for the reception because he was needed at the EOC, but it was a reason to celebrate, and for a brief couple of hours we all felt normal. Dick gave Steve a three-day pass for a honeymoon before he had to report back to the unit. As it turned out, the timing of their wedding could not have been better; Dick and the unit were gone by the following weekend.

Journal Entry

Watching Steve and Pam get married, I couldn't help thinking back to when Dick and I got married. Our wedding was postponed because of a deployment, so months later, when we finally got married, we were on cloud nine to have that behind us. We had nothing but new horizons ahead.

You never know when you begin your marriage how it will play out. You assume it will be long and full of love and that you and your spouse will grow old together. I'm trying hard to live in the moment, but I feel the clock ticking. I know that it's almost time for Dick to leave, and I understand that in order to move forward—in this case, get through the deployment—the sooner Dick goes and does his thing, the sooner he'll come back to me. It's pretty simple, when you think about it: You have to get over the hurdle—you have to meet the demon head-on, stare him in the eyes, see what he's got in store for you—before you can get to the other side. Fortunately, the fear of the unknown is often scarier than the actual event.

5

Time seemed to stand still for a while. We kept thinking Dick was leaving, but then another day would go by, another night, and it was so difficult to keep things normal. We did the best we could. Dick played tennis with the boys; we went to the movies; we went to Dairy Queen for ice cream—anything that we would normally do in the summer, anything to avoid the reality of the situation. It was a grueling waiting game that seemed to drag on for weeks, but it was really only a week.

By August 16, Dick and his unit were literally just waiting for the Air Force planes to pick them up. The Apaches and other aircraft had been taken apart for the flight; the Apaches had their blades folded and their horizontal stabilizers and wing stores (for weapons) removed—basically, anything that protruded. The other types of aircraft had similar modifications done, all to maximize the number of helicopters that could be loaded into the belly of the C-5 cargo planes. It would take approximately thirteen of those planes to transport Dick, his soldiers, the helicopters, some vehicles, and other essential equipment to Saudi Arabia.

After a couple of bad days during which I had a hard time

focusing on anything other than Dick's leaving, I finally felt calm and a strange sense of peace came over me. I noticed that the knot in my stomach was almost gone. My life was in order, I had the love and support of my family and Dick's family, and we had two good sons who seemed to have grown up overnight. Most important, I had the love and respect of an incredible man. Sure, I wanted to hang on to him forever, but that was out of my control. I was ready to get the show on the road.

By the time Dick got the call that the planes were en route to Campbell Army Airfield, with an actual estimated time of departure, I think we were all more than ready. Certainly, the boys and I did not want him to leave, but it reaches a point where you have such a constant fear of the unknown nagging at you that you just want it to be over with. Also, as much as I had been dreading the goodbye, I needed to bring some normalcy back to my sons and to my own life. It would be a new normal, but I was ready to create it for my family. Everything I had been through as an Army wife had led me to this point in time.

My pep talk to myself got me through the goodbye and into bed that night, so that somehow the boys and I slept well. But when the airfield commander called me early the next morning to tell me that Dick and his guys had departed during the night, I hung up the phone and the floodgates opened up. In those initial moments when I knew that he was gone—and not just somewhere in the United States where we could call each other, but on his way to Saudi Arabia and possibly combat—I was all the things I said I wouldn't be. I was scared and overwhelmed and wondered how in the world I was going to make it. I was a crying mess. I wanted one more kiss, one more hug, and began to regret that Dick's and my last "rendezvous with destiny" had been a few days prior. That morning after he left, I regretted everything. All I could think was that something might happen to him and that we might not have another chance for any of the "big stuff."

I put on my game face, something Dick had taught me, and after the boys and I ate breakfast and they were on their way to play tennis with their buddies, I went over to see our brigade commander's wife. Our brigade commander had changed out, and Colonel Tom Garrett had taken over for Colonel Dave Loftin just a few weeks earlier. We had known Tom and Betsy Garrett for years, so it was an easy transition for everyone. Betsy was a great listener, and her husband was on the flight with Dick, so I could pour my heart out to her. She got it. That was all I needed that first day, to know that I wasn't alone and that I had someone to talk to, someone who understood.

When I got home, I called our parents to let them know Dick had left. I purposely waited until after my crying jag. Over the years, I had learned to be careful about how much I shared with our parents and how my emotions affected them. It was harder on them if they had to worry about me. I wanted to set a positive tone because I knew that in the coming months, I would be *their* shoulder many times. Besides, it was Dick we needed to worry about, not each other. It didn't mean that there were no tears that day, but I really worked at sounding upbeat.

And then Gail called from Idaho. I was so relieved to hear her voice. "Vicki, did Dick leave yet? I've been so worried about all of this."

"He left a couple of days ago. Gail, I thought I was okay with it all, I thought I was ready to say goodbye, but I wasn't. This time is different."

"I feel so sheltered out here in Boise, I wasn't paying too much attention to the news, but then when I heard the 101st Airborne was deploying, it became so real. I keep asking Tom if I should come back early, and he's kind of downplaying it. What do you think, Vicki—is the whole division really going?"

"It's pretty surreal here. Its feels like a different post right now, with all the energy, the hustle and bustle, the traffic, the transport vehicles, and the news crews. Gail, I can't imagine all of this activity for nothing. I've never seen anything like this. It's not just a unit or two; it's definitely the entire division that's going. When are you coming back here?"

"Next week, right before school starts."

"Good, because I'm hanging on by a thread here! I need to get through this with you."

One of the hardest things about being a wife and/or mother is letting go of someone you love. I'm not talking about saying goodbye at the airport before a business trip or a training exercise or sending your kid off to college. I'm talking about watching your loved one leave you to go far away, when you have no way to reach them, no guarantee of their safety, and no clue when they might return. That August when Dick left, I was pretty sure he would be in a dangerous situation the minute he arrived at his destination. We were told he would be going to Saudi Arabia to set up operations for a possible conflict and to deter aggression. President Bush had made it clear that the United States was not going to allow Saddam Hussein to stay in Kuwait, so most of us on the post were pretty sure that something was going to happen in that region of the world. All of that added to my fears and concerns.

As the 1-101st was among the first to go in, Dick tried to prepare me for what to expect in the first weeks.

"Vicki, there will be no coms. I will somehow get word back to you and the families that we have arrived, but it will be difficult at first. I will write letters just as soon as I can. The rear detachment commander will put out the address for us once the APO [army post office] has been set up. I know it's not much, but it's out of my control. I have no idea what we're walking into over there."

"It will be like when we were dating and you were at West Point while I was still in school in Vermont," I said. "Your letters meant the world to me! And then that year you were stationed in Korea and we had to rely on letters again because long-distance calls were so expensive. I would send you pictures of baby Clint and write you long letters describing everything he was doing."

"Yeah, I remember. Somehow it worked; somehow we got through it."

In many ways, I knew what to do, what to expect. Dick and I had gotten to know each other through letters and had relied on them throughout our dating years and at different times in our marriage. But this was harder than I had thought it would be, so different from other times, when he at least could call soon after he arrived at his destination. I needed a letter; I needed to feel connected to him.

The boys started school, and the same day we had our first commanders' wives meeting of the season. Our monthly information exchange coincided with the school year; we took a break during the summer months, as many of us traveled and there was always a big turnover in the units. Gail and her kids had just returned from vacation the day before, but I hadn't seen her yet. I knew we would have to wait to talk because in a crowd of more than seventy women, we wouldn't have the chance. We agreed to meet at her house after the meeting.

Meetings were a way of life if you were a commander's wife or command sergeant major's wife. The monthly meeting was designed to inform, disseminate information, and keep us all up to date on everything having to do with the division, the tenant units, and Fort Campbell. In turn, each of us put out the information to the wives in our unit. If you could not attend or had chosen not to participate, then you delegated someone in your unit to attend on your behalf. It was old-school—it had been done that way for decades—and it worked, for the most part. The meetings also created camaraderie among the commanders' wives and kept us in touch with each other. During the summer months at Fort Campbell, there might be as many as twenty-five changes of command at the battalion and brigade level, so the September meeting was an opportunity to meet and welcome the newcomers.

But that particular day, as I listened to Major General (MG) Peay, the division commander, speak to our group, I had full clarity about my role not just as an Army wife but as a commander's wife. I looked around the room; I knew most of the women. Maybe because Dick was already gone and each of their husbands would be leaving in the coming weeks, my fellow Army wives felt like kindred spirits, and I was filled with a deep sense of purpose.

I was sure the others were having similar realizations. It was a sobering moment when we realized we were there not for social purposes but for the good of the soldiers and families in our husbands' units. It was no longer about potlucks and fundraisers or how we'd spent the summer and who had a new hairstyle; we were entering a whole other level of what it meant to be Army wives.

That meeting had to do with supporting the soldiers and their families, helping them get through a deployment, keeping them connected and informed, and, God forbid tragedy struck, being there to help the families deal with it. All the things I had learned up until that point would come into play, and in the coming weeks and months, I would learn much more about the Army—its supporting agencies, the compassion of our communities, and the kindness of human beings. The accidents and losses Dick and I had already been through over the years, coupled with Chuck's accident just months before, kept me focused on the important things so I could be prepared, just in case.

Journal Entry

August 30, 1990
Today is Dick's and my fifteenth wedding anniversary. I thought his absence today wouldn't bother me, but it does. I don't have anything

tangible to connect me to him—no flowers, no date night, no gift, no phone call, nothing. When your future is so full of uncertainty, you reflect on what was and you miss those special times that you take for granted so easily. You think about holidays and your loved one in a new light, realizing how fleeting it all is.

Why do we get so caught up in thinking love is something tangible, when in reality it's the most wonderful feeling in one's heart? I definitely feel Dick in my heart. So, if we can't be together on this particular day, big deal! Maybe it's time to put on my big-girl panties; if Dick can do what he has to do, then I can do what is asked of me. But I still think I'm entitled to feel a little sad today.

6

Before I got a letter from Dick, I saw him on CNN. I was at the battalion headquarters, working on my first newsletter to the wives, and we heard something about US Apache helicopters in Saudi Arabia. But that was all. When I got home that afternoon, the phone was ringing. It was my mom, out of breath, saying, "Dick is on CNN! Turn on your TV!"

That was before cordless phones, so I had to hang up in order to go into the den and watch the TV. Moments later, there was Dick Cody himself on the screen. I jumped up and down, laughing and crying at the same time. I couldn't get past how handsome he looked. And he looked so normal, like he was just out in the desert for a training exercise and then had decided to give a little interview on CNN—as if he did that every day.

I ran back to the kitchen to call his parents. They had seen him as well and said that the segment had been on *Headline News* a couple of times. I ran back to the den, found a VHS tape, put it in the machine, and sat there waiting, knowing that *HLN* repeated its top stories on the hour and half hour. Sure enough, there he was again! I was so excited on a number of levels. First of all, he was safe, at least for the moment. Second, he looked so cute in his desert camouflage uniform with the floppy hat (one that I had never seen). I was also pleased to see that he was clean shaven, which was a mystery to me, since he had no access to running water or showers. He was so well spoken, I was bursting with pride. I just kept asking myself, *Is this actually my husband?*

And so it was for the next hour. I ran back and forth between the phone in the kitchen and the VCR in the den. The boys came rushing in from school, all excited because some of the teachers had seen their dad on TV. We replayed the tape multiple times. The interview continued to run on multiple networks throughout that weekend, so we had plenty of opportunities to see Commander Cody. I finally calmed down and didn't squeal each time I heard Dick say his opening line, "We are here to deter aggression. And as attack pilots, that is what we will do." It was such a morale boost for my kids and me, for my family and Dick's. It was also great for the unit, because it meant they were all okay and the world knew about the elite Apache helicopter unit from the 101st Airborne Division. I rode that high for the next few days.

Clint and Tyler were attending the same school for the first time in a few years. I was so glad they were together at this particular time. Leaving his elementary school was a big change for Tyler, and now that their dad was gone, I noticed a new closeness between him and his brother. They seemed to be doing great, all things considered. I was lucky to be a stay-at-home mom; it was a time of transition, and the three of us counted on each other more than ever. As the rest of the division left and more and more of their friends' dads departed, the boys felt more comfortable. However, during the first two weeks of school and the early days of the deployment, Tyler especially had a more difficult time.

"Mom, when our teacher asked us whose dad is deployed, I was the only one to raise my hand. I felt so alone," he told me.

I tried to reassure him: "Everyone else is preparing to leave, too, and soon all you kids will be in the same situation. I know it's hard right now, but it will get easier."

"And what about soccer? I don't even have a coach yet, and we're supposed to start practicing next week."

"Let me see what I can do. I've got a lot of skills, Tyler, but I have no clue how to coach soccer!"

I talked with our rear detachment commander to see if Youth Services had contacted him about volunteers. Living on an Army post, our sons had grown up being coached by soldiers or their dad. Soldiers make great coaches, as they are often young and far from home and they miss their own siblings. Coaching gives them a chance to be with kids again. It's a win-win for everyone. Dick always had plenty of volunteers from his unit, but that fall we moms and kids felt the impact of having so many soldiers gone from Fort Campbell. We had lost an important part of our volunteer pool.

After making some calls, we eventually got enough coaches for the soccer season. Even with the entire division deployed, each unit had a couple of soldiers who stayed back to run the rear detachment, and the post itself had a number of soldiers serving in support units. When the rest of the division left, in mid to late September, things began to settle down for most of us, as we got accustomed to an Army post consisting mostly of moms and kids.

I was worn out and spending way too much time on the phone with other wives. Each night, right after I tucked in my sons, I fell into my own bed, but so many of those nights I ended up getting phone calls. I would be yawning while talking, just trying to get the person on the other end through some minor crisis. I felt pulled in a million directions. I really just wanted to talk to my family and Dick's, as I sensed they needed reassurance from me. My mom and dad and Dick's parents called me almost daily. Our siblings began checking in with me more regularly than usual, too. Every day, someone was calling me. Our family had always been close, but during that time, our bond grew even stronger. Hearing their voices, knowing they were there for Clint, Tyler, and me, brought me tremendous comfort. I don't know what I would have done without the love of our family.

Then the first letter came. I immediately noticed that my name and address were in Dick's handwriting but the return address was in someone else's writing, which read, "Not my return address. APO NY 09283." I tore it open, deciding I would figure out the strange return address after I read it.

I had never felt such relief. Even though I had seen him on TV and knew he was okay, getting that first letter was monumental in terms of morale for the boys and me. I knew then that we would start getting mail; I knew then that I could get through it. Just like that, we were off and running in our new normal.

August 19, 1990, 2400 hrs.

Vicki, Clint, and Tyler,
Hi from Torrejon, Spain! We arrived here after an eight-hour flight. Upon arrival here we were greeted by the base wives group and the Boy Scouts! They had set up a large concession for us, complete with toiletries, food and baked goods, and writing supplies. It was so heartwarming and meant so much to me and my soldiers. They offered to mail our letters home, which is why it is not my return address on the envelope. We will take off soon for the long flight to Dhahran, Saudi Arabia.

The troops are doing good, just very quiet and focused. Don't worry about me. I am fine. We are all fine.

You guys take care. Love you all very much! I will write when I hit the sand!
Dick/Dad

Journal Entry

We wives are going through what resemble stages of grief. First stage: Is this really happening? I don't want to do this. I can't do this. Next: the weepy, cry-over-anything, especially when someone is nice to you, stage. No one gets through this one without crying, and sometimes in public places. Finally, comes acceptance.

When I read Dick's letter today, happy tears and sad ones mixed together ran down my face. Sometimes the very thing we spend so much energy anticipating either falls short of what we expected or comes with a caveat. His letter gives me comfort that he is safe right now, but it also makes his absence real. His letter forces me into the acceptance stage of the grieving process.

7

I finally started getting "actual" letters from Dick the first week in September. I estimated, based on the date on which he wrote the first one and when I actually received it, that it took about ten days for it to get to me. Once I had that figured out, things were easier for me, because I knew what to expect. That first letter from Saudi Arabia was my lifesaver. I read it over and over again till the paper was worn out and I had it memorized, searching for any possible clues or secret information that might be between the lines. I carried it with me, in my purse, for the next few days. It made me feel close to him, like I had a piece of him.

The mail was sporadic, but at least it was getting through. Some days I would receive a couple of letters, and then I'd go days with nothing. It was a while before I knew whether he was getting my letters, and I worried about that. It was hard to write a letter and not know when or if it would make it to Dick. The boys and I just kept writing and sending, hoping they would eventually reach him. If Dick's letters meant so much to us, I could only imagine what ours meant to him. He was the one living in hell.

King Fahd International Airport

Dear Vicki, Clint, and Tyler,
We arrived in Dhahran, Saudi Arabia, on August 18 after a ten-hour flight. The flight was rough, as we were packed in like sardines with all of our combat gear. We spent the first two days getting the twelve Apaches unpacked and put back together. We were exhausted, and the heat was oppressive, but my guys did great preparing the aircraft for flight. It takes an hour or two to put the Apaches back together, and when the rest of the aircraft arrived, the process went faster; the OH-58s and Blackhawks are easier and were ready in minutes. I was so proud of my crew chiefs and mechanics for how fast they turned things around—no easy task in 130-degree heat!

We then flew the aircraft to King Fahd International Airport (KFIA), which is still under construction but will be our home for the time being. It has multiple long runways and taxiways, which are essential for all of the aircraft that will eventually be flying in and out of here. The Air Force showed up with every A-10 they own and of course took all the best ramp space!

We are living in the unfinished parking garage. There are workers of all nationalities working around us. Add to that all the military forces that are showing up, and this place is bustling, but it's about to get even busier in the coming weeks.

You can't imagine how miserable the heat is, and we have nowhere to go to get relief. My biggest challenge has been to keep water and shade available for my crews.

I flew north out of our base camp, through the desert. Nothing but a huge Death Valley. I've never seen anything so vast in my life. Occasionally you'll see a few camels but literally nothing else.

The world situation is getting worse from our immediate perspective, and I believe that war is imminent. We have really backed Hussein into a corner, one that he may not be able to get out of.

I hope you three are coping with my absence. I know that this is hard on you and the other wives and families. My hope is that you will help each other get through it—that is what we are doing here. I promise to write more later.

Got to get back to work. Do not worry about me, I always fly safe. I am taking care of myself and everyone in the task force.

I love you all very much,
Dick/Dad

By mid-September, Tom Greco and his infantry battalion were leaving, and many others were preparing to depart. I was already a month into Dick's absence, and saying goodbye to Tom, who was like a brother to me, dredged up the "letting go" angst all over again. It was another person to worry about. I was sad for Gail; I knew exactly how she would feel that night when she went to bed and how she would feel the next morning. The first few days were the hardest.

As the rest of the division left, Fort Campbell, Kentucky, gradually took on a different look and feel. First, commercial truck convoys left with equipment; then unit convoys drove their own equipment. Even the trains were loaded up. All of them were heading south to the port of Jacksonville, Florida. Throughout the day and into the night, I could hear huge military planes and chartered 747s landing and taking off from Campbell Army Airfield, carrying cargo and troops.

It had been so busy during those six weeks that it took to move the division that we had gotten used to the extra hustle and bustle. But by the end of September, it was suddenly very quiet on our post. There were no lines at the post exchange (PX), the barber shop, or the shopette, and the gas stations were nearly empty during the week. We didn't have to wait in line at the drive-through window at Kentucky Fried Chicken, Taco Bell, or Burger King. The businesses just outside the gates—pawn shops, military-clothing stores, tailors, check-cashing joints, tattoo parlors, bars, and liquor stores—suffered as well. They counted on the business of approximately eighteen thousand soldiers stationed at Fort Campbell.

There was no traffic going on or off post during rush hour. In fact, there was no rush hour. Our post, which had previously had a daytime population of about forty thousand, had dwindled to a few thousand. There was a skeleton staff at our hospital, since many of the Army doctors and nurses had deployed, and we still had civilian government employees and the maintenance crews needed to run an Army post, but in the evenings and on the weekends, it was just a few thousand moms and their kids. Most of us had never experienced anything like it.

There was a certain comfort in that environment, though, like we were all in it together. We all had the same fears and concerns, and we all just wanted to get through the days until our husbands came back home. We wanted safety in numbers. I'm sure Dick felt the same way once the rest of the division arrived in Saudi Arabia, knowing he had the mighty 101st Airborne to watch his back. For the past six weeks, my biggest fear had been that Saddam Hussein and his huge Republican Guard would plow right across the border that Dick and a few other units were protecting and destroy everything in their wake.

Journal Entry

When you take away all the technology and the instantaneous communications that we are accustomed to, it's amazing how much a letter can mean to you. I've always felt like Dick was more open with his feelings in his writing, and that his letters show a softer side of him.

You really can get a person's tone and tenor from a written letter. You can feel their love, their humor, their sadness, and any other emotion. And a letter is tangible. You can save it, you can read it over and over, you can touch it and sniff it, and you can envision the person writing each word. It takes time to handwrite a letter, and you need paper, a pen, an envelope, and a stamp. You appreciate that the person took the time to write it. You write a letter not knowing when or if the person will receive it. It may be days or weeks, but you still put your heart into it, like you are talking to the person and they are going to respond right away. To me, nothing else compares.

8

Our rear detachment consisted of LT Ken Brown, a brand-new second lieutenant, fresh out of college and flight school; Master Sergeant (MSG) Cantrell; and Sergeant (SGT) Bingham. Ken was a sweet kid who arrived just as the unit was deploying, so Dick had him stay back to be the rear detachment commander. Since it was his first duty assignment, he didn't know much about the post and supporting organizations. We had been stationed at Fort Campbell before, so I knew my way around the post and the Army in general, but we were in an ever-evolving situation, uncharted territory, and there was so much I had yet to learn. I felt like I was having to teach the LT while I was learning as well. Luckily, MSG Cantrell knew more than any of us and was a real gem.

I began stopping by the battalion headquarters a couple of times a week. I knew that was the pulse of the unit and where I would learn what the issues were and what I could do to support the families in our unit. Many problems for Army families involve money. At that time, the Army was still using an antiquated system in which some soldiers actually received their pay in cash. Dick had warned me before he left that it would take time for the Defense Finance and Accounting

Service (DFAS) to catch up with such a large-scale deployment and that there would be pay issues the first couple of months.

Boy, was he right. The problems began that first payday, at the end of August. Wives were lining up at the rear detachment, saying they had no paycheck, no money. The soldiers had also been told to leave their checkbooks at home with their spouse or a parent if they were single. They were not supposed to bring the checkbook on the deployment, and yet some had done just that. I made a point of showing up midmonth and end of month to get an idea of just how bad things were.

For many officers' wives, the pay issues were merely an inconvenience. We were short some money but knew that it would get sorted out eventually. But for many of the lower ranks, those issues were significant.

For our September FSG meeting, we had a couple of guest speakers. After I spoke and shared what I knew about the battalion and what was going on over in Saudi Arabia, I turned it over to a lieutenant colonel from the division's rear detachment. I was hoping that if the wives got answers from the top, from a higher-up "green suiter," rather than from me or our young LT, it would allay their suspicions and calm the rumor mill, and things would settle down. The LTC briefed us on pay issues, mail, phone calls, and other administrative things. But as soon as he finished his talk, the questions were like rapid fire directed at him.

"Will they be home for Thanksgiving?"

"What about Christmas?"

"What do you mean, they won't be home for Christmas?"

"My best friend's husband, who's in the MP [military police] battalion, said they'll be home before Christmas."

"I heard the first ones in will be the first ones out."

"When will our husbands get combat pay?"

And on and on it went. I tried hard to remain neutral and not roll my eyes. I reminded myself that, other than the recent, four-month training in California, many soldiers and families had never experienced a deployment. Operation Desert Shield was high profile; all eyes were on Saudi Arabia, Kuwait, and Iraq, courtesy of a twenty-four-hour media blitz. It was impossible not to speculate and wonder what was ahead of us, but I understood the logistics of the deployment and, based on the news reports, I was pretty sure it was going to be a lengthy one. I couldn't figure out what part of Dick's statement, "We will be gone six to twelve months," these families did not understand. But I forced myself to be patient with all of the millions of questions, knowing that we were dealing with different experience levels and emotional levels, diverse backgrounds, and many other variables. I couldn't expect everyone to process events the same way.

Our next speaker was a psychologist who talked about what we were experiencing and how to deal with stress and emotions. He told us about all the services available for us and our children if we needed them. His calm, relaxed demeanor reassured us all, and I could feel the tension in the chapel ease just a bit.

As people were preparing to leave, a wife raised her hand and in a soft, tentative voice said she was down to her last $20. She had no food in the house and no warm clothes for her children, *and* her husband had taken their checkbook with him to Saudi Arabia! Her two young children were sitting quietly next to her. Suddenly, the chapel was silent and the other wives around us stopped what they were doing. The wife started to cry, and then I felt tears running down my own face. My heart began pounding, I wanted so much to fix things. I told her we would figure it out and get her some help, but my gut reaction was to reach in my purse and give her some money. I looked at MSG Cantrell and saw him motioning me not to. Ever so gently, he stepped in and said he would handle the pay issues. He drew her away from the crowd, and I watched as he took down her information.

After everyone was gone, MSG Cantrell came over to me and said,

"Ma'am, I know you just wanted to help and your intentions were pure, but you can't start giving money to everyone in need. It will never end, and it will set a precedent."

"But she has no money! What can you do?"

"I will get her into AER [Army Emergency Relief] first thing Monday morning. They will give her money and food vouchers until we can get her husband's checkbook back. I gave her some money for the weekend. I can handle these kinds of things, and it's better if it comes from me, rather than the commander's wife. "

"I'm so angry at her husband for putting her in this position. What was he thinking?"

"I know, ma'am. Trust me, I will make sure that soldier's first sergeant gets the checkbook from him!"

I understood what MSG Cantrell had said to me, but I couldn't stop thinking about the woman with no money or food. What irritated me most was all the other whining and complaining that went on during the meeting, about stupid things like why the guys couldn't come home for Thanksgiving, when right in our midst was a wife who desperately needed help. I was so thankful she had come to the FSG meeting. What courage it took for her to tell us about her situation.

I saw the need for a meeting every four to six weeks, with a briefing from rear detachment and possibly a guest speaker. Each of the companies met regularly for potlucks and social gatherings, but having the whole battalion together was necessary as well. And I needed to let rear detachment handle the briefing portion; that way, they were the messenger, not I. And then I could focus on being the "team mom."

I learned a valuable lesson from MSG Cantrell that night. He was right, and I was thankful that he stopped me before I made a mistake. I was so used to having Dick guiding me when it came to Army stuff. For now, MSG Cantrell would be my "true north."

August 30, 1990
King Fahd Airport

Hi Vick,

Happy anniversary! I wish more than ever that I could be with you right now. Wow, fifteen years is a long time, but it goes by so quick! I can't remember a time not loving you—seems like you and I have been together all of my life. You are my best friend in the world.

This will be a quickie (no pun intended!) before I go off to fly for the press corps. They are here to do a story on the "elite" Apache unit from the 101st Airborne Division. Should be exciting!

Thank you for your letter, got it yesterday. Tell Clint and Tyler I enjoyed their letters as well. They are so funny! They are growing up so fast.

I am worried about pay issues. We are coming up on our first payday since the deployment, and I expect all kinds of problems. Be prepared to hear about it from the wives. Keep me posted on that.

Sorry you have to go through this again. I know it is not easy, but I know you will manage, like you always do. I promise I will fly safe and come home to you as soon as I can. Hug the boys for me.

Love you more than ever,
Dick

Journal Entry

He remembered our anniversary! I had already moved on, but it sure was nice to know that he wrote to me on the actual day. I never doubted him; I'm just trying to get used to a different way of life.

*During times like these, you have to remind yourself of what "is,"
rather than what "is not," even when everything in your gut is telling
you to want more. So much in life is out of our control—like when Dick
and I had to postpone our wedding because of a deployment, or when
Dick left for Korea for a one-year tour when our first son was just days
old, and the list goes on and on. You have to learn when to relinquish
the controls, when things are so far out of your purview that nothing
you do can change them, and then you have to figure out how to make
it work for you.*

*Our current situation does not change my love for Dick or his for
me. Maybe that should be my mantra.*

9

We still had no personal phone lines, but I got to talk to Dick a couple of times when I was in the battalion headquarters on a government-issue phone. We both knew that we needed to keep our conversation official, since it wasn't a personal phone line, but he had told MSG Cantrell that he needed to talk to me periodically about battalion issues. Dick realized just how much was going on back home and some of the things the rear detachment and I were trying to deal with. The call was awkward, because we got disconnected every few minutes, and then it would take a few minutes for Dick to call back. It sure wasn't easy, but it was better than nothing. We had no privacy—each of us had people around us—so we didn't say "I love you," but I was able to tell him that the boys and I were doing just fine. I knew he needed to hear that, and I just needed to hear his voice. He sounded so good. We talked about battalion stuff, and I told him about the rumors that took up so much of my focus and, of course, about the pay issues. I asked him when they might get phone lines for all the soldiers. During our conversation, I felt some of the weight lifted off my shoulders. Dick and I had always been a team when it came to his Army career, and I had missed my teammate those first weeks of the deployment.

Then one morning I got a call. As soon as I said hello, the woman on the other end, in an accusatory tone, said, "I don't think it's fair that you get to talk to your husband and nobody else does. Who do you think you are?"

My heart was pounding and my mouth dry as I replied, "Yes, I've talked to my husband, but our conversations are not personal; they have to do with the battalion."

"Well, it's not fair, and you shouldn't be able to talk to him."

I felt attacked, but I knew that I was not going to be able to convince her that my conversations with Dick were for the good of the group. I wanted to play the "rank" card and remind her that I was the commander's wife, but I knew that would make it even worse, as she probably expected me to do just that. Not knowing what else to say, I simply told her, "Well, I'm sorry you feel that way."

And then she hung up on me. I put the phone down and of course started crying—big, choking sobs. I was worn out from working so hard on behalf of the wives and families, spending hours each day on the phone and hours at the headquarters, helping the rear detachment put out fires. And then, in an instant, one anonymous woman unhinged me. It wasn't just her words that haunted me; it was her accusatory tone. I felt maligned, scrutinized, misunderstood, and unappreciated. Maybe I was naive to think that people understood my intentions.

When I called Gail and told her, she said, "Vicki, if you think that's bad, I had a wife file an IG [inspector general] complaint against me, saying I wasn't doing my 'job'! Do you know that many of the wives think we actually get paid to do this, to be a commander's wife?"

"Yes, I've heard that one, too." We just had to laugh at the situation, and I felt better after I talked to my friend.

I spoke with Dick soon after that incident, and he was really pissed. He tried to reassure me that I was doing a good job, but we both wondered who the "rat" was. Someone on his end had heard him talking to me and had gotten word back to his wife or someone else. I guess I wasn't the only one getting a phone call.

Much like what Dick was going through on the other side of the world, I was learning what I was good at and what I needed to work on. I had good people skills; I was able to relate to people from all walks of life. I was empathetic and sympathetic, caring, and approachable—qualities that my parents instilled in me and that most people liked about me. But those same qualities at times made me vulnerable. Because I was open and honest and treated everyone with respect, I assumed I would be treated the same way. I guess that was shortsighted of me, but I had no reason to feel otherwise. It was such a stressful time for everyone during those first weeks and months of the deployment that stress brought out the best and the worst in people. It wasn't just the phone call from the anonymous wife that got under my skin; it was a few wives, who acted selfish, complaining, whining, and being subversive within the group by stirring the pot and feeding the rumor mill. It was like having a large family that I had to referee, console, please, and entertain while moving forward.

I also had wives who confided things in me, claiming an emergency, so that I would get a message to Dick so they could talk with their husbands. Their ulterior motive was always to get the husband back home. Each time, their situation turned out to be a lie, which left me stuck in the middle and forced Dick to get involved. I was embarrassed that I believed every sob story. I gave myself a good talking-to and vowed never to let that happen again. I also learned to steer all of those types of things to MSG Cantrell.

More than one wife claimed to have had a miscarriage, but when she was told that her doctor must send the message to her husband through the Red Cross, she suddenly had no medical issue of any kind. We had a wife who was suicidal, and while I was on the phone with her, MSG Cantrell and LT Brown were on another line with the hospital, working to get her admitted immediately. We continued to

have families with money problems, so we started a food pantry in
the storage room in our battalion headquarters.

We had a wife, a soldier herself, who was caring for her stepson,
and while she was out one evening, the teenage stepson got a loaded
gun and began shooting in their neighborhood. The local police were
called, and when the stepmother returned home, she was arrested for
child endangerment. It was late on a Friday night when LT Brown
had to go to the jail and bail her out.

As consuming as life inside Fort Campbell was, I made a point of
reading the local newspaper and watching the news so I knew what
was going on outside our gates as well. Soldiers had left their pets;
one soldier actually left his minor, teenage kids with just a credit
card and some mattresses in an empty apartment when he deployed.
Story after heartbreaking story highlighted the need for family care
plans, financial planning, and, above all, leadership's involvement
with their soldiers' lives. So I took my role seriously and wanted to
know about all the problems, however big or small, ridiculous, triv-
ial, or serious. But that left me emotionally drained, and as hard as I
tried to shield myself and not absorb everyone else's troubles, I didn't
succeed. Dick always told me I needed to have thicker skin; I wished
someone would tell me how to grow *thick* skin.

Camp Hell, Saudi Arabia

Dear Vicki,
We have set up a forward operating base (FOB) up on the
Saudi–Kuwait border, so I'm up here for a few days. I'll keep
a company up here and rotate them every so often, and I'll fly
back and forth to check on them. There is absolutely nothing
up here but desert, as far as the eye can see. The flying is intim-
idating even for me, as I think, "Where the hell would I land
if I had an engine failure?" The old test pilot in me is always

searching for a possible landing spot, but I would hate to have to shut it down in the middle of this desert!

We call this Camp Hell for obvious reasons, mainly because of the extreme heat. If the living conditions are sparse at King Fahd Airport, this gives that word a whole new meaning! There is nothing here. We live in tents, we eat MREs [meals ready to eat], we have no running water, and I sleep with my loaded weapon on me. This is an outpost for nothing more than watching/waiting for the enemy; some call it a speed bump if the enemy comes through. I rotate my guys every two weeks, as you can't stand it for any longer than that! We are here to support 5th Special Forces Group and a brigade from the Saudi National Guard, and at the moment, we are a reaction force and deterrent to a possible Iraqi invasion of Saudi Arabia. Once we get the rest of the 101st here and some "heavy" divisions on the ground, I fully anticipate our mission to change.

The morale of my guys appears to be high, especially given the living conditions. But I keep a close eye on everyone, as do my company commanders.

We should have the new phone lines pretty soon, so I will be able to start calling the house. Bill Witt arrived yesterday and brought me two of your letters that he carried with him. Sounds like you have everything under control; I knew you would get things organized. The fact that you are getting so many calls from wives means they trust you and look up to you. But I feel bad about the wife who was mean to you about our phone conversation. I know how vulnerable you are right now and I know there are others who give you a hard time, but here's some advice from your best friend in the world. You are doing a great job, and the majority of the wives and families feel that way. Trust me, I've had many soldiers (both single and married) tell me that they are thankful for all you are doing back there for the families. Try not to let the few in the group who maybe don't get it, who don't care, who don't know you, get under your skin and hurt your feelings. I've dealt with this my entire career. I learned a long time ago that for all the people who like my leadership style, there are always some who think I'm a complete jerk. Focus on the things that really matter, and remember that all of this is exaggerated under these circumstances. Years from now, you won't even remember the negative things. Always remember how proud I am of you!

I love you,
Dick "No Mercy 6"

Journal Entry

When you put a group of people together in a stressful situation, personality differences, egos, and emotions compete and complicate things more than usual. I have a great group of spouses here. The majority of them are kind and caring, hardworking, respectful, and able to get along with one another. It really is just a very few who cause problems that affect the group dynamics.

Maybe I am too involved, but I can't turn away from what is going on. I keep asking myself, "How in the world can I continue to take on other people's problems?" Some of the problems are fixable, but others are sad and have no easy answer. How do I keep a balance, something that I have always been able to maintain but am struggling with right now?

When you reach a point of feeling like enough is enough, it's time to change your tactics. Sometimes you have to take a step back from the situation and not only take a closer look at the situation but also take a hard look at yourself. That might mean admitting that you can't *do it all and you can't be everything to everyone. Maybe it is time to reprioritize and reset your goals.*

My peers and fellow commanders' wives continue to be the best source of strength and knowledge for me, as they are all experiencing similar feelings. I am not alone.

10

Approximately eight thousand miles away, in Dhahran, Saudi Arabia, Dick was dealing with far more significant issues, ones that I could not imagine.

When Saddam Hussein invaded Kuwait in August and claimed the oil-producing monarchy as Iraq's 19th province, he caused an international outrage. He readied his forces for what many assumed would happen: an invasion of Saudi Arabia. If he succeeded at that, Iraq would have a stronghold on more than half of the world's oil reserves, which would destabilize the entire Persian Gulf region and disrupt the world economy. At first, the United Nations and Arab League called for his immediate withdrawal. Then came economic sanctions. When none of that worked, the United States took a harder stance and, with the blessing of Saudi Arabia's King Fahd, President George H. W. Bush launched Operation Desert Shield, sending US air and ground forces to Saudi Arabia. He gave a deadline of January 15, 1991, for all of Saddam's forces to leave Kuwait.

The United States assembled an international military coalition with thirty-four nations—representing the largest since World War II. General Norman Schwarzkopf, a four-star general and commander of United States Central Command (CENTCOM), would be the commander of coalition forces. As early as August 10, the war planners presented General Schwarzkopf with the initial draft of an operation code-named Operation Instant Thunder.

General Schwarzkopf and his planners knew that any invasion on our part using Air Force strikes and eventual ground forces would have to begin with a surprise attack to take out the key radar sites leading into Baghdad. The best way to do that without risking the lives of ground troops was to do it from the air, specifically with helicopters. Initially, the planners considered using special-operations aviation units for such a mission.

By the time Dick and his Apaches arrived on the scene, his unit was already being considered for the top-secret mission, even though it was a conventional Army aviation unit. All of this was going on behind the scenes. Since Dick had not been in combat or fought in an actual war, I was clueless about how these things started and played out.

I was a child of the 1960s, born in the '50s, in college in the '70s. Growing up in Burlington, Vermont, I had a small frame of reference about the military and war, except for what I studied in school or saw in a movie or on TV. The Vietnam War had a huge influence on my generation in terms of music, social unrest, and the fact that we could watch footage on the nightly news. The news coverage—not only the horrors of the war, but the effects causing divisiveness and fueling anger and protests back home—shaped the fabric of our lives and, in some ways, tainted how we viewed our military. It was the first time I saw soldiers being portrayed in a negative way, so unlike the treatment of veterans from the previous wars. I did not understand the term "baby killer" in relation to American soldiers, or the terrible way they were treated when they returned home, or how Americans could denigrate our flag. The very things that we were taught in school about decency, respect, and patriotism seemed to be laughed at, spit at, stomped on, and burned in the volatile '60s and '70s. I knew one person from my high school who joined the Marines, went to Vietnam, and was killed in action. I was proud of him for his service, as was my hometown. And then I met the man I would marry as he was embarking on a career in the Army.

Through six years of dating and fifteen years of marriage, I watched my husband and his fellow soldiers epitomize selfless service to our nation. I had nothing but pride and respect for the career they had chosen. Over time, the Vietnam War faded into the background and I stopped thinking about all the negative images, unless I was watching a movie or reading a book about those years.

But that fall of 1990, I struggled with what all the talk of war meant to my husband and his unit. Would it be like the Vietnam War? Would it be like what I had seen on TV or in a movie? How does a war start? Who fires the first shot?

With Dick not around to explain things to me, my mind conjured up what I thought might happen, all of it based on my view of the world and what I watched on TV or read. The way I saw it, there were maybe four possible scenarios, and I didn't like the first two. If Saddam Hussein decided to cross the border into Saudi Arabia, the US Army would be pinched. At that time, Saddam had the fourth-largest army in the world, with nearly one million men. In August and September of that year, our military had a fraction of that covering the Saudi–Kuwait border. It took weeks and months to get all of the coalition forces in country and ready, so if Saddam had invaded early on, it would have been devastating. Equally scary was the threat of chemical weapons being used on our military. There was a lot of talk about that in the news because of Saddam's track record.

Both of those scenarios were too dark and scary, so I kept those thoughts in a compartment in my head and forced myself never to go there. There was always diplomacy; maybe economic sanctions, embargoes, and threats would work, but I wasn't holding my breath on that one. If combat was going to occur, the scenario that worked best for me was one in which Dick and his Apache unit, along with the 101st Airborne Division, backed up by the entire US Army, Air Force, and Marines, got the first shots in and gained the upper hand early, pushing Saddam's Republican Guard back to Baghdad and overthrowing him. The United States would be victorious, and maybe the troops would be home by next spring. I liked that and focused my thoughts on a positive ending to the story.

I was counting on Dick's letters to give me some idea of what to expect. Our phone conversations were careful because of operational security (OPSEC). Since the beginning of our marriage, Dick had drilled into me that you never knew who was listening, so I never asked him anything compromising while on the phone. For a different mission, ten years prior, we had made up code words for just such occasions, but when he left that August, we didn't really talk about those. I always knew if Dick needed to tell me something, such as he was going off on a classified and dangerous mission, he would simply say, "Take my motorcycle out of the garage."

In my letters to him, I tried to think of clever ways to catch him off guard and glean some information from him. For example: *Clint had a great soccer game, scored two goals! Do you think there is going to be a war? Tyler scored as well. What did you mean about working for another boss? Has your weather cooled off?* But it didn't work. I was frustrated and finding it increasingly difficult to respond to not only the other wives' questions but those of our own families in Vermont. Every phone call from our parents or siblings began, "What does Dick say about the situation? Does he think we're going to war? When does he think it will begin?"

Every time I thought things had settled down with the other Army wives, something would trigger a reaction and it would start all over again. One evening I hosted the monthly coffee for our commanders' and first sergeants' wives at my house. We were eating and enjoying each other's company, doing a little business, when someone mentioned seeing our guys on the news. I put the TV on. Big mistake! We heard the words "Breaking news: A Blackhawk helicopter from the 101st has crashed in Saudi Arabia."

When everyone looked at me like, *What the heck?* I reassured them that if it were ours, I would have been called. I could tell they didn't believe me, so I called CW4 Joe Pisano, in the division rear detachment, but he couldn't tell me anything. With that, our lively little group became quiet and somber. Soon after, women began to leave. I felt deflated, like we could never get away from our fears. Something that caused us worry was always being reported. The great thing about instant news is also the curse, especially for military families back home. And for pilots' wives, it only added to the strain that we endured every day.

Because our unit had multiple types of aircraft, any report of a helicopter crash involving the 101st Airborne Division was enough to stop us in our tracks; we feared the worst until we got the details. It was just human nature. Many of us had lived with this stress for as long as we had been Army wives, but it never got any easier to hear a word like "crash." Accidents were not some abstract notion; they were a very real possibility.

King Fahd Airport

Hi Vicki,
Sorry I haven't written in a few days—I have been on reverse cycle, going to meetings, and meeting myself coming and going. I have been getting your letters and the boys' as well. I love hearing about everything you're doing. I especially like the way you try to get me to talk about what's going on over here. You're funny!
We had a visitor here recently: Old Stormin' Norman

himself! He came to meet with MG Peay and planners from the 101st Airborne and some other "key players." He walked up to me and put his arm around me, and as we were walking, he said, "Cody, I like your style. I like what you're doing here. . . . Now, stay away from the press!" I said, "Roger that, sir!"

Not sure if he remembered me from years ago when I was in the 24th Infantry Division and he was my commanding general, but I sure remembered him. He is still a very imposing guy! We had a good meeting and I got to brief some "stuff."

If you remember the old scenario that Ned and I were involved in ten years ago, you'll have an idea of what I am "practicing" in addition to my 101st duties. Nothing to worry about—honestly, I have it all under control. From what I hear, the news is trying to forecast what they believe will happen. There is not much I can share with you; you'll have to be patient and trust me.

I meant to tell you, we have an OH-58 company attached to us, the E Company Stingrays, from Fort Lewis, Washington. The commander is CPT Tim Gowen, a good guy.

I am sending a couple of guys home with medical issues. Most were existing before the deployment, just made worse with the living conditions here. One of them is Mr. Mike Dousette, a warrant officer, very mature and capable; he will be a big help to you as the new rear detachment commander. LT Brown will be coming over here; I know how much you like him, but I need him here. He is a brand-new pilot and needs to be getting some flight time and experience. And I'm sending Brownie [Spec 4 Mitchell Brown] home, much to his dismay. He's been pretty sick and spent time on the hospital ship but isn't getting better, so he needs to come home. I know you and the boys will love having him back there.

I really miss you. I miss your face and . . . everything. I miss

watching Clint and TJ playing their various sports, and shoot-
ing hoops with them and coaching them. I miss coming home
at night and getting "debriefed" by you on the day's events,
both good and bad!

Tell the wives everyone here is okay. The entire unit is doing
great and being well cared for. I'm working on a newsletter
for the families but have rewritten it three times already, as
I don't want to say the wrong thing and cause you any prob-
lems. I will fax it to the office, and you can review it before I
send it to all.

Take care, and I'll try to give you a call this week. And yes,
I am flying safe!

Love you,
Dick "No Mercy 6"

Journal Entry

Being on your own is lonely, but maybe there is something to be gained
from that. Things slow down just a bit, and perhaps you have more
time for yourself and for self-reflection. (I will be the most self-aware
person by the time Dick's Army career is over!) When you are tested,
you learn what your strengths and weaknesses are, and when you don't
have your sounding board, you figure things out on your own. I some-
times surprise myself with what I am capable of accomplishing when
forced to. Maybe all of this character building is for a reason; maybe
I will need these strengths years from now, although I can't imagine a
more stressful situation than the one I am in right now.

11

One of the things that I always loved about Dick was his ability to adjust to any surroundings and not just adapt but turn it into a positive experience. He was good for me in that way, and I always strived to be more adaptive myself.

The site where he and his soldiers were living, the parking garage still under construction for King Fahd Airport, was formerly a military air base. Remnants of that base still existed and included basketball and tennis courts, which gave Dick the opportunity for some team sports for him and his guys. He always found a way to play sports wherever he was. They formed basketball teams, and Dick and a couple of his lieutenants decided to start playing tennis, as well.

People often wondered how Dick maintained his happy-go-lucky demeanor, his positive and upbeat attitude, while juggling a number of balls. It was true: Dick was one of the most even-tempered people I knew, and it took a lot to upset him or stress him out. I think part of it was his nature, but I believe sports were one of the most important things that he did for himself and those around him. He played every one with such intensity, focus, and determination that his worries or stressors disappeared. Every unit he was in, whether as the commander or as a member of the unit, he formed up, played on, and sometimes coached the team. And it worked, not just for his well-being but for that of everyone else who played.

This deployment to Saudi Arabia was no different. I shipped him two tennis rackets and a couple cans of tennis balls. He went through balls faster than I could ship them, so then his dad, another avid sportsman, began sending tennis balls by the case.

I got my second wind in October and felt like the boys and I would be able to get through the deployment. I sensed that my positive attitude was having an impact on the other wives as well. I was impressed with the wives' creativity and ingenuity in thinking up fun things to do and planning for the holidays. We did bake sales, bingo nights, potlucks, and fundraisers to help supplement our food locker. We thought ahead to Christmas; with 350 soldiers in the unit, we couldn't buy for everyone, so we thought of things to make. Each company did its own thing. The goal was to have something for everyone, whether married or single, on Christmas morning. We knew we would have to ship the boxes in late November, so we were busy planning in October. It was fun, kept us busy, and was team building.

I had my hobbies as well. I went to aerobics class regularly, I took some arts-and-crafts classes, and, of course, I had plenty of volunteer work. The boys' school asked me to help form up a parent advisory council, made up of spouses of all ranks from various units. We met once a month with the teachers and administrators at the middle school. I was so impressed with the leadership at the school for initiating the idea so early in the deployment. They truly cared about our kids and wanted to make sure they understood and met their needs. They listened to our concerns, processed our feedback, and, most important, gave us a voice. It was very innovative for that era, and it made a difference in the school experience for our children during a very stressful time in their young lives. Being involved in different aspects of our Army community gave me a sense of purpose.

We had gotten our first VHS camera earlier that year, a big hulk of a thing that was the size and weight of a carry-on bag. That fall, the boys and I made videos to send to their dad. Clint and Tyler, along with their buddies Scott Greco; Jeff and Luke Van Antwerp, whose dad was another of Dick's West Point classmates and commanding the engineer battalion; and sometimes Scott's younger sisters, Jessie and Meg, thought up scenarios for me to film. With the camera hoisted on my shoulder, I was director, producer, and filmmaker extraordinaire.

Most of their scenarios involved a military mission and/or a hostage rescue in Iraq. They used their toy Apache helicopters for flying scenes, and they rummaged through closets for clothing and in my kitchen drawers for useful tools and props. Clint, using his dad's call sign, No Mercy 6, was pilot and rescuer; Tyler played the hostage. Their buddies had supporting roles as pilots or bad guys. I thought it was important for them to act out things that were most likely going through their minds. Their videos always ended with them walking off into the sunset, arm in arm, singing the 101st Airborne song, "Rendezvous with Destiny." The boys shared the same camaraderie with their fellow Army brats that Dick had with his soldiers and I had with the wives. Dick and his guys enjoyed watching the videos, and it gave us an outlet for our creative juices.

I had never witnessed such patriotism as I did that fall. I watched on TV as truck convoys and Army vehicles made their way south along Interstate 24 from Nashville to Chattanooga, then Interstate 75, through Atlanta and on to Jacksonville; citizens lined the overpasses, waving American flags and cheering the convoys. I've often thought about that time and wished my husband and his fellow soldiers could have seen the American people rallying for them. I wonder what it was about that particular period that united us and brought out that sense of patriotism in so many people. That feeling of support carried on through the winter months and was a morale boost for all of us.

Around the beginning of October, I noticed that Dick's letters no longer had a postage stamp; instead, in the upper-right corner of each envelope, he wrote the word "Free." I had never seen that before and thought it was pretty nice of the US Postal Service to give the soldiers a break. I wondered if the Postal Service had done that during previous wars.

The mail and the phone service were the most important things for all of us. Dick was able to call our house once or twice, and I relished being able to talk more freely. He always had people around him on his end, but I at least had privacy on mine. Like the phone lines, the mail continued to be sporadic, so I was afraid to become dependent on either form of communication. But it sure was nice to hear his voice.

King Fahd Airport

Hi Vicki,

I love getting your letters! You are right: I have no one to really unload to. Tom Garrett is a great brigade commander, a good listener, and we are very close. I go to him a lot, but there are some things no one can help me with. I always heard that being a commander can be lonely, and there are times right now when I feel very much alone. My company commanders are doing great, as are the company first sergeants. But I've got some issues and need to make some personnel changes for the good of the unit. It's like what you are dealing with: personality conflicts, some people not pulling their weight, and all of it magnified over here. These things wouldn't be a big deal back at Fort Campbell, but when you are training to possibly go to war, I have to think safety and mission first! I'm probably going to ruffle some feathers, but that is nothing new for me! Don't mean to bother you with this stuff; I know you have your hands full. I miss having you to talk to at the end of the day. I will figure all of this out.

There have been so many accidents and mishaps over here already. Not in our battalion, but in many of the other aviation units. It's stupid stuff. I have a tight rein on my pilots, and I'm sure there are some who think I am a micromanager, and I'm sure some of my men are sick of me already, but I don't care. I will do whatever it takes to keep my guys safe. I refuse to lose anyone in a training accident; the worst is yet to come! We need to be disciplined at all times and not just when we get the call to move out. Tell the wives that their husbands are flying good and with caution and to try not to worry.

You are doing a great job with the wives. That's a great idea that you set up a food locker in the battalion headquarters. I'm sure that will help a lot of families. But most importantly, you are taking such good care of Clint and Tyler.

Take care of yourself and hug the boys for me, and remember I love you very much!

Always,

Dick

Journal Entry

As hard as it is sometimes, I just have to keep moving forward. The world did not stop turning when Dick deployed. It would be so easy to let his absence stop me in my tracks, but to allow that would be a disservice to me and to our sons and would set the wrong example for the other wives. Life is to be lived. We can't just sit on the sidelines and watch it pass us by—where would we be at the end of the day?

Every circumstance has a silver lining, even the ones that seem most difficult at first, and I intend to get something good out of this situation. I want to be stronger for it, and I want to enjoy this time and these stolen moments with my boys. And if, at the end, all I have is Dick to pat me on my back, then I'll pat myself as well, for a job well done. Army life is not going to get the best of me.

12

No sooner had the phone lines gone up than they came crashing down, and what a mess it was. It wreaked havoc not only on the soldiers in theater but on the families back home. Some were able to make calls, some got to talk multiple times, and some didn't get a call in. You can imagine what that did for morale. My phone rang nonstop during the day with complaints. In a letter to Dick, I told him it was almost better if they never got the phones back up. It caused more trouble than it was worth. I was getting used to the ups and downs of letter writing and its sporadic delivery, but it was a little more consistent than waiting for a phone call.

Despite all the communication hurdles, Clint and Tyler and I did our best to carry on. I did notice that they were cussing more than usual, so one day I made a "cuss can" for them. Being the artsy-craftsy person that I was, I decorated a coffee can with pretty paper and labeled it "Cuss Can: 25 Cents for Cuss Words, 50 Cents for the 'F' Word." I explained that they needed to think about what they said, never cuss in public, and, overall, just limit their bad language. The coins in the can began to build up, and I realized that the majority of their allowance was going into the can, but I also noticed an improvement in their language. Then I made a fateful mistake one night: I was short on change for a pizza delivery, and I raided the cuss can. They watched in silence, but I could see the wheels turning in their minds. A week later, on allowance day, I heard a commotion in the kitchen, swear words flying, and the clink of coins going into the cuss can.

"What are you guys doing?" I asked when I came in.

"We're just swearing."

"I can hear that, but why are you doing that?"

A moment's hesitation, and then Tyler said, "There's a lot of money in there; can we go out for Mexican tonight?"

I just looked at them. How could I get mad at them? They were the best friends I had at that moment, and I had to laugh at their ingenuity. Later that night, as we ate our tacos at Chi-Chi's, I said to them, "All you had to do was ask me to take you out to dinner."

Clint replied, "Yeah, but it was fun to swear."

I was lucky to have school-age kids; their busy schedules helped the time pass quickly. The weekends were consumed with sports; Tyler had soccer games at Fort Campbell on Saturdays, and Clint's games were on Sundays. Clint and Scott Greco played on a traveling team in Clarksville, so, every Sunday after church, Gail and I packed up our cars with chairs and drink coolers and headed out to locations all over middle Tennessee: Hendersonville, Franklin, Nashville, and as far south as Chattanooga. It was a great way to spend the weekends that fall. Even more important, it felt freeing to get out of town and away from the house, for quality time with my two boys. Because cell phones didn't exist back then, I could really get away from it all—I was totally unplugged from the phone and the TV and could put my stress and responsibilities on hold, if only for a few hours. People can't do that with today's technology. Our cell phones are always with us, and while they're great for keeping us connected, they also serve as a distraction, often preventing us from being present in the moment.

For Dick and his men, Sundays meant "no boot" day. It was the only day of the week he allowed his soldiers to be out of uniform and to wear sneakers. Other commanders were more lenient, letting their soldiers wear whatever they wanted when they were off duty and on the weekends. Dick knew there were complaints behind his back, but he never wavered when it came to doing the right thing. He saw what went on in the less disciplined units: mistakes, accidents, injuries, even deaths. He said to me more than once, "Discipline and standards should never take time off, and the duty day never ends, especially in the combat zone. Sloppy in appearance, sloppy in your work." In the aviation business, you can't afford any mistakes due to lack of discipline. But on Sundays, after various church services were offered, Dick and his men played sports and relaxed just a little bit.

Dick's greatest challenges continued to be extreme heat and sandstorms, both of which wreaked havoc on the helicopters. Living in the unfinished parking garage posed unique challenges as well. There was nowhere to go to get relief from the heat. They were living in open bays, no walls or windows, just four concrete levels of open garage spaces. The Air Force lived in air-conditioned billets with showers and hot meals. Dick and his guys never understood the difference between them and the Air Force pilots. They took the same oath and had the same mission to fly their aircraft. It's pretty hard to do the mission and fly if you can't sleep because of the heat. There had always been competition between the services, but during that time, the way the Air Force lived created a whole new level of friction.

Dick finally found a way to give his guys some relief. The King Fahd Airport complex was so huge that it had large ducts, two or three miles' worth of tunnel space that ran underneath the runways, to house all the electrical wiring. The ducts were the coolest place at the airport, and once they were discovered, Dick knew they were the place for his pilots to get their crew rest, a requirement before flying. The ducts were aptly nicknamed the Bat Caves and became the most coveted billets in town.

When Dick did mention these things to me, he never did so in a complaining way; he was very matter-of-fact in his depiction of his living conditions. I would have been complaining up one side and down the other if I had been the one living over there—which is why you don't find me in the ranks of our Army. I could do without certain creature comforts, maybe even live without potato chips and other favorite foods, but I could not and would not want to live out in the elements, in sand and 130-degree heat, sleeping on a cot, eating MREs, with no showers, no TV, no phone, no walls, and no privacy. I am thankful for the brave men and women who voluntarily protect our nation and are so willing to sacrifice for the greater good, but that would not be me. I know my limitations, I know my needs, and I know what I am good at. I like being on the sidelines, cheering Dick on. I am perfectly happy and content there.

Camp Hell, Saudi Arabia

Vicki,
A short note, as it is been hectic here. We are now into what we in the military call "mature theater," which means "all forces in country." As you can imagine, with all the various Army and Air Force units, it is crowded, and the pecking order of who is doing what, where, and when changes daily. We have been doing a lot of "what if" scenarios. But, as I've mentioned before, I work with some "others," so I have my own chain of command to report to besides our division commander, MG Peay.
There are now six Apache battalions in theater, and, whether anyone admits it, there is competition between the

attack battalions. I'm too busy to worry about that. Besides, Expect No Mercy continues to lead the pack in flying, maintenance, and tactics. I am so proud of my guys; everyone is giving 100 percent. I have the best pilots and crew chiefs of any unit here.

How are you doing? I know you are probably getting harassed over the phone issues. It was nice while it lasted, but, unfortunately, with this many people in one location, the phone lines couldn't handle the volume. I guess there were sixty thousand calls in twelve hours and the lines crashed. It could take two weeks to fix, so right now the phones are for military use only. Tell the wives to be patient, and remind them that I am more interested in preparing for war than trying to fix a problem that is above my pay grade! (Just kidding!) I know this complicates things for you, but there is nothing any of us can do. We can't count on phone lines at this point.

I feel guilty that you have to take care of all these things, and you are great to not complain. I want you to know that I realize how hard it is on you and I am truly sorry for putting you through this. I promise we will take a long vacation when this is over!

I have the entire task force moved forward right now. We are the only aviation battalion forward, in full force. Most of the other units are still in training mode, but we are locked, loaded, and ready for whatever is ahead. We have been doing actual "live" fires, the only attack battalion so far to do any. As you can imagine, this boosts the morale of the guys.

I've been getting my guys familiar with the terrain. It is tough flying, as I've said before, with nothing to key off of. The sand shifts constantly, causing the terrain to fluctuate, making it difficult to gauge distances and altitude. You really have to rely on instruments. Brian Stewmon and I make a good crew.

Even though he is young, he is a technical whiz in the front seat; then I have the air sense and experience in the backseat. We work well together, so don't worry about me. I am super careful. I also keep my eyes on every one of my pilots.

Got to run—I get to shoot Hellfires today! Me + Brian Stewmon = Super Team!

Love you and miss you a lot.

Always,

Dick

Journal Entry

When you and a loved one are on different paths, maybe one of you facing more challenges than the other, it is so hard not to think about and worry about the other person. You want to fix it, make it easier for them, but you can't. This is one of those things you have to let go of and simply accept.

The thing is, sometimes the other person is not struggling the way you think they are; sometimes the struggle is within yourself. In this case, the struggle is mine. If Dick knew how much time I spend obsessing about his living conditions, he would think I was being ridiculous because he gets to fly an Apache helicopter, shoot rockets and Hellfire missiles, and be part of history in the making. To him, he is living his best dream!

13

The clock was ticking for Saddam Hussein and his Republican Guard, and by November he had still made no move to exit Kuwait. It was pretty obvious to most Americans that we were headed for something. Still, I couldn't fathom an all-out war. Even though I had been married to a career Army officer and he had been deployed before, it had never been for an actual war. I had little frame of reference for something like a World War, the Korean War, or even Vietnam. From what I knew about Vietnam, there was a steady and continued buildup of forces sent there to keep the North Vietnamese (communists) from taking over South Vietnam. No one single action started that war, and by the time I was old enough to take an interest in it, it was winding down and had become the most controversial war that the United States had ever been involved in.

Fast-forward to August 1990, when the single action of Iraq invading Kuwait set off a chain reaction that led us to war because President Bush, the United Nations Security Council, and Congress decided Saddam Hussein's army must leave Kuwait. President Bush issued the ultimatum "Be out of Kuwait by January 15, or we will take military action." His order with a deadline was something that I, and many in my generation, had not witnessed before.

The media was poised and ready for any upcoming conflict or action. Journalists were stationed throughout the Gulf region, some even embedded with units, giving us instantaneous news. It would be the first time we had had twenty-four-hour news access during a war or conflict, and the networks sure were going to make the most of that. It was like a new prime-time TV series called *A Line in the Sand*, *Conflict in the Gulf*, or some other clever moniker, and they managed to fill the time with armchair quarterbacks and analysts who helped fuel the speculation, making it hard not to watch. The media had a captive audience in us; most of us were glued to our TVs, even when there was nothing new going on, because we had been told that on or around January 15, something *big* was going to happen. Pop some popcorn, turn on the VCR, settle in your comfy chair, and watch the war begin, right there on national TV!

Thanksgiving was approaching, and many of the wives had plans to leave Fort Campbell for the long weekend. It was too far for the boys and me to go to Vermont; besides, we were going there for Christmas. But we desperately needed to get away. We went to Atlanta to visit some old Army friends, Rick and Jane Lester. We had been stationed together in Savannah when our kids were young. Rick, a highly decorated Vietnam Cobra pilot, had been Dick's boss for a short time at Hunter Army Airfield in the mid-'80s. We were stationed together again in 1987–'88 in Seoul, Korea. So we shared a history, and the Lesters offered the perfect sanctuary for the boys and me that Thanksgiving.

I love road trips—always have. Something about getting out on the open road, with a new adventure on the horizon—and, at that particular time, getting away from responsibilities and phone calls— always puts me in my happy place. The five-hour drive was pure bliss, and by the time we arrived in Marietta, I felt like a new person. It was the best weekend, for a number of reasons: being with old friends, making videos to send to Dick, shopping, eating, and sleeping in, and, most of all, taking a vacation from my worrying.

The highlight for Clint and Tyler and me was going to an NBA game in Atlanta: the Atlanta Hawks versus the Philadelphia 76ers. The 76ers were Tyler's favorite team because he loved Charles Barkley. There was a big showing of patriotism at the game that night, and on the loudspeakers before the national anthem, they paid tribute to servicemen and women who were overseas.

After the game, it was a dream come true for the boys when Rick took us courtside and we got to meet some players. Rick approached Charles Barkley, with Clint and Tyler in tow, and said something to the effect of, "These boys right here, their dad is in Operation Desert Shield, defending our freedoms; could they please get a picture with you?"

I will never forget Charles Barkley's reply: "Come here, boys. I would be glad to get a picture with you. Please thank your dad for what he's doing over there."

Next thing I knew, Dominique Wilkins and a few other players who overheard what was going on gathered around Clint and Tyler, offering to have their pictures taken, too. With Rick's Polaroid camera, we had instant photos, which the players then signed. Every one of them told the boys to thank their dad for his service.

As I stood there watching, I had an unprecedented experience. It was the first time in Dick's career that I felt support from perfect strangers and as if what he was doing really mattered. Clint and Tyler had not witnessed that either. It was an unexpected reward that made the boys and me realize what Dick had chosen to do with his life was not only appreciated but maybe making a real difference in the world.

We returned to Fort Campbell totally rejuvenated. I will always be thankful to our good friends and the perfect weekend we spent with them.

King Fahd Airport

Dear Vicki,

Did you get your birthday gift? I hope you like it. One of the workers here took me to a guy who makes jewelry at the market outside the gates. We had to "sneak" off base, as I'm not really supposed to leave, but I wanted to find something special for you. It is a gold cartouche with your name in Arabic.

I hope you and the boys had a good trip to see the Lesters. I thought about you a lot and was worried about you driving that far in holiday traffic. I know you are more than capable and a good driver, but it is hard to be so far away from you, especially if anything ever happened. You probably don't realize this, but we all worry about our families back home.

The chow hall did a really nice turkey dinner with all the fixings for us. We actually sat at real tables to eat! Then we played Ping-Pong and various other games and sports—anything to pass the time. I worry about my soldiers; holidays are tough on all of us, but somehow, morale seems to be pretty good. We stay so busy the majority of the time. There are always aircraft to fix, we wash our Apaches every couple of days because of the sand, and just the launching of and flying the aircraft keeps everyone hopping. You know how when Clint and Tyler were little, you used to try to wear them out during the day so they would sleep at night? That is basically what I try to do with my soldiers: keep them all busy so they don't focus on how crappy it is. I continue to be amazed at soldiers' adaptability, ingenuity, and resourcefulness. When we need something, they build it; they can take a piece of plywood and make partitions around their parking spaces to create a room. They are always working on something. I have some very artistic guys who create logos for our T-shirts, posters, and letterhead. Some guys play their guitars. All in all, it's not too bad.

The day after Thanksgiving, it was business as usual. I have now moved up to the border again. I don't want my guys to get complacent, so we do lots of drills and practice different scenarios. I really sense we are on the brink of something, and I just want us to be prepared.

The weather has improved. It is cool at night and in the early morning until about 10:00 a.m., when it gets up to 90 degrees—a huge improvement from last month! It is pretty quiet here at night, and the sky is literally filled with stars! I have never seen so many. Wish I had paid more attention in school when we studied the solar system, so I would know what I'm looking at. I guess back home I'm too busy to notice these things, and living in urban areas, you don't see the night sky like this.

Always know that you are in my thoughts, and because of that, I take no unnecessary chances. I will come back in one piece. I promise!

Love you and miss you, and also, I appreciate the way you have stood by me all these years.

Always,
Dick "No Mercy 6"

What I was oblivious to during that time was that Dick's mission planning was in full swing. When he mentioned, "We are on the brink" in his letter, I thought we had been on the brink since he had left that August, so I didn't sense that anything was different. Maybe I had let myself get lulled into a false sense of security, since nothing bad had happened yet. We were approaching Christmas, and I was naive enough to think that nothing would happen before the holiday. Again, my mind was conjuring what was more palatable for me to handle, since the thought of a war starting during the holidays was too much for me, the boys, and all the families at Fort Campbell.

Journal Entry

When you are surrounded by people who live the same life as you, you don't think that you or your loved one is doing anything special. It's not that you take it for granted; it's more like you just expect it—it is the way it is. Only when you take yourself out of that environment, maybe take a step back, do you see things in a different light.

What the boys and I felt at the basketball game was so special for us, and what someone like Charles Barkley gave to us was more than a photo op and an autograph. He validated what their dad had chosen to do and was thankful for that service. People should know that when they pay tribute to, express gratitude for, or even acknowledge a soldier's service, they are supporting the soldier's family—the spouses, the kids, the mothers and fathers who stand beside them and sacrifice as well.

But for me, my greatest validation comes from my husband. I am the luckiest woman in the world.

14

The Expect No Mercy battalion had garnered the attention of the top leadership in the coalition. What I didn't know until much later was that back in September, when Dick first met General Schwarzkopf, he was already being considered for a highly classified mission. Prior to that meeting, Dick had met with COL Jesse Johnson, the commander of Special Operations Command Central (SOCCENT), a part of Central Command of which General Schwarzkopf was the commander. COL Johnson had been part of Desert One, the failed rescue mission to free the Iran hostages back in April 1980, resulting in injuries and loss of life when the Navy Sea Stallion helicopter crashed in the dessert. His experience with those types of missions had taught him valuable lessons, and he vowed that type of disaster would not happen again.

Dick also had experience in that arena; he had been part of a follow-on mission that was to be a second attempt to go back into Iran to get the hostages, using small attack helicopters. It was October 1980 when Dick, a young captain at Hunter Army Airfield in Savannah, Georgia, got the call to be part of that mission, along with his close friend and fellow pilot Ned Hubard. He and Ned left

Hunter Army Airfield immediately, and for the next four months Dick helped modify and rebuild OH-6 Loaches (Little Birds), turning them into gunships. When the aircraft were finished, they trained in the Arizona dessert. The training was dangerous, intense, and so classified that very few in the Army even knew of its existence. Their mission was canceled right before newly elected President Reagan took office and President Jimmy Carter's diplomatic efforts secured the release of the fifty-three hostages. Dick came back home to me and our two young sons feeling deflated. I was so thankful to have him home safe that I didn't fully understand his disappointment and his unusually quiet mood.

In trying to describe his ambivalent feelings, he said, "Vicki, can you imagine working on something, risking so much, practicing a mission for months, and then never getting to do it? I've been living on the edge with this group of pilots, doing the most daring flying I've ever done. It was scary, it was invigorating, and it was exciting. And then it ended. It would be like if you were a quarterback on an NFL team and you trained for the Super Bowl and then never got to play, or the game got canceled."

"I think I understand, Dick. Really, I do. But for me, I'm just glad you came back home to us. I've never been so worried about you. I have to think that for whatever reason, it was not your time, and that maybe something terrible would have happened. I know you will get your chance someday."

Exactly ten years later, Dick Cody was going to get his second chance. He was going to do the mission of a lifetime, which would put him and his unit in the military history books.

The timing was right; the stars were aligned. Dick had the right aircraft, and his battalion was the best in the business. His leadership and certainly the four months spent training in the California desert had resulted in a cohesive team, a true band of brothers. For all its varying backgrounds and experience levels, 1-101st Aviation

Regiment was a pool of limitless talent, and Dick knew how to tap into that. From the pilots and crew chiefs to the maintainers, wrench turners, refuelers, truck drivers, and mechanics, every soldier gave 100 percent for the good of the team. By the time the Expect No Mercy battalion hit the sands of the Saudi Arabian desert, they were working together like a synchronized Indy 500 pit crew.

Dick knew every aspect of his unit and took the time to get to know every person. He had flown with each of his eighty pilots at different times; his knowledge of their strengths and weaknesses was invaluable when he needed to make decisions for upcoming missions. His hands-on leadership style, his vast knowledge of aviation, and his vast flight time and test-pilot time all played a role in how well he and his unit succeeded in the coming weeks and months. Everything he had been through in his fifteen-year career—every accident, every mishap, every training exercise, every challenge—only made Dick Cody stronger. He used all of that to push himself, and if he saw an obstacle in his way, he figured out how to get around it. In doing so, he instilled the same "can do" attitude in his soldiers.

So, in September 1990, when Dick met with COL Johnson and the plan was laid out and the objectives set, he couldn't believe the scenario *and* his good fortune. He had to contain his excitement so as not to appear overeager for such an important mission.

After further discussion, COL Johnson asked Dick, "Can you accomplish this with your Apaches?"

Without hesitation, Dick replied, "Yes, sir. Absolutely!"

"Are you sure? Total destruction?"

"One hundred percent, sir!"

And just like that, the ball was rolling—a ball that would gain speed and momentum and culminate in a history-making raid.

But I knew none of that back then; I was clueless. Dick's letters were upbeat, and he was so good at keeping secrets. He had to be. From time to time, I would pick up a clue or nuance in a letter, but

I could never fully put the pieces of the puzzle together. More than once, he referred to "1980–'81 . . . Remember what Ned and I were doing." I realized then that I had never truly understood that mission. I thought it was about hostage rescue, but there were no hostages in Kuwait or Iraq, so how could I possibly know what Dick was involved in now? I spent countless hours speculating with my closest friends, and sometimes speculating with me, myself, and I. It was one of life's great mysteries, just looming out there in front of me, and it drove me nuts not to be able to figure it out. I thought back to all the times I had worried about Dick and then reminded myself, *I have complete faith and trust in this man.* I felt the same about his battalion.

AA (assembly area), Cadiz

Hi Vick,

I'm up here fighting a rehearsal battle with the EPAC [Eastern Provincial Area Command] forces. This area is pretty nice, surrounded by three hills, but it still looks like the moon! We road-marched all of our vehicles up here three days ago. They got caught in a sandstorm and had to camp out and wait it out! The troops thought it was exciting!

Before I left King Fahd, I got letters from you and the boys. It was great! The mail had been stuck for the past two weeks. Nothing came in for days, and then all of a sudden it was like a windfall! I love reading your letters; they give me such a clear picture of you and the boys and everything going on back home. You really are a good writer. I think you could be an author someday! The boys have inherited that from you, because they express themselves so well. You have done a great job with them. They make me laugh with the things they say. Your letters are the highlight of my days.

I've been doing a lot of thinking and have had to make

some big decisions that I can't even share with you. I can't really talk to anyone. Vicki, I feel so blessed to be commanding this battalion. It is head and shoulders above any other unit here. CSM Ehrke has such a good grasp of the soldier side of things, and we work well together. I've got the best staff: Howard Killian is perfect as my XO, Dave Moore as S-1, Russ Stinger as S-2, Mike Davis is the best S-3, and Miracle Solley as S-4. They all work well together and have my back, which helps me as I find myself coming and going (working for different bosses, if you catch my drift).

After the few changes I made earlier, things are working out just fine in all the companies. My company commanders, Dave Parker, Newman Shufflebarger, Doug Gabram, Jorge Garcia, Blaine Hodge, and our new guy, Tim Gowen, are doing great, and each one has built a solid team. Everyone is a superstar with so much talent, it's difficult to choose one over the other. Someday I'll explain what I mean by that, but who'd have thought that would be a problem? I guess I just have to trust my gut.

A few weeks ago, I had Task Force Normandy flying with the Air Force, moving most of the task force to a base camp up north. Of course, this is just practice. . . .

I got to see Tom Greco and Bob Van Antwerp the other day. They are doing good. Every time I go to the division headquarters, I see old friends and buddies from my West Point days and other units I've served in. It's like old home week!

Gotta run! I miss you all the time, especially at night.

Hug the boys for me!

Love you,

Dick

The words "Task Force Normandy" caught my attention, as Dick had not mentioned that before. I wasn't sure of its significance and didn't realize what a big clue he was giving me. I thought maybe he was referring to a task force, a group within his battalion, that went on patrols or did something up on the border at Camp Hell. How was I to know that I was supposed to connect the dots between *his* Task Force Normandy and the D-Day invasion in World War II when the 101st Airborne Division jumped into Normandy? That was a stretch for anyone's imagination, and Dick gave me far too much credit to figure that out. The clue was lost on me.

It was getting harder and harder for me not to ask him questions when we did have a phone conversation, but I had been trained well, since I was a young Army wife, never to ask or talk about sensitive things, like missions or troop movements, on a phone. But it was killing me.

Journal Entry

Have you ever been in the dark about something? It's kind of like in a dream when you're trying so hard to find a way out of something or to figure out something that's nagging at you. You just can't quite put your finger on it, but you know it's important. You sense there might be some danger just around the corner, and yet you have no control over what's coming.

It is hard to be patient, hard to ignore this feeling of mystery, because it involves the person I love most in this world. Then again, so many times in life, we don't get to know the answers ahead of time. Maybe there's a reason for that; maybe knowing what's around the corner is far more stressful than living with the mystery.

15

Each letter from Dick was a small gift, and every time I opened an envelope, it was like opening a window into his life "over there." Whether his news was mundane or exciting, it didn't matter to me, because he was giving me a piece of him. And he ended each and every letter with his love for me.

Some of his letters were more of the same, maybe something he had written about the week before, maybe just a short note on a piece of his blue Expect No Mercy notepaper. Other times, he sent pages about his maintenance philosophy, which by then I knew by heart. We had always been each other's sounding board, and the distance did not change that. We unloaded our feelings, concerns, triumphs, joys, and disappointments in our letters to each other. It ceased to matter how long it took to get a response to a question; when I was reading his letter, I was listening to him, and when I was writing to him, I felt like he could hear me.

There were times when we couldn't help ourselves and wrote things of a sexual nature. Our phone calls were never too intimate, because Dick always had people around him. In a letter, I could be more daring, dropping an innuendo, an insinuation, a come-on. At first, I was too intimidated to write something personal, thinking someone might read it, but then I thought, *So what? We're consenting adults, married for fifteen years, still very much in love; I can say whatever I want in a letter, and if someone other than Dick reads it, too bad!* Not that I would write anything graphic, but since Dick and I expressed every other kind of feeling in our letters, it was just one more way to share some of the intimacy that we were missing out on. Nowadays, people have personal iPhones, even in a combat zone, so they can talk to their significant other regularly and any way they choose: phone sex, sexting, FaceTime. All we had back then was good old-fashioned, handwritten letter sex. One time I mentioned something to Dick in a note, and then, about two weeks later, one of his letters began, "The sky is the limit, Vick. Whatever you want, you got it. . . . I'm all yours!" Because I had written a few letters in between, I couldn't remember exactly what I had asked for or promised him, but whatever it was, the smiley face he drew let me know he was happy.

Dick was using emojis long before they were a smartphone feature with hundreds of options. His letters were sprinkled with smiley faces, and he used them in just the right way. When he wrote something serious that he must have thought would concern me, a smiley face at the end of the sentence was meant to defuse it. And any mention of sex would include a smiley face. It was unexpected and endearing from a guy who was hard-core, tough, and so "hooah."

His letters to Clint and Tyler were a mixture of stories about his Apache helicopters; advice about sports, like "Don't forget to dribble with your left hand"; encouragement about school; and words of love: "Take care of each other. Be good for your mom."

Until that year, I never realized Dick's capacity for writing letters. By October, he was corresponding with a number of schools, and that was above and beyond the letters coming in from his very large family and mine. When he told me of all the letters he was receiving, I realized what a great time manager he was. Anyone who wrote to

Dick got a letter in return. Given his duties and responsibilities as a commander, I couldn't imagine where or how he found the time to write; I could barely manage to send off a letter to him once or twice a week.

Earlier that year, a major motion picture called *Firebirds*, starring Nicolas Cage, Tommy Lee Jones, and Sean Young, had been released. The movie took place at Fort Rucker, Alabama, and highlighted the intense training that Apache pilots go through and the capabilities and use of the newest attack helicopter in the military. It generated a whole new interest and curiosity about Army helicopter pilots, and Apache pilots specifically. Dick, Clint, Tyler, and I were first in line to see the movie, which for Clint and Tyler further validated that what their dad did was very cool. Their love of and fascination with helicopters had begun at an early age, but with the advent of the Apache helicopter, so began their quest to become Apache pilots themselves one day. There was even a toy Apache helicopter with Dick's name on it, based on his Expect No Mercy battalion. By the fall of 1990, when the deployment and Dick's TV interviews were all over the news, Dick became something of a character, right out of a movie. People began writing to him specifically, but also to "Any Soldier, 1-101st Aviation Regiment." The letters were passed on to the soldiers, and pen pal relationships formed.

Two of the teachers who were writing to Dick began to write to me as well. Their efforts had generated an interest beyond their classrooms, and more children and parents wanted to get involved by sending care packages with donated items for the soldiers. These teachers and their classrooms had become invested in Dick, his soldiers, and their welfare.

Dick asked me to send one of his toy Apache helicopters to the class he was corresponding with in Fairlee, Vermont. I received the following letter from their teacher, Judy Hatch.

October 30, 1990

Dear Mrs. Cody,

My class and I would like to thank you for the toy helicopter you sent. When we received the letters from your husband and his soldiers, I called our local TV station. They were excited about our story and sent a film crew to our classroom. As they were filming the children and the letters, which we put on the bulletin boards, your package arrived! It was perfect timing, and they ran the story on the six o'clock news, along with your letter to us!

A few days later, the newspaper wrote a story about the children and the letters. Needless to say, the children are thrilled to have their story in the news.

In our last letters to Commander Cody, we sent pictures of the children and some bright-colored leaves from our trees. I'm sure your husband misses the fall foliage here! We also made a banner and took a picture of the kids holding it and will send that to the unit.

Your husband and his men are truly wonderful for writing to us. The children now have real heroes, and not some silly Teenage Mutant Ninja Turtles from TV! They say the Pledge of Allegiance with meaning and respect now. They know where Saudi Arabia is on the map, and they've been watching the news and reading the newspaper. I can't express the change I've seen in them. They know the meaning of patriotism, thanks to your husband.

We all hope and pray that everyone will come home safely. We are constantly thinking of them.

Thank you again,

Mrs. Judy Hatch

At our next FSG meeting, I read the letter to the wives so they would know about the bonds forming between our soldiers and perfect strangers—a testament to the support and patriotism in our country.

King Fahd Airport

Hi Vicki,

Please excuse the typing. Not trying to be impersonal, but I can get the words out faster and with more clarity when I bang away on this machine. Plus, my hand gets tired from all the letter writing!

How's everything going? Thanks for the packages, I needed everything you sent. The laundry here is slow, and they lose socks, underwear, and T-shirts on a regular basis. I was down to my last pair of undies the other day—not good in these conditions!

My parents sent some gallon jugs of Vermont maple syrup, so our cooks made French toast for everyone. The troops loved it! I get so many packages now, as do all my soldiers. We pass things around and share our goodies, since there is no way to eat all the stuff that comes in.

I am now corresponding with schools in Rhode Island, Kentucky, Indiana, and Vermont. The schoolkids who write to us call us the "Apache guys." God love them—their letters are so cute! They are well informed and quite concerned about the welfare of the soldiers over here. They are fascinated with the military and ask the darnedest, sometimes funny, questions about soldiering, the desert, our mess hall, the tents we live in, camels, and, of course, the Apache. It has been so good for our soldiers to know that they are appreciated and supported by people back home. The soldiers talk about their pen pal friendships and the cute things the kids say and the pictures they draw for them. The letters also give my soldiers a chance to talk about what they do in the Army.

Along with all the schools, there is also a family from California who saw me on the news and wrote to me. They have two boys, so I sent them some of our Apache patches. I'm getting so much mail now that I typed up a letter on the computer with some blank spaces for personal notes, just so I can keep up and still write back to everyone.

You probably saw on the news that they are sending an additional one hundred thousand troops here. They are still arriving, and, from my perspective, we will need them all. The guy to the north (Saddam) missed a golden opportunity last August when we first arrived here. He could've rolled right through us in a few days, as we did not have enough troops or ammo to stop him. He can't do that as easily now, but if he decides to go for broke, he could inflict some major casualties before we defeat him. So we are thankful for the influx of troops!

Got to run and prepare a briefing for the division commander. Take care of yourself, and give the boys a big hug for me. Tell them I will write them tomorrow.

Love you and miss you more each day that we are apart.

Always,

Dick

Journal Entry

We all need human connection, in whatever form it comes in. Essential to our well-being, it fulfills us and lets us know we are not alone. For just a moment, think about what it would be like if you did not have all the technology that connects us today: the ability to call anywhere in the world anytime you wish, to look at the person you are talking to via FaceTime or Skype, to text or email dozens of times per day without even thinking about it. Try to imagine you have only a landline, maybe no answering machine, so if you are out of the house, you might miss a call you've been waiting for from your loved one who is far away. Worse yet, your kids haven't talked to their dad in four months! Your only form of connection is through written letters and an occasional phone call. You do whatever it takes to make it work, so as not to lose that precious connection with your loved one, and somehow that effort fulfills you in a way you never thought it could.

The schoolchildren's letters to the soldiers let them know they are thought of and appreciated, and in return, the soldiers' letters to the children give them a glimpse into another way of life, satisfying a need in both parties and creating that human connection.

Dick's and my letters to each other keep us going, and whether we write of love or pride for each other or share sexual innuendos for a later time, they sustain us when we have nothing else and give us something to look forward to.

16

Dick called our house the week after Thanksgiving, after the boys and I returned from our road trip to Atlanta. He called in the morning, and after we talked for a few minutes, I asked him if he could call back in the late afternoon. I knew it would be after midnight for him, but the boys had not talked to him since he had left in August. Amid their school and sports schedules and the unpredictability of the phones, they had never had an opportunity.

I didn't tell the boys when they got home from school, in case something came up. They were outside, playing with their buddies, filming their next video to send to Dick, when the phone rang. I answered it and then called out the back door, "Boys, your dad is on the phone!"

They came rushing in, out of breath as they reached for the phone. I listened as Clint and then Tyler recounted our recent trip to Atlanta, the basketball players they had met, the autographs and pictures. They each talked about school, soccer season, and the upcoming start of basketball. Each one asked their dad how he was doing and when he thought he would come home, questions about a few of the Dick's pilots who had befriended them, and, of course, how the Apaches were holding up in the desert. They talked for a short while, then handed the phone back to me and raced back outside. I could hear the excitement in their voices as they told their friends who they had just talked to.

I was crying when I got back on the phone. Something about watching Clint and Tyler while they talked to their father dredged up tears just below the surface, the ones that I tried so hard to keep at bay when I talked to Dick. And I swear I noticed a little catch in his voice when he said to me, "Vicki, they sound so grown-up! I don't know what I expected, but I didn't expect them to be so mature about all of this."

"I was thinking the exact same thing as I watched them talk to you. When did our boys become so squared away?'

"We are so lucky, Vick. But I know it has to do with you and how you are handling this situation. Your positive attitude has impacted them."

"I feel like they've grown up overnight, or at least since you left four months ago."

Then we got down to business, talking about Christmas plans, as we never knew when or if we would get cut off and when Dick would be able to call again.

That evening, while eating dinner, the boys and I talked about the phone call with Dick.

"Dad sounded good," Clint said. "Except for that delay when I talked, he sounded like he was somewhere nearby."

Tyler added, "Yeah, I thought he would sound different, but he sounded like Dad."

That phone call in late November was reassuring for all of us; it gave Dick peace of mind that the boys were doing just fine in his absence, and the boys got to hear their dad's voice. They hung on to that pick-me-up for days afterward.

The soldiers whom Dick had sent home for medical reasons were a welcome addition to our rear detachment, and by November, they had settled in nicely. CW3 Mike Dousette took over as rear detachment commander when LT Brown left, and we bonded immediately. I felt as if I had known him for years and could turn to him for anything. Like MSG Cantrell, Mike Dousette was mature, soft spoken, and nonthreatening and seemed to know just how to handle things. In the coming weeks and months, I would need his guidance more than ever. We also welcomed back CW2 Jamie Weeks and SGT Mitchell Brown, affectionately called Brownie.

Dick and I and the boys were especially fond of Brownie. He and Dick played tennis regularly, and then Brownie started coaching and mentoring Clint and Tyler. At twenty-one years old, he was like a big brother to them. When we heard of Brownie's return, the boys and I were thrilled. However, Brownie wasn't as happy about the circumstances.

When he stopped by our house the day he returned, he gave me a big smile, but I could feel the disappointment in his body language when we hugged. He then had to answer my barrage of questions about everything having to do with Dick, the unit, King Fahd Airport, the deployment, Saudi Arabia, the soldiers' living conditions, and anything else he might think would be of interest to me. He was the first and only person of whom I could ask these questions, someone who had actually been there.

"Mrs. Cody, I didn't want to be sent back here. I feel like I let your husband down, and the unit, too."

"Brownie, you know Dick doesn't think that. No one does. You can't help your medical situation. You were really sick, and you need to be back here, where you can get treatment when you need it."

"But the unit is my family and I want to be with them, especially if a war happens over there."

"I understand, but it is what it is. Besides, we can really use your help back here in the rear detachment!"

When the boys came in from school and saw Brownie, they nearly knocked him over as they rushed to hug him. They had quite a few questions as well.

I realized that having Brownie back was like having a little piece of Dick with us. The boys immediately began planning how Brownie could coach basketball and how they could play tennis when the weather was good; it was like a long-lost friend had come home to them.

As we began the month of December, I felt like things had settled down with the wives and our Family Support Groups. Our meetings and gatherings had become routine, and living without our husbands had become the new norm; we were getting by.

The company commanders' wives and first sergeants' wives were doing great things in their companies. Back in October, my B Company commander's wife, Lori Gabram, herself a lieutenant and Army nurse, got orders to deploy with the hospital. I had grown very close to her, as had the wives in her company, and I worried about who would fill the void. But there was always someone willing, and Kay Drew, wife of LT Tom Drew, stepped up and offered to be the representative for B Company. I was so grateful for Kay, a young wife with a baby and also a full-time teacher, who took on the duties and kept things running in that company. I never took for granted the sacrifices that all the commanders' wives (Sandy Parker, Chris Shufflebarger, Susan Garcia, and Bonnie Hodge) and first sergeants' wives (Annie Schon and Sherrie Huenink) made during that time.

So many volunteers gave of their time and energy for the good of our unit, making it enjoyable for me and for many others.

We had mailed the Christmas goody boxes to Dick and to his soldiers before Thanksgiving. The wives and I had been busy all during October and early November, making up the items that would go to all 350 soldiers; we used olive-green Army issue socks as stockings and filled them with toiletries, treats, and little handmade ornaments. Each of the company commanders' wives sent an artificial Christmas tree to every company.

For Dick, the boys and I put together a typical goody box; the only real gift we had for him was a picture of the three of us that we'd had taken at Olan Mills, which I put in a frame. We wrote cards and notes to him. I put in some issues of *Corvette Magazine* (and stashed a couple of *Playboys* in there, too), and the usual underwear, socks, shirts, and toiletries. It wasn't anything special, and it was hard for me not to be able to send something exciting, but it was from the three of us and that was all we could do. Again, I reminded myself that life isn't about material things. Besides, I knew Dick would like the picture of Clint, Tyler, and me.

Just as I did, most of the wives had plans to travel back to their hometowns, so preparing for the holidays gave all of us a nice distraction; I could almost pretend it was going to be a typical Christmas. And, for some reason, I still didn't think the war would start before the holiday.

And then someone at Department of the Army (DA) decided it was time to brief everyone on mass casualties and notification procedures. I thought, *Oh, please don't do this to us now—not right now. Things have been relatively quiet and peaceful; can't we just keep them this way for a little longer?* I'm sure DA wanted to cover that base in case something happened during or right after the holidays, but it was just such poor timing. I felt a heavy weight on my shoulders the minute I walked into the first meeting.

I understood the need for a game plan. I understood that the wives needed to know how the process worked. Back in 1985, when our family was stationed at Fort Campbell, a plane carrying soldiers from the 101st Airborne Division crashed on its way home, killing all 248 soldiers onboard. The Gander crash was the biggest air disaster in military history and the largest loss of life in a single event in the Army. No one saw it coming; there was no plan for such a tragedy. Hundreds of families had gathered in the field house that morning for the welcome-home ceremony. Since the news was already reporting the accident, the leadership knew that they needed to notify the group as a whole, right then and there. They had chaplains and counselors on hand, but most of the wives and children ran from the building, dispersing to their homes. It was the worst possible scenario, and every single one of us learned from that horrible experience. From DA on down to the local level at every Army post, plans for a mass-casualty notification were put in place. But we also needed to understand the notification process on an individual basis.

I met with Mike Dousette at the headquarters before we spoke with the wives. He had the guidelines from DA Casualty Assistance and was required to brief us on certain things. For example, if a soldier is injured, the notification is made by phone; if a soldier dies, the notification is made in person by an officer from the unit and a chaplain. Who is primary next of kin? Who is secondary next of kin? Things of that nature. Just the mention of the terms "casualty assistance" and "notification"—reminders that our spouses were in a dangerous place and of how we would be notified in the event of an accident—was emotional for all of us. It wasn't that none of us ever contemplated that possibility, but hearing someone talk about it out loud made it real.

I anticipated some resistance from the wives, given their varying ages and experience levels, so I asked Mike, "Do we really need to do this right now? You know this will stir up a hornet's nest with the wives."

"I understand, ma'am. And yes, I think we can delay giving out some of this information, as DA has given us until early January. But I suggest we meet now with the commanders' wives and first sergeants' wives to give them a heads-up, give them the basic briefing, and get feedback from them. Then we can proceed from there."

"I agree. Let's wait until early January to meet with the support groups from the individual companies. For this particular subject, I think it will be best to meet in smaller groups."

"Yes, ma'am."

What we couldn't put off, and what we needed from each wife before the holidays, was up-to-date contact information, where they were spending the holidays, and how long they would be gone. Even asking for those details made some people angry, like it was an invasion of their privacy. I didn't get it; I *wanted* the rear detachment to know how to get ahold of me in case of an emergency, especially while the boys and I were away.

I was counting the days until we left for Vermont. I was tired of being in charge of so many people. I just wanted to be me for a while, surrounded by my family.

King Fahd Airport

Hi Vick,
This is the last letter I will send to Kentucky. From here on out, I will send letters to Vermont. I know you and the boys must be getting so excited to go home. I am so glad our families are in the same location and that you can be with all of them at the same time. I know they are all looking forward to seeing you and the boys.

How are you doing? Your letter in one of your recent packages gave me the impression your morale was low. Like you, I have good days and bad days. On the bad days, I think about you and the boys and how I need to get back to the three of you. In order to do that, I have to focus on the job at hand and get my guys and myself ready for what's ahead. Somehow, that gets me through it.

I got all of your Christmas boxes, and also the boxes for the soldiers, so you don't have to worry; everything arrived. I will try and hold off opening until Christmas, but you know how I am!

We sent out the Christmas video that PA [Public Affairs] made of all of our soldiers and their Christmas greetings. It came out really good, and I think the wives will enjoy seeing their husbands. It will go to rear detachment, and they will make copies for each of the companies. You should have that any day now.

We have been doing more live firing and rehearsals. Just want to make sure my guys are ready before we get into the holidays; we can't let our guard down.

I meant to tell you, my crew chief, Spec 4 Bobby Gage, named my aircraft Ol' Rigormortis, and he stenciled it on the outside of the cockpit. Brian and I think it's pretty cool.

I need to go but will write more tomorrow. I have to pre-flight my "bird" before we go out to fly and shoot Hellfires tonight.

Don't worry about me. I always fly safe.

Always,

Dick

Journal Entry

Confronting the "elephant in the room" is always difficult, because most likely the elephant is something that makes you squeamish, that makes your palms sweat and your mouth go dry. Who wants to face something uncomfortable? Nobody. It is far easier to pretend, ignore, and avoid than to face something. But don't you think that by acknowledging and talking about the elephant, you can then work on a game plan, and that just maybe, by having a plan, you will feel some control?

I, for one, do not want to be caught with my pants down when and if the shit hits the fan. I want to think ahead to what I might do, where I would go, how I would manage if something bad happened to my husband. Once I've got my plan, I'll put it away and pray I never have to use it.

17

The 101st Airborne Division, originally an airborne division back in World War II when its troops parachuted into combat, became an air assault division during the Vietnam War, the only one of its kind in the Army. "Air assault" is the term used for a helicopter-borne fighting force; it uses the firepower, mobility, and total integration of helicopters to maneuver on the battlefield. Dick's Apache unit, along with the other attack helicopter battalions in the division, would lead the way for the air assault when the ground war began.

Dick's "day job," and his primary mission with the 101st Airborne Division, was to prepare his unit for the ground war that would probably begin in January or February, given the fact that Saddam had not left Kuwait. Dick's pilots and crew chiefs, every soldier in the unit, had a role to play, as 1-101st's mission was key to the overall success of the division's air assault. They spent their days and nights rehearsing and fine-tuning every aspect of the mission plan for the division.

But at night Dick went to meetings with his other boss at a different headquarters, to plan the highly classified mission that he had named Task Force Normandy—the mission that I would not figure out until much later. Keeping two bosses happy and never compromising one mission for the sake of the other was a lot to juggle for a battalion commander.

Task Force Normandy was classified not only to the world but to most of the Army as well. It was what they call compartmentalized, meaning only those involved were privy to the details of the mission, and even then, you knew only your part in the plan. Dick's brigade commander, division commander, and assistant division commander had been briefed on the mission because they were Dick's immediate chain of command; otherwise, no one else knew about the mission, including Dick's own staff and the rest of 1-101st.

As early as September, Dick had drawn up the mission plans, and by mid-October, he had picked the crews that would be part of it. The mission would require eight Apaches with eight crews of two pilots per aircraft. The difficult part of his decision making did not stem from a lack of talent, as all of his pilots were proficient enough to fly the mission, or from desire, as he knew his pilots would trample each other to be first in line to volunteer for such an undertaking. His dilemma was that he could take only fifteen pilots (besides himself) out of eighty.

Dick's vast experience and years spent in aviation units, and, certainly, all of the accidents he had witnessed, had taught him the importance of crew mix. Crew mix is about pairing the right two pilots to fly together. It is not always the most senior ranking or the pilots with the most flight time that make the right combination; personalities and compatibility figure into crew mix as well. The unit had acquired a number of brand-new pilots the previous year, some of them young warrant officers who had gone from high school to flight school. What they lacked in flight time, they made up for with technical proficiency in all the weapons systems. Having grown up playing video games and using computers, this new generation of pilots was tech savvy beyond their years, and the control panel of the Apache was like one big video game screen.

The four-month training exercise in California the previous year had given Dick the opportunity to observe and fly with each of his pilots, so he had a realistic sense of each individual's strengths and weaknesses. By the time they landed in Saudi Arabia, Dick was comfortable with all of his crew mixes. He had specifically picked Warrant Officer 1 (WO1) Brian Stewmon, one of the pilots who had been in the helicopter accident at Fort Hunter Liggett, to be his copilot, right after the accident. Knowing how traumatic surviving a crash can be, and since Brian was just out of flight school, Dick thought it made sense for the most senior pilot (Dick) to be paired with one of the most junior. When they flew together from California back to Fort Campbell, Dick's instincts proved correct; he and Brian were a perfect fit for each other.

The Apache helicopter is a tandem-seat helicopter, with a front seat for the gunner and the backseat for the pilot doing the flying. Dick was rated in both front- and backseat flying but flew most of his hours in the backseat as the pilot in command. The cockpit is tiny and narrow, even smaller than the inside of an Indy race car. You spend a lot of hours strapped into that small space with your copilot, fostering a bond and closeness that some compare to a marriage. The relationship requires complete trust and synchronization because of the inherent dangers of flying such a complex aircraft.

Knowing that he could not reveal the Task Force Normandy mission ahead of time and that he was sending them into harm's way, Dick selected crews who he was sure would accept the dangers unconditionally. He tried not to think about who in his task force was married or who had kids, because everyone had family. He would take just one of his company commanders with him, leaving the other four behind.

It was a tough call for him, but he could not be in two places at once and he had to consider what might happen back at King Fahd Airport after he did what he was going to do. Since no one knew what repercussions his mission might generate with the enemy, he had to make sure he left behind a strong combat force to ensure that the rest of the unit could carry on in his absence. With his two majors, Killian and Davis, and four strong company commanders back at King Fahd, Dick knew the unit was in good hands.

What was always in the back of his mind as he made his decisions was the promise he had made to all the families back in August: "I will bring everyone home."

Task Force Normandy began rehearsals, and while none of them knew exactly what they were practicing for, they sensed it might be something more than just preparing for a ground war. Living with his soldiers in close quarters, Dick heard the speculation and rumors circulating among not only his Normandy crews but everyone in the unit. They saw their commander coming and going at odd hours, and they knew he was working on something above and beyond the missions for the division. Since the basic mission of any attack helicopter battalion is to provide air support to ground forces, and as the January 15 deadline was approaching, many speculated that Task Force Normandy would be flying cover support for some other unit, maybe an Air Force special-operations mission.

Dick took his Normandy crews to a meeting at SOCCENT in December. When they met COL Johnson for the first time and saw the Air Force special-operations unit in attendance, they knew they had been selected for a highly classified mission, one whose targets they would not see until twenty-four hours before they launched. They also realized the mission was above and beyond the one they were rehearsing with the rest of their unit.

The next and probably biggest obstacle that Dick faced was a logistical one involving the helicopter itself. The internal fuel tank on the Apache holds enough fuel for about two and a half hours. They had a certain distance to cover and would need four to five hours of fuel time, meaning the Apache could not complete the mission with one fuel load. The logical solution was to set up a forward area refuel point halfway to the objective site, where the Apaches could stop and refuel, but Dick and COL Johnson believed that was too risky. It would require involving more people in the equation and sending troops and fuel trucks out into the desert at night, plus the risk of refueling in the dark, all while preserving the element of surprise against the enemy. Dick was adamant: "No way are we doing a refuel point! I will figure out another way, but I will not put my people at even more risk and possibly compromise the mission. End of discussion!"

As a test pilot, Dick always thought outside the box and liked to take things as far as he could with aircraft modifications. If there was a need, he would figure out a way to satisfy it. He had been doing that since he graduated from the test-pilot course as a captain. He loved flying the brand-new Apache helicopter but thought the Army had not tapped into all of its capabilities and full potential. Back in July, before he ever knew of a deployment to the desert, Dick decided to experiment with auxiliary fuel tanks, deploying the unit from Fort Campbell, Kentucky, to Vidalia, Georgia, using an external fuel tank attached to the side of the aircraft, to see the range he could get. It worked, giving him extra fuel time, but he did not know if the auxiliary (aux) tank would work in a combat setting while firing live rockets and missiles and possibly getting shot at. Also, the tank was not crash-worthy.

During a planning session with his Normandy crews, LT Tim DeVito reminded Dick of the tests they had done in Vidalia. After calculating, reconfiguring, and coming up with every possible scenario, LT DeVito came up with a plan for using the external (aux) fuel tank on one side, next to the rockets, and two wing stores for Hellfire missiles on the other side of the aircraft. They were walking a fine line involving weight and balance, but with some adjustments they were sure it could work. The helicopter would have to be test-flown before they let the pilots fly it.

One day in mid-December, Dick and his most senior pilot, CW4 Chip Hall, strapped themselves into the cockpit of the Apache, with approximately 1,500 pounds of jet fuel in the aux tank, sitting in between the rockets and the cockpit, and flew out into the desert. The recommended gross weight of the Apache is approximately seventeen thousand pounds; with the added weight of fuel and weapons, it was almost twenty thousand pounds, which made the aircraft aerodynamically unwieldy. But the test was successful; they fired rockets and missiles without a glitch. I could only imagine the relief that Dick and his copilot felt when all systems worked, the fuel tank did not interfere with the computerized weapons systems, and nothing ignited the tank!

Dick never let on about any of this, not on the phone or in his letters with his innocuous comments about "going out to fire missiles tonight!" He never hinted at the level of danger and the fire that he was literally playing with. And he had the nerve to tell me he didn't take risks? What part of flying out into the desert, with an external fuel tank next to your rockets, in an overweight helicopter, doesn't sound dangerous? If I had known all of this was going on, I would have kicked his ass for being unnecessarily rash. Things could have gone differently that night, before the real mission ever launched, and I could be writing a whole different story today.

However, looking back now, I am glad I was protected through my lack of knowledge, some naiveté on my part, and Dick's blasé attitude. By the time I received his letter, his exploits were history. His successful test flight was the same day the boys and I were flying up to Vermont. I was the happiest I had been in months, getting away from Fort Campbell and all its stresses, and knowing our families were waiting for us.

King Fahd Airport

Dear Vicki,

As I write this letter, you and the boys are on your way to Vermont. I feel good knowing you will be with family for the next two weeks.

Enclosed is an article, "The Case for Destroying Saddam Hussein." I thought it was interesting and right on target. I agree; we need to take this all the way to Baghdad. I don't want Clint and Tyler to have to deal with this someday when they're grown up! I'm ready to get on with the task at hand and do our part to topple this guy's regime!

I've been working on some things and pretty much have them resolved. Remember the Vidalia missions last summer using external fuel tanks? I got permission to do some modifications on the Apache, and it was just the solution we needed. The aircraft is so versatile that no matter what we do to it, it still flies great. I test-flew it and then sent the data back to McDonnell Douglas. They were so excited to see how far we have taken their aircraft. I'm sure every Apache battalion will want to do this now, as it gives us greater capabilities, especially in combat. Fingers crossed that it continues to work for us.

I hope to talk to you when you arrive in Burlington. Have fun skiing. Wish I could be with you.

Love you always,
Dick

Journal Entry

Ignorance really is bliss. I wonder if we sometimes inherently defend ourselves against the scary things in life. Do we really not pick up on clues, or is that our way of protecting ourselves? Or is it God's interven-tion on our behalf?

Dick sure is dropping enough clues that you would think, for a smart girl, I could figure out this puzzle. Maybe deep down inside I don't want to know just yet; maybe it's simply enough right now for me to take care of myself and the boys and the families of Expect No Mercy.

18

Dick grew up in Montpelier, Vermont, and I in Burlington. Because we moved around so much and never put down roots in any one location, Vermont was still our home. It was where the four of us went whenever Dick had leave, or where the boys and I went during Dick's frequent and lengthy training exercises; to be with family in good times and bad. So making the long trip, just the three of us, was not unusual.

But the trip that December 1990 was different. Dick was deployed to a combat zone, and I had no way of getting in touch with him, not even to let him know we had made it to our destination. I was tapped out from dealing with casualty assistance issues and people bickering about why they had to let us know where they were going. Being a single parent is exhausting enough, but I had been carrying an added burden, one of my own doing: I'd been feeling responsible for many other wives and family members. I needed downtime and some nurturing, and I wanted someone else to be in charge for a while. What better place to do that than with my family and Dick's? I knew that seeing them would give me the shot of adrenaline that I needed. And the boys were excited to see their grandparents, aunts, uncles, and cousins. Even though I had seen my mom the previous April, we had not been to Vermont in a year. I had never been so glad to see my parents waiting for us as we got off the plane. *Home at last!*

Soon after we arrived, our first order of business was to visit the elementary school in Fairlee. When I had mentioned to Judy Hatch that we were coming to Vermont for the holidays, she invited my sons and me to visit her classroom and school.

The morning of December 20, the boys, my mom, and I set out on a short road trip and an adventure in a part of Vermont that I had never been to. About two hours southeast of Burlington, the small town of Fairlee (population: 921) sits on the New Hampshire border, just off Interstate 91. Even though I had my mom and the boys to talk to, the drive still seemed to take forever.

"I don't know about you guys, but I can't wait to see this school and meet the kids who have been writing to your dad."

From the backseat, in unison, Clint and Tyler said, "Me, too!"

When we pulled up to the small elementary school, the first thing we saw was a huge banner that read WELCOME, MRS. CODY, CLINT, AND TYLER. Judy Hatch and the children were there and cheered us as we got out of our car. I turned to my mom and said, "Wow, I did not expect this!"

Signs and posters of support for our soldiers lined the hallways. As we entered the classroom, I immediately recognized Dick's hand-writing; letters from him and his soldiers were mounted on the bul-letin boards. At that, I felt tears welling up.

All eyes were on us as Judy introduced us. And then, each student sweetly came up to me and handed me a yellow rose. The class pre-sented my mom with a poinsettia plant. I wanted to wrap my arms around the whole group collectively, right then and there.

"Thank you for your warm welcome and for inviting us to your school," I began. "I can't wait to get to know you and show you the things that I brought with me, but Mrs. Hatch tells me it's time for lunch. I promise as soon as we get back, we'll have time to talk and you can ask me your questions."

In the cafeteria, teachers and administrators came up to me and said, "You're Commander Cody's wife! We are so happy to have you here!"

I don't know what I expected, and certainly my mom and the boys had no clue either, but from the minute we arrived at Fairlee Elementary, we were treated like royalty. A reporter from the local newspaper took pictures and notes, one of the sixth-grade students videotaped our visit, and a film crew arrived later to film a segment for the evening news. I had to chuckle when the boys whispered to me, "Are we famous?"

Back in the classroom, Judy asked me to give the children a brief overview of Army life: the Army post where we lived at Fort Campbell, information about Dick and his soldiers, what it was like in Saudi Arabia, Apache helicopters, and things of that nature.

With a degree in elementary education, I knew how to tailor my talk for third graders, but there was so much I wanted to cover. Assuming they had little frame of reference about Army life, I jumped right in with the basics about living on an Army post, moving frequently, and what my husband's job was. Because I was so passionate about Dick's profession and having Clint and Tyler there with me, talking about our life as an Army family was easy.

I then showed the students a short video that Dick had sent, so they could see him and his soldiers and their living conditions at King Fahd Airport. I told them how much their letters meant to my husband and his soldiers, and how the soldiers shared their letters with each other. Dick had also been sending me rolls of film that I had developed and put in a scrapbook, along with newspaper clippings. The kids gathered around me while I showed them the scrapbook, and they looked at every picture, stopping me if I went too fast.

They also had no trouble asking me rapid-fire questions.

"Does Commander Cody like to fly the Apache?"

"Yes, he loves flying it. He thinks it's the best helicopter he has ever flown."

"How long did it take him to learn to fly it?"

"He was already a pilot, but he went back to flight school for about four months to learn to fly the Apache."

"Do you think there will be a war? When do you think he will come home?"

"I'm not sure what is going to happen, but my husband said he might be gone for a year. We hope it's not that long."

To Clint and Tyler, they asked questions like, "What's it like to have your dad gone for so long? Have you ever been in an Apache? Where have you lived?"

Clint replied, "I miss him a lot, but he has to do his Army job."

Tyler chimed in, "He's gone a lot, but when he's home, we have fun. Sometimes we go to his hangar, and we get to climb in the helicopters. The Apache is so cool."

"Wow, that must be so much fun!"

When the children went to gym class, Clint and Tyler with them, Judy took me around to the other classrooms to meet the teachers, the children, and some parents who had come. I knew that Fairlee was a very small community with no military presence and probably not a lot of diversity, so I wasn't sure what I was going to encounter. Would they be antimilitary, antiwar, and did I represent not only something that was foreign to them but something they did not support? I had a flashback to the negative image of Vietnam soldiers and the war protests of my youth and wondered how I would be greeted, what kinds of questions I would be asked.

Judy interrupted my thoughts and said, "Vicki, these parents are so anxious to meet you. They have never met a lieutenant colonel's wife, so you represent something unique to them. More than a few parents have asked me how they can help, if they can send something to your husband and his men."

My fears were totally unfounded. In each classroom, I was met with kindness and warmth and questions that showed sincerity and curiosity. As I answered them, I thought, *It's the unexpected gifts that give us the greatest pleasure. If only Dick and his soldiers could witness this.* I thanked them for their patriotism and support.

When the day ended and we said our goodbyes, I realized my mood had lifted. After everything that had gone on in recent weeks back at Fort Campbell, the visit to Fairlee put things in perspective for me. I felt the embrace of perfect strangers and witnessed genuine patriotism at a little school in a small town in Vermont. It was a such positive experience, rich in human connection, as my sons and I came out of a very challenging time.

On the ride home, we talked about the day's events. Mom was the first to speak. "Vicki, you know how proud we all are of Dick, but seeing how that school feels about him was really something. I'm so glad I was with you today."

Clint remarked, "Those kids think Dad is a hero. I was surprised."

"Yeah," Tyler said, "they knew all kinds of stuff about Dad and his Apaches. It was pretty neat."

Clint and Tyler had always thought of their dad as *their* hero, but that day they saw him as a hero to other people—people who had never even met him.

Those two weeks in Vermont were just what the three of us needed. It was the usual controlled chaos, with all the buildup and preparation for Christmas: last-minute shopping; driving back and forth from Burlington to Montpelier to see siblings and cousins; spending time with both sets of grandparents. Dick and I were lucky that our families lived just forty-five minutes apart. Our tradition had always been to spend Christmas Eve with my family and Christmas Day with his.

I stayed busy right up until Christmas Eve, but when I took the boys and their cousin Ashley to afternoon Mass at St. Mark's church, a flood of memories, of our wedding and Clint's christening, came rushing to the surface. It was the first quiet and reflective time I'd had since we had arrived in Vermont. As we sat in the packed church, I kept saying to myself, *Do not start crying now. You can do that later!*

That evening, after dinner with my family, I gave the boys their Christmas gift early: new ski equipment. My brother, Dicky, a ski instructor at Stowe, and his fiancée, Patti, who worked at Rossignol, helped me pick out the right skis for the boys. The look of surprise on Clint's and Tyler's faces was a nice distraction, and for a brief moment, things seemed almost normal to us.

Christmas Day was more difficult than I had thought it would be. I had done so well the night before at my parents' gathering, which consisted of my sister and her three daughters, Dicky and Patti, and a couple of my parents' neighbors. It wasn't a big group, and not everyone had a partner, so I didn't feel like the odd person out. But when we got to the Codys' on Christmas morning, there were all of Dick's six siblings, their spouses, and ten grandchildren.

The Cody family is a lively and fun group, not a quiet one in the bunch, and the boys and I were swept up in all the hubbub of their Christmas traditions: downstairs to the basement den to watch all the kids open gifts, then back upstairs for the big meal; then the adults opened their presents.

I had our big video camera up on my shoulder to film the kids. The minute I looked through the viewfinder and took in the scene, all the happy couples watching their children, it was like watching my life without my husband. I could not control the tears that began pouring down my face. I quietly backed out of the room, with the camera still in front of my face, turned, and raced up the stairs.

I lugged that heavy camera up those steps for all it was worth, sobbing and just wanting to get away, but I ran right into Dick's parents, Bob and Jan, who were standing at the top of the stairs. I looked at them and said, "I don't think I can do this." I then saw that Dick's mom was crying as well.

Jan and I went into the other room while Dick's dad went on downstairs. It was the first time in months that I let myself give in to what I was feeling, which was that everyone there had their loved one except me, even as I wondered, *How in the world can I feel lonely when I'm surrounded by family?*

Dick's mom was no stranger to the dangers of Dick's career choice. His parents had worried about him and felt all the same stresses that I had over the years and through many separations and deployments. But until that day, I don't know if I had ever stopped to think about what it was like for a mother to send off her son.

"Jan, I can only imagine what this must be like for you," I said. "You have your whole family downstairs, but one of them is gone. It must be really difficult."

"When you came rushing up the stairs, I had just said to Bob, 'I don't know how I will get through today.'"

"That's exactly how I feel!"

"Vicki, all we can do is pray. It's in God's hands, and I truly believe Dick will be okay; he is so strong and capable."

Dick's family had a strong sense of faith; his parents attended daily Mass. I knew Jan was right, and it was comforting to know that she understood how I was feeling in that moment. We dried our tears and joined the group downstairs. Amid all the excitement and activity, they hadn't even realized I'd been gone.

Clint and Tyler held up their gifts to show me. "Mom, look what we got!"

"Wow, this is so cool! Thanks, Nana and Doo!"

And then it was okay. Christmas was still going on with or without me, and certainly without Dick, but I was surrounded by love. Period.

King Fahd Airport

Dear Vicki,

Merry Christmas! I'm sending this letter early to Vermont so you will have it on or around Christmas Day. I'm sorry this is all I have for you this year, but I'm sending it with all my love. You are my best friend in the world, always have been, always will be! I doubt I would be as successful as I am without your love and support.

The tape of you and the boys is great. I have watched it over and over! You all look so good. I'll try to make one to send you guys.

I wanted you to know that everyone who writes me tells me what a great job you're doing. I never doubted you; you've always handled whatever the Army threw at you. I am so proud of you, especially for taking care of the families in the unit. You are a special lady.

I hope you and the boys have a good time with your family and mine. I'll call my parents' house on Christmas Day. Give my love to your parents, Chris, and Dicky. I love you and miss you every minute of every day.

Always,
Dick

Journal Entry

We can't be strong all the time. We can fake it—suppress, deny, and avoid our emotions—for only so long. Eventually, there is a trigger, a tipping point, and it all comes pouring out. My tipping point was when I looked through the lens of the camera and saw the scene for what it was. In that moment, there was no denying my situation. I was just glad I had somewhere to run to; I did not want to be "that person" who put a damper on everyone else's happiness.

It's okay to "take a knee" sometimes. Admit that you need a time-out, a shoulder to lean on; then readjust and move forward. Trust me, you'll feel better for it!

19

I had known the Cody family since I was sixteen years old. When Dick and I met, in 1969, his oldest sister, Diane, was just out of college and his brother Bill was my age and in high school. The younger siblings, Cathi, Robin, Bobby, and Lauri, ranged in age from six to thirteen years old, so I watched them grow up. By 1990, they were all married, and most had kids of their own. I shared a lot of history with the family, and what I always loved most about their dynamic was the way they all looked up to their brother Dick.

When he called on Christmas afternoon, the phone was passed around to everyone. I watched his parents and each sibling talk to him, and I heard the uncertainty and fear in their voices. They were uncharacteristically subdued and serious. As each handed the phone to the next one, I saw their tears.

The boys and I took our turns, and then I went upstairs to talk on another phone. I had never felt so overcome with emotion. I rarely cried on the phone to Dick, as I knew it did no good for either one of us, but that day I couldn't help myself.

"I'm sorry I'm crying, Dick. I've been so emotional all day."

"That's okay, Vick. I know this is hard, and I'm sorry there's nothing I can do to change it or make it better."

"It's not your fault. It's loneliness; it's my fears; it's what we're facing in the coming weeks; it's not wanting to hang up because I never know when I'll talk to you again. It's a million little things, and at the same time it's only one thing: I just miss you."

"I feel the same way. I'd give anything to be there with you and the boys."

I decided to change the subject. "How was your day? I know it must have been lonely for all of you there. Did you get a decent meal?"

"The chaplains got together and did a nondenominational service this morning, and then the mess hall had a big meal for us in the afternoon. Under the circumstances, it was fine. I'm so glad you were able to get the boys' ski equipment! They sounded excited when I talked to them. Thank your brother and Patti for helping with that. When do you think you'll go skiing?"

"We hope to go two or three times, weather permitting. We made plans to take Cousins Jason and Todd with us."

We talked longer that day than we had the entire time Dick had been gone. I can't imagine how much that phone call cost his dad, but it sure was nice to have privacy and no time limit. I was doing better by the time we hung up.

That Christmas Day, I took a knee more than once. In fact, I took enough knees for the entire family. Each time I did so, I got back up and wiped my tears, and by evening I was finished with my pity party. While the kids ran around and played with their new toys and the grown-ups sat by the fireplace, Dick's brothers, Bill and Bobby, entertained us with hilarious stories about their big brother, Dick. We ended the day on a high note, our sides aching from laughter.

Skiing with the boys also helped me get over the whole psychological Christmas hurdle. It was a huge part of our lives, and so good for the soul.

Ringing in the new year was anticlimactic. I spent the night with my sister, Chris, while our parents took care of our kids. After dinner out and an early movie, we had big plans for girl time: stay up late, play cards, do our nails, and catch up on everything. The reality was, we fell asleep by nine thirty. But that was okay, too, because I didn't care about watching the ball drop at Times Square and seeing everybody kiss their partner. I just wanted to get through the last of the holidays and get on with 1991, sensing how much lay ahead for me and my children and the rest of our country.

A few days prior to our departure, I was in Montpelier and had a conversation with Dick's brother, Bill, hoping to see if he knew what Dick was up to. We had gone to Cody Chevrolet, the family dealership, to look at a Corvette I'd seen. Like Dick, Bill had graduated from West Point, but he had served his commitment and then gone back to Montpelier to help run the family business. It was after-hours, so Bill, my boys, two of his sons, and I were the only people there. The kids ran around while he and I talked about the car and how I could get it and surprise Dick when he returned home.

"I have this feeling Dick is going to do something dangerous and out of the ordinary, but I don't understand and can't figure out what it is," I said to Bill.

"I know, Vicki. I get the same feeling. He has alluded to something and keeps saying to watch the news; he said that again when we talked the other day."

"Bill, I haven't said this to anyone, but I'm so afraid something will happen to him."

"I know you're worried, but Dick is the best in the business. He's a tough guy, and he'll be okay. But I have no clue what he is up to."

I had not admitted to anyone else that I was afraid for Dick. I didn't want to worry our parents, but saying it out loud to his brother that night was like admitting it to myself.

Saying goodbye at the Burlington airport was never easy. All of my family were there. My mom was crying, and my dad had a worried look on his face. I know they wanted to help me, shield me, all the things a parent wants to do for their kid, but they couldn't. No one could. When we hugged, I kept saying to them, "It will be okay. We'll be okay. Try not to worry about us. I can handle this." As I walked away from them, I had that feeling of being totally on my own again. I talked a good game for their benefit, but deep down I was shitting bricks.

Weirdly, I couldn't wait to get away from Fort Campbell and be with my family, but after two weeks, I was anxious to go back to Kentucky. While we were in Vermont, I worried many times that something would happen in Saudi Arabia while I was disconnected from my safety net, far away from my Army post and my Army family. I wanted to be with people who were going through the same thing I was.

The good thing about getting away is that it gives you a fresh perspective. I felt reenergized and ready to help our rear detachment commander finish up the last of the notification/mass-casualty briefings for the wives. In early January, Mike Dousette and I went to each of the company FSG meetings. I steeled myself, figuring those gatherings would stir up emotions among the wives. For the most part, they were receptive and compliant, but in every meeting there were one or two wives who just didn't want to accept the what-ifs. And that was really what we were talking about: What if something happened?

I sat back and observed Mike as he explained the procedures, in his gentle and nonconfrontational way, and then handed out information sheets. He asked the wives to fill out the sheets with their religious preferences, including the name of a specific priest, rabbi, or chaplain whom they would want to have with them in a crisis, and also the name and number of a close friend or relative nearby whom they could call for support. We also reiterated that we needed to know how to contact the wives if they traveled somewhere. Because of what had happened during the Gander crash, when we'd had none of that information, we knew how critical those first minutes and hours are after a notification occurs.

One wife tossed the papers back at Mike and declared, "Do not come to my house to tell me that something has happened to my husband! I will not answer the door!"

I decided it was time to speak up. "Listen, I'm in this just like you all are. None of us wants to talk about this or think about something happening to our husband. But we need to know certain things, just in case. That's all this is—information that we *might* need someday— and providing it doesn't mean something bad will happen. It should make you feel like you have a little bit of control should you ever need assistance."

"Well, I'm not going to answer my door if you come."

"The reality is, if something happens to your husband, someone *will* call you or come to your door. Wouldn't you rather hear it in person than see it on the TV?"

"I'm not going to answer my door."

This woman was obviously going to get the last word in, so I let it go, but I was thinking, *Now is not the time for childish and stubborn behavior. Can't we just get through this?*

For many of the wives, it was the first time they were facing certain truths, so some of them were crying. Much as I wanted to cry right along with them, I was more pragmatic. Maybe because I'd had more experience dealing with life and death in an Army setting, I had become good at compartmentalizing. From the time Dick had graduated from flight school, and in every aviation unit we'd been in, we'd seen what could happen in an instant: crashes and accidents that involved deaths. We lost so many friends in the '80s that whenever the phone rang at night, I feared the worst. But early in our marriage, I came to grips—I had no choice—with the reality of being married to an Army aviator. I forced myself to face it, as scary as it was. And now, all these years later, I was having to revisit those scary thoughts while seeing them through the eyes of the young wives in our unit. As a commander's wife and mother figure, I hurt like they did, and I hated that they had to confront something so unsettling. I never wanted to see them cry. During that meeting, any feelings of rejuvenation that I'd had after our trip to Vermont evaporated, leaving me feeling extra vulnerable.

One day over lunch, Gail and I talked about the notification briefings and how our wives were handling it. Gail and I always had such fun together, finding humor in just about anything. She was not one given to emotional displays and always had a steady demeanor, but the serious look on her face let me know that she was scared.

"Vicki, do you realize that if something happens, like a large assault on our ground troops, Tom could lose lots of soldiers—like, maybe hundreds?"

"I know, Gail. I know how dangerous it is for the troops on the ground, and I worry about Tom and his unit. It's different for Dick and his guys. They can get shot down or crash, but unless there's a chemical attack or their tactical area gets overrun, aviation units have fewer casualties."

"What will I do if we have dozens of casualties all at once?"

"Gail, I promise I will be there if you need me. I will do anything to help you, if it comes to that."

We were quiet. Then I looked at my friend and said, "Who would've thought we would get to this point, where we would be talking about this subject?" I just couldn't stop wondering, *When did life get so serious?*

King Fahd Airport

Hi Vicki,

It was great talking with you, the boys, and my whole family. I'm sorry you had a rough time on Christmas Day. Believe me, it was no picnic over here! We just have to remind each other that we love each other and that we'll get through this, no matter how rough it gets.

My mom and dad were bragging to me about Clint and Tyler and how grown-up they are and how well they're handling my absence. They loved seeing your interview on the local news! I'm so glad you went to Fairlee; thank you for taking the time to do that. I'm sure it meant so much to Judy Hatch and all the kids.

I can't tell you much about what's going on here, but I think you can read into what Secretary Cheney and General Powell have been hinting at and advising the President on. We are very concerned about OPSEC right now, especially since the phone banks are back up and running. So when I do call, do not ask me anything! I try to give you hints in my letters. One thing I can tell you: My pilots and I will earn our air medals and combat patches! We are ready and focused, and I feel good about our role.

I better get going. I'll write more later. Take care, and don't worry about me.

Love you and miss you,
Dick

Journal Entry

When we face a really big challenge in life, we're lucky if we get to take it in in increments. That way, we can accept it and get used to it one dose at a time. But we don't always have the luxury of time, and sometimes we get hit with the full brunt of an event all at once, with no warning.

I'm glad that we were given the installment plan for this event; we've had five months to get used to the idea of war. It could have started in August, the minute our husbands got off the plane, when they had no backup and we wives were not prepared, but it didn't. We got used to their leaving and to being on our own. Next, we figured out how to communicate when we had hardly any options, and then we got through the holidays. I'm surprised that we've adapted, but we have. And now we're forcing ourselves to think about mortality. Again, we're processing that and preparing ourselves for the next increment: war.

20

The newspaper headlines were enough to scare anyone, especially those with a loved one deployed to Operation Desert Shield. Throughout December and into January, the top news stories were all about impending war:

"Bush Warns Saddam: 'United States Poised for War.'"

"'We're Ready Now,' Says Schwarzkopf."

"Congress Allows Bush to Wage War."

By mid-January, the headlines were even more alarming:

"War? Only God Knows."

"Iraq on Borrowed Time."

"Saddam Assails Bush, Fahd, Warns of Holy War If Attacked."

With each passing day and each new headline, my feelings of dread grew worse. So I did what I always did when things felt out of my control: I took control of what I could—my little piece of the world. For me, that meant housekeeping: tidying up my house and also taking care of loose ends within our FSGs. Once the briefings were finished and only a fraction of the wives had attended, I told myself that I— we—had done all we could to prepare. I couldn't hold everyone's hand. I checked in regularly with the company commanders' wives, who in turn checked on their wives. After the intensity of the recent briefings, it sounded like everyone was quiet and hunkered down.

Then I got the flu and was forced to stay in the house for a few days. I was exhausted, both by my illness and from all the negativity and talk of war. We commanders' wives had meeting after meeting to attend, and I began to feel as if they were generated just to give us something to do, but they were redundant. Getting sick was my body's way of telling me, *Enough!* Secretly, I was glad, because I had that nesting feeling and all I wanted to do was be home with my boys and wait for January 15.

Dick was doing the same thing I was, only with big global ramifications. He was putting the finishing touches on his mission, checking on his guys, getting daily weather and intelligence (intel) briefings, and waiting for the go-ahead. On January 10, Task Force Normandy conducted their final rehearsal. There was nothing more for them to do.

And then he called on January 12, a Saturday afternoon. I thought that was unusual, because he usually called on weekdays. Luckily, the boys and I were home because I was still too sick to take them anywhere. I always let them talk to their dad first; it gave me a few minutes to collect my thoughts. Since I never knew when Dick would call, I liked to have at the ready my questions and the things I wanted to tell him.

The boys were looking forward to the start of basketball, and that was most of their conversation.

"Dad, we start practice next week. Guess who my coach is? Brownie!" Tyler said. Clint was equally excited about his coach, Tyrone, another soldier from our rear detachment.

The boys finished talking, and then I got on. Dick sounded great, like nothing big was going on. Just days away from President Bush's January 15 deadline, I was stressed to the max and just wanted to get the show on the road. I couldn't figure out how he could be so calm, given the situation, but thank goodness he was, because if I had known ahead of time that he was calling to say goodbye, I might have come unglued.

I knew that I could not ask him any questions about what he was up to, so instead we chatted about normal things, like the kids, school, and sports. But then his voice turned serious and he said, "Vicki, I might not be able to call for a while." He paused and then added, "I need you to take the motorcycle out of the garage."

Boom! A jolt of reality hit me. He had used our code words, the ones we had come up with back in 1980 when he went on his clandestine mission with Ned Hubard. We hadn't spoken those words in ten years. I don't recall even talking about our code before he left that August. He knew I would never forget it, and I hadn't, but it came out of the blue, and it meant he was going somewhere to do something dangerous.

In that moment, I thought, *Okay, Vicki, this is not a surprise; you've been wondering about something like this for months. You know what you need to do.* I replied, as nonchalantly as possible, "Okay. I just wish I knew why."

"Just watch the news."

"Hey, Dick, you know you don't have to prove anything to me. I'm proud of you, enough for a lifetime. Promise me you'll be careful."

"You know I always am, Vick."

I couldn't just leave it at that, though. I had to defuse the situation. So, I added, "Dick Cody, you better not let anything happen to you, because I will kick your ass when you get home!"

We both burst out laughing. At that very moment, what else could we do? I had had my fill of seriousness, and I sensed he had as well. We always had the ability to laugh, at ourselves and with each other, and that day was no different. I had a sinking feeling that this was more than a typical goodbye but was determined to sound normal. "Fly safe, Dick. I love you!"

"I love you, too."

I hated to hang up, wanting to linger a little longer, but there wasn't much left to say. My mind was telling me, *There's no need to drag this out. He's got a lot on his plate, and you don't want to make it more difficult than it already is.*

When I went into the den, the boys were watching TV and acting like nothing was out of the ordinary. I took my cues from them, thinking I would process my conversation with Dick later, when I went to bed. We put a movie in the VCR and escaped into one of our favorites, *Adventures in Babysitting*.

In bed that night, I felt calm, like I had when Dick first deployed. I knew I was approaching another hurdle and was curious to see what it was; I hoped to get some answers to the questions and speculation that had been crowding my thoughts for too long. I still believed that Task Force Normandy was a mission "in support of" an Air Force mission. I never dreamed that Dick's mission was *the* mission.

For the next three days, I did nothing but clean the house. Coming out of my sickbed, I just wanted to get everything in my life in order. I baked and cooked, cleaned closets and mopped floors. I worked until I was exhausted. But I always had the TV volume on high so I could hear any breaking news while I was in another room.

My phone rang continually throughout those days. People from all parts of our life—family and friends, both Army and civilian— were calling to check in with me. Each one asked the same questions: "Does Dick think there will be a war? When will it start?"

I speculated right along with them, talking about the latest head-lines and saying I thought the war would begin sometime soon. But I was always careful about what I said on the phone and never revealed that Dick had called me to say goodbye. I could hear his voice in my head saying, "Vicki, remember OPSEC!"

I didn't know that when Dick called us that day, he and his crews had just come from the final mission brief with COL Johnson at

SOCCENT. Also in attendance were Dick's brigade commander, COL Tom Garrett, and division commander, MG Peay, who had yet to be briefed on the exact details of Dick's mission. The mystery of what Dick had been planning and what he and his crews had been training for came to light as he briefed the mission's basic details and timeline. What he omitted were the actual targets; that information would come later. But it was enough for everyone present to know that it was a history-making mission and the most dangerous one the flight crews would ever go on.

Then COL Johnson addressed Dick and his crews: "I was part of a failed mission in Iran, back in 1980, that ended in disaster. I will not allow that to happen again. There is no room for error, no room for failure; too much is riding on this, and too many lives are at stake. I have guaranteed General Schwarzkopf 100 percent, and that is what I need from each one of you. If you are not willing to die to complete the mission, raise your hand now."

The room fell silent as reality set in, but no one raised his hand.

As the meeting was coming to a close, COL Johnson took Dick aside and privately told him, "I need you and the task force in place no later than the fourteenth."

"Roger that, sir!"

Dick's division commander, MG Peay, walked over to him and said, "You're going to do it, Dick. The 101st legend continues. Start the war, but don't be the first casualty!"

King Fahd Airport

Hi Vicki,

Happy New Year! I hope the rest of your time in Vermont was good for you and the boys. I feel so grateful that we have family we can depend on to help us get through these times. Everyone back home is so impressed with the way you have weathered this storm and how well you have brought up the boys in my absence.

Every day that you are in Vermont, I try to imagine what you are doing and where you are. I sure wish I was there with you all. How was the skiing?

This has been a tough deployment for us, but I have to think that it's for a higher reason, something bigger than we are, and that we will be better for it. You need to know that I am firmly committed to getting every one of my guys, including me, through this thing and home safe. This is such an important mission. Like I said before, I do not want my sons to have to face this when they grow up. The world is at a critical juncture. All of the third-world, heavily armed countries and nations need to know without a doubt that the US and the United Nations will not tolerate a dictator taking over another country.

It's been a long day, one headache after another. Sometimes I get so tired of being caught in the middle between two competing headquarters. I just want to do what I'm supposed to do, without all the politics! I am keeping a journal, taking good notes. This will make one hell of a book someday!

I better go for now; I need to get some sleep.

I love you and miss you, and I will come home to collect on all those promises you made!

Dick [smiley face]

I was still getting letters that Dick had written to me during the holidays, so I could almost pretend that nothing was amiss. I continued my daily routine, but the knot in my stomach was the size of a baseball.

Journal Entry

Sometimes you reach a point where there is nothing left to say. Every part of you is telling you to hang on a bit longer, but at the same time you know what you need to do: let go gracefully. It's the right thing to do.

I did not want my last conversation with Dick, regardless of the outcome, to involve me crying or whining about the situation at hand. Whatever he's up to, he needs to be completely focused, with no excess baggage from me. For the record, I stepped up to the plate that day, in a big way. I did it for Dick, but I also did it for me. I needed to know that when things got tough, I could be counted on.

Dick takes command of 1-101st Aviation Regiment
(Expect No Mercy) June 1989, Sabre Army Airfield,
Ft. Campbell, KY, courtesy 101st Public Affairs

Receiving line at Dick's Change of
Command ceremony, courtesy 101st
Public Affairs

Dick with his mother, Tyler and Clint,
courtesy Vicki Cody

Dick on the flight line at KFIA, Saudi Arabia,
August 1990, courtesy Dick Cody

Dick talking to his soldiers at their new "home" in the unfinished parking
garage at KFIA, Saudi Arabia, Aug. 1990, courtesy Dick Cody

Dick in his room/office, a closet in the parking garage at KFIA, courtesy Dick Cody

Mail drop box at Camp Hell, Saudi Arabia,
courtesy Dick Cody

Dick and the "Expert No Mercy" basketball team at
KFIA, courtesy Dick Cody

Dick and Tim De Vito having just received their tennis
rackets, ready for a match at KFIA, courtesy Dick Cody

Dick and his soldiers enjoying a game of cards on a
"no boot day," courtesy Dick

The boys and I, our Christmas gift to Dick, courtesy Olan Mills

Banner made for Dick and his unit by Mrs. Hatch's third grade class at Fairlee
Elementary School in Vermont, courtesy Judy Hatch

Gathering at my house for FSG leaders Front row from left: Sandy Parker, unknown, Bonnie Hodge, Sherry Heunink, me, Susan Garcia, Lori Gabram Back row: Annie Schon, unknown, Denise Davis, Carolyn Killian, Kay Drew. Missing from photo Chris Shufflebarger, courtesy Vicki Cody

Me with First Lady Barbara Bush, February 1991, Ft. Campbell, KY, courtesy White House

Task Force Normandy on the afternoon of Jan. 16, 1991, Al Jouf Airfield, Saudi Arabia   courtesy Dick Cody

TF Normandy sand table rehearsals prior to the mission,
courtesy Dick Cody

TF Normandy sand table rehearsals,
courtesy Dick Cody

Dick with his company commanders and staff before the war
Front row from left: Major Killian, Dick, Major Davis
Back row: Captains Garcia, Gowen, Parker, Shufflebarger,
Gabram, and Hodge, courtesy Dick Cody

Dick with his crew chief Spec 4 Bobby Gage and co-pilot WO1 Brian Stewmon,
standing next to Ol' Rigormortis, courtesy Dick Cody

Dick with West Point classmates, Tom Greco and Bob Van Antwerp;
just after the cease fire in northern Iraq, courtesy Dick Cody

Dick and Tom Greco

Welcome Home at Campbell Army Airfield, Spec 4 Mitchell (Brownie) Brown
in background, April 6, 1991, courtesy Bill Cody

Dick's welcome home gift, courtesy Vicki Cody

Receiving the Commander's Award from MG and Mrs. Peay, DCSM
and Mrs. Weiss on the left, courtesy 101st Public Affairs

After Dick's change of command, June 1991,
courtesy Vicki Cody

Clint next to his Apache, September 2001, Ft. Rucker, AL,
courtesy Clint Cody

Tyler next to his Apache, Iraq 2003, courtesy Tyler Cody

Clint and Tyler, northern Iraq, 2003, courtesy Tyler Cody

Clint and Scott Greco, Iraq 2003, courtesy Clint Cody

Dick promoting Clint to CPT in Iraq, 2003, courtesy Dick Cody

Dick and Tyler next to Ol' Rigormortis, Ft. Campbell, KY, 2005,
courtesy 101st Public Affairs

21

On January 14, nine Apaches and a Blackhawk took off from the safety of their parking garage "home" at King Fahd International Airport. Task Force Normandy was headed to Al Jouf, a staging area in northwestern Saudi Arabia, approximately 640 nautical miles (nm) away and approximately 100 nm south of the Saudi–Iraqi border. It would be their "safe house" while they awaited their final orders.

Task Force Normandy was made up of two teams of four Apaches. The White Team was led by LT Tom Drew with CW2 Tim "Zeke" Zarnowski, LTC Dick Cody with WO1 Brian Stewmon, CW2 Thomas "Tip" O'Neal with CW3 Dave Jones, and CW3 Ron Rodrigues with CW2 David Miller. The Red Team was led by CPT Newman Shufflebarger with CW3 Tim Roderick, WO1 Jody Bridgforth with CW3 Jim Miller, WO1 Tim "Vinny" Vincent with CW2 Shaun Hoban, and WO1 Jerry Orsburn with CW4 Chip Hall.

Dick had added the ninth Apache for backup just in case something went wrong, and a Blackhawk helicopter, nicknamed *Goodwrench*, loaded with tools, spare parts, mechanics, sleeping gear, and MREs.

There had always been a special camaraderie among the Expect

No Mercy soldiers; other units saw it, felt it, and envied it but could not describe it; it just was. The days leading up to their departure, a tremendous energy overtook 1-101st as everyone did their part in getting the task force prepared and ready to launch. The crew chiefs inspected every inch of their aircraft—not just the ones that were leaving, but all of the aircraft—in preparation for an inevitable war. They weren't sure when they would have to move out with the division to their FOBs. And now that Dick was leaving, the soldiers were apprehensive about where he was going and why and when he would return. Sensing this, and because, as their leader, Dick believed that trust and respect worked both ways, he made a risky decision to let them in on as much as he felt was necessary.

At their afternoon formation on January 13, far away from any other units, Dick gathered his battalion around him and told them to take a knee.

"I am leaving tomorrow with Task Force Normandy. We will be gone for about four days. Because I have complete faith and trust in each of you, I am going to entrust you with some information. But you need to understand how serious this mission is and what is at stake. You cannot tell anyone what I tell you—it will put our lives in danger. For the next few days, I need you all to stay together here in our area. Don't go over to the other units, and don't talk with your buddies there; you can talk amongst yourselves here. I don't care what you hear, what questions anyone asks you—you can't talk about this. I am counting on each one of you, and I know I can trust you." He then gave them a sanitized briefing of the mission and concluded, "When we get back, we will all prepare for the next phase of this deployment. Expect No Mercy!"

The next morning, as Dick and his two teams flew over the sprawling tent city that was home to the eighteen thousand soldiers of the 101st Airborne Division, those on the ground were oblivious to the history-making aviators on their way to the division's next "rendezvous with destiny." If they heard the hum of the blades and looked up to the sky, they saw nothing out of the ordinary. Hundreds of aircraft flew into and out of KFIA daily. There was nothing to clue them in to what was different about that particular formation of helicopters and what was going to take place in a matter of days. It was just another day, just another flight of helicopters going out for some training. And that was exactly what Dick wanted them to think.

But the soldiers of 1-101st knew differently. As they watched their commander and fellow soldiers fly away, they felt like a vacuum had sucked the energy out of the battalion, if only for a short while. However, it wasn't as if everyone could sit around and goof off just because the boss, the "old man," was gone, so it was back to work, business as usual. In Dick's absence, Major Mike Davis, the ranking officer, was in charge of the battalion. For a major, that was a huge responsibility, even under ordinary circumstances. Now that Dick was gone and the air war was about to begin, Mike Davis would have to keep the battalion prepared and focused for a possible retaliatory strike.

If, in fact, the air war was beginning on or around January 15, no one could predict what Saddam Hussein might do. Would he retaliate with an attack against the 101st Airborne Division? The division counted on 1-101st and its twenty-four Apaches for critical air support. The absence of nine of them for four days left the division vulnerable, which was why Dick's bosses, Garrett and Peay, had to know what he was doing. They wanted reassurance that he would return as soon as possible from the mission to support the division.

I've often wondered what was going through Dick's mind as he took off that day, leaving the rest of his battalion behind. The unit was his family—the soldiers were like sons to him—but he had a mission to do and couldn't be in two places at once. Knowing him like I do, I'm sure the minute he took off, he was laser focused on what was ahead—not what was behind. He has a keen ability to make decisions and not look back—no second-guessing, no regrets. I, on the other hand, would have had a million thoughts swirling through my head: *Did I teach my soldiers everything they need to know to survive? Did I tie up all the loose ends? How will my soldiers manage if something happens to me? Did I select the right crews to take with me?* I would also be worried about pressing matters like where and when my next meal would be; the accommodations at our destination and whether they would include a bed, pillows, and bathrooms; and if I would get my coffee in the morning. I probably would have had a migraine from the pressure of the situation. Plus—and this was the biggest reason why I could never be in the Army—I would have been shaking-in-my-boots afraid.

It was cold and rainy that day, with heavy showers and less than a mile of visibility—not the best conditions to fly in. The flight to Al Jouf would take approximately seven hours, with a stop partway to refuel. The men flew low, using no radios, to avoid detection from not only enemy radar but coalition forces as well. They landed at King Khalid Military City (KKMC) to refuel, completely unannounced. A large number of helicopters already operated out of KKMC, so the Apaches did not look too out of place.

After a quick stop, they were back in the air for the final leg of their journey. They flew west, even though it was a restricted area at that point. No units or flights were allowed west of KKMC—almost like a "no fly" zone. US and coalition forces had not yet moved that far west, so anyone who flew in that area would be unprotected from the enemy, not to mention ill equipped if they had a mechanical problem and had to put the aircraft down. The United States did not want anyone near the Iraq border until it was time. But Dick and his task force were immune to any of those rules because of their mission.

It was another four hours to Al Jouf, and now they flew even lower, nap of the earth. "Nap of the earth" (NOE), used in high-threat areas, means flying very low, using geographical features like valleys and folds as cover, and flying with the terrain, rather than over it. Because they were getting closer to the Iraq border and worried about radar there, they flew NOE.

If they thought the desert and the area surrounding KFIA was desolate, the western part of Saudi Arabia was even more so. There were no towns, no villages, nothing but mile after mile of monotonous, flat desert terrain and an occasional camel. When they were 100 nm west of KKMC, Dick made a radio call to each flight crew and instructed them to test their lasers and fire some of their weapons, just to make sure all systems were working. They must have felt the same relief Dick had back in December, the first time he tested the weapons systems with the Apaches' new configuration and auxiliary fuel tanks.

They rolled into Al Jouf at about 5:00 p.m., making just one radio call on their approach to land. Al Jouf was a one-runway forward staging base, with a tower and taxiways. The Air Force had taken over the few buildings there and would be using it as a staging area for search-and-rescue helicopters once the air war started. After Dick and his crews secured their aircraft just off the runway, a couple of unmarked trucks came and took them to a small compound where civilian contractors had once lived.

Their accommodations were less than ideal. What they had been told were nice billets were actually just small concrete huts with a kitchen and a bathroom. No hot water, no beds or furniture, just a couple of folding chairs. They would sleep in sleeping bags, ten to a room. Someone remarked that at least there was a toilet, a real luxury for them. But the real slap in the face came when they were told there was no security and that they would have to secure their own area, taking shifts during the night. It was comical to them; there they were, about to embark on a history-making mission, and they couldn't even get a good night's sleep and a hot meal.

That evening, after they had cleaned out their huts and settled in,

Dick came in with LT Russ Stinger, the S-2 (battalion intelligence officer) who had come with them to Al Jouf. Dick and Russ were carrying maps and folders and spread everything out on the floor. Dick handed each pilot his target folder. The men of Task Force Normandy realized that they were finally going to find out where they were going. They devoured their folders, which included exact targets, locations, flight routes, code words, satellite photos, intelligence updates, and a joint operations mission brief. The whole enchilada was right there for them to feast on. LT Stinger had done an amazing job gathering and preparing all of the intel data, the most critical piece of the mission. It was completely quiet in the room as Dick watched his pilots absorb the material in their folders.

They then gathered around two large sand tables on the floor, one for each target. Dick talked and answered questions, and the pilots made comments as they began practicing scenarios using the new information they had. The sand tables were exact replicas of the topography of their target sites, complete with buildings, structures, even vehicles. A few of them remarked that their folders and the sand tables looked exactly like what they had been rehearsing for months back at KFIA, but in practice, they'd been shooting at structures; now, it looked like they would be shooting at radar sites. It dawned on them that since the war had not yet begun and there had been no shooting, maybe it was on them to *start* the shooting. They made the connection between Task Force Normandy and the 101st Airborne's Normandy invasion in World War II. By taking out critical radar sites, Task Force Normandy would fire the first shots and officially start the Gulf War, and with that, Operation Desert Shield would become Operation Desert Storm.

Seeing the full weight of the mission register on each of their young faces, knowing what he was asking of them, Dick figured he should give them a few minutes alone to digest what he had just unveiled to them.

"I'm going outside to smoke a cigar," he said. "If anyone wants out of the mission, join me outside. No questions asked."

He stood outside the hut, wondering if anyone would appear. He also realized he did not have a cigar and began pacing. The door opened, and when Dick turned, he spotted Tim Zarnowski. Zeke was the last person he had expected to see.

"Sir, how's your cigar?"

"I'm all out, Zeke."

That did not surprise Zeke, as he had provided his commander with one when they were at KKMC. He pulled out two cigars and handed one to Dick. As they lit up, Zeke said, "Sir, it's a good mission. We're all in it."

Dick had been carrying the full weight of the mission for months, and while he had been counting on everyone to feel the same commitment, he would never have assumed that. Ultimately, the burden of responsibility would always be on the commander and him alone, but now that he knew everyone was in, some of that weight was lifted. It was now on fifteen other pairs of shoulders as well. He and Zeke went back inside, and then it was back to the sand tables. They worked late into the night, and finally Dick told them they all needed to try to get some sleep. The next few days would be long and tiring.

I don't imagine there was much sleep to be had that night, given the poor living conditions and how much the men had on their minds. The pilots had to have been exhausted, but their fatigue must have been mixed with adrenaline and anticipation. They had sleeping pills from the flight surgeon, but even those couldn't still their nerves.

Back home at Fort Campbell, I received a letter that would be Dick's last one for a while. Again, I was struck by the fact that I was getting mail that he had written at the beginning of January, when now, based on our last phone call, I figured he was on the move. Little did I know that he was already at a safe house.

King Fahd Airport

Dear Vicki,

It was great talking with you and the boys. Things are about to get busy here, so I was glad we got to talk. We are packing up our stuff in anticipation of action. It also gives me an excuse to clean out my area and get my guys to do it as well. You wouldn't believe how much stuff we all got during the holidays. Plus, we just seem to accumulate things, and I don't know where they come from. It's not like we can go out shopping. The only things I've bought from the little PX here are a camera and a cassette player. I got some Elvis tapes and listen to them daily. Probably drives my guys nuts, but you know how I love Elvis!

Anyway, I sent two boxes home: books, pictures, and other stuff that I won't need in the coming weeks. Once things get started over here, we will move to FOBs and can't take much with us.

So many of my West Point classmates are here that it is like a reunion. Of course, I see Tommy Greco, Bob Van Antwerp, Hank Kinnison, and John Hamlin regularly because they are in the 101st, but Mike Deegan just showed up, as well as George Webb and Frank Hancock. It's great to see familiar faces from my school days, and I know we will look out for one another.

I had a good meeting with MG Peay, and he finally understands what his "loose cannon" has been juggling these past months. We gave him a full briefing on Task Force Normandy. I assured him that I have both missions under control and have postured my battalion in such a way that we will be able to fully support the division's mission.

I hope you have plenty to keep you busy in the coming

*weeks. It's going to get a little crazy before it calms down. I
keep telling myself that with each passing day, we get closer to
resolving this and returning home.*

   I miss you a lot, Vicki!

   Love,

   Dick

Journal Entry

*My courage is waning. The deadline is here, and I'm afraid of what it
will mean for all of us. I talk about patience, inner strength, balance,
acceptance, and facing life's challenges, but I'm not feeling any of that
right now. Something is just a little bit off in my universe, and I know
it has to do with Dick.*

   *Where do we get men and women whose bravery surpasses their
own well-being? What makes someone put his country, his fellow man,
before himself? How do you decide you will do whatever it takes for the
greater good? How do you get courage when supplies of it are running
out and crunch time has arrived? The men and women who wear our
nation's uniform inspire me every day. I think about my husband and
his fellow soldiers and what is surely ahead, and I decide I need to be
more like them.*

   *When wallowing in self-pity and wishing away the fear isn't work-
ing, it's time to accept what might happen and live with it.*

22

January 15 arrived without any kind of fanfare. What did I think—there would be trumpets blowing and a parade to signal the start of the war? Did I think it would begin on the actual deadline, as soon as I got up and had my coffee? I managed to stay busy that day, but I had a hard time concentrating on anything. I went to my morning aerobics class but felt uneasy being away, so I went right home afterward. My house, the phone, and the TV were my lifeline if something happened. So I cleaned out some more closets, made phone calls to check on the commanders' wives, and chatted with people who called me. I had been talking to my parents and Dick's almost daily at that point, but for the next few days I got calls from many others: our siblings, friends, acquaintances, and Army contacts from previous assignments, thinking of Dick and praying for him.

I thought about Dick every minute of the day, wondering what he was doing. I had a nervous energy that felt more like anticipation than fear. A couple of times, I caught myself and wondered, *Should I be afraid?* The problem was, I wasn't sure what I was supposed to be afraid of.

The news coverage was frenetic, a barrage of sound bites.

Last-minute peace efforts with UN Secretary-General Javier Pérez de Cuéllar and Iraq's Foreign Minister Tariq Aziz went nowhere. In a radio address to Iraq, Saddam Hussein said, "Any last-minute peace overture is up to the United States." In another interview, he reiterated that he was "ready to fight to keep conquered Kuwait."

It was obvious to the world that war was inevitable. Maybe President Bush was giving Saddam a way out by waiting another day or two, or maybe he wanted to surprise Saddam by attacking *after* the deadline.

The boys came home from school, did their homework, and played with their friends. At dinner that night, Clint asked me, "What do you think Dad is doing right now? I thought President Bush gave the deadline, but now nothing has happened."

"I'm not sure, Clint. I think there is going to be a war, but I don't know how or when it will start. Probably pretty soon, though."

Tyler chimed in, "But what about Dad? What will he do with his Apaches?"

"I think the Air Force will go in and bomb some things around Baghdad to get it started; then I think Dad and his unit and all of the 101st will move in to push Saddam's army out of Kuwait. I've never been through anything like this before, so all I know is what I hear on TV and read in the newspaper. Try not to worry about your dad. He'll be okay—he flies an Apache!"

After dinner and homework, we watched *The Wonder Years* on TV. The day was over, a day that we had all feared, and nothing bad had happened. But that still did not solve the mystery of what was to come.

That same day in Al Jouf, Dick and his crews tried to fight off boredom. They were so secluded at their safe house, they didn't have many options for distractions or entertainment. A couple of guys played their Game Boys; Dick had scored some decks of cards from the Air Force, so some played games with those. Someone always kept a radio, so they listened to the BBC at night. It was a relaxing day, in its own way, but the waiting was the hardest part for them, because they were ready to do what they had come to do. Keeping that edge once you're in the zone is difficult. They knew that once they got the go-ahead, they would shift from boredom to a heart-thumping rush of adrenaline in seconds.

Dick was busy going back and forth between the safe house and the Air Force headquarters that had been set up at the airfield, getting intelligence and weather updates. That night, they did more sand table rehearsals, making small changes where necessary and tweaking their plan. It was getting late.

"Guys, try to get some sleep," Dick said. "You can sleep in tomorrow morning, as it will probably be the longest day of all. But remember, we are here to start the war."

On the afternoon of January 16, Dick and all of his crews were on the flight line, doing their final prep and checking everything on their aircraft, putting data in their computers and fixing their kneeboards—small boards that they would strap to their knees and that contained important navigation and target information, codes, radio frequencies, emergency procedures, and so on.

As Dick and Brian were sitting in their aircraft, going over last-minute details, a rental car sped across the tarmac toward them. An Air Force colonel hopped out and asked Dick to join him.

"We have received H-hour [the start of the war] from the CINC [commander in chief]. . . . It's January 17 at 0300 hours. Your mission is a go!"

That meant their mission would commence at 0238, H-hour minus twenty-two minutes. They had twenty-two minutes to complete their mission, get in and get out, before the largest Air Force armada in history began bombing the shit out of Baghdad, Iraq.

Dick walked down the flight line, stopping at each aircraft. He gave each crew the thumbs up and said, "It's a go! H-hour is 0300; we

are H minus 22. Let's go back and try to get some rest and eat something, if you can. We'll meet at 2100 hours for a final mission brief."

When they walked into the briefing room that night, none of the
usual joking around went on; the atmosphere was serious business.
Task Force Normandy was a joint operation, since it was using Air
Force Pave Low helicopters for support. The Pave Lows, nicknamed
Jolly Green Giants in Vietnam, were long-range helicopters used
for special operations and combat search and rescue. The Pave Low
crews and their commander, LTC Rich Comer, were at the briefing.
Dick and Rich Comer had become fast friends during the months
of planning back at KFIA. The two of them briefed the pilots that
night.

Because of the stealth nature of the mission, which required the
Apaches to be in complete blackout and radio silence, and because of
their location in the desert, they could not use satellites for navigation. They would use their night vision systems while the Pave Lows
relied on their terrain-following radar and GPS to guide the Apaches
toward their targets. It was added insurance for the Apache pilots.
The Pave Lows would also provide search and rescue if anyone got
shot down.

It was probably that part of the briefing that got everyone's attention. The pilots had had the past twenty-four hours to get used to the
enormity of their mission, but when they were briefed by the para-
jumpers (PJs) in their combat uniforms, with grenades and knives
strapped all over them, telling them "what to do if you get shot down
in enemy territory," the anxiety level cranked up another notch or
two. But at least they had the assurance that if anything went wrong,
the Pave Lows would get to them and the PJs would extract them. For
most of the pilots in the task force, that was a first.

Like a coach with his football team in the locker room before the
big game, Dick struggled for something inspirational to say to his
crews. Looking at his men, a dream team of superstars who, even

at their young ages, were ultra-professional, he realized anything he had to say at that point was redundant.

"You've practiced this mission to perfection. The plan is sound, the aircraft are ready, and the chance for failure is small. I know you can do this. I know *we* can do this."

Task Force Normandy's mission was to fly into Iraq, destroy the early warning/ground control radar systems, and open up a twenty-two-mile-wide air corridor, allowing Air Force and coalition aircraft to penetrate and successfully attack targets deep in Iraq. The Apaches were the perfect aircraft to do the mission because they could fly low, below most radar, and come in stealthily. Their sleek design made them difficult to see at night, which was when they preferred to fight. The entire plan depended on the element of surprise; if the enemy got word of the incoming Apaches, they would be shot down in an instant.

The targets were two radar sites, twenty-six miles inside Iraq and sixty miles apart. Each team would head for their target and, in synchronicity, fire their weapons, destroying everything at the site: the various types of radar within it, barracks, buildings, generators, vehicles, and all personnel. That was no easy feat, considering that they could communicate only within their cockpits. No radio calls between aircraft were allowed until well after the mission was complete and the code words said. They had to count on timing and on nothing getting in their way. If they did not destroy the sites 100 percent, just one phone call from the enemy meant the incoming Air Force bombers would never stand a chance. It was a brilliant, if not ballsy, mission by any standard—something that no one had attempted since the Doolittle Raid in World War II.

Task Force Normandy took off from Al Jouf in the pitch black of night, each Apache weighing almost twenty thousand pounds and fully loaded with rockets, Hellfires, and all the fuel it could carry. The White Team took off at 0100; the Red Team departed six minutes later. It was approximately a one-and-a-half-hour flight from Al Jouf to the target sites in Iraq. Each team had two Pave Lows with them to help them navigate to the border. The Apaches flew fifty feet off the ground, at 120 knots, in complete silence.

On the way to the target, Dick saw a flash about a mile away pass in front of them. *Oh, shit,* he thought. *People know we're coming!*

Brian came on the radio and asked, "Sir, what was that?"

"Probably an SA-7 [shoulder-fired, surface-to-air missile]. Those Pave Lows are loud and flying pretty high; border patrol might have heard them and shot into the dark. It never locked onto us, so we're okay."

More of the same happened along the route, most likely Bedouin tribes using small arms, border patrols hearing the rotor blades in the distance and firing blind. They couldn't see an Apache unless it flew directly over them, and by the time they saw it, it was usually too late for them to react. The small-arms fire couldn't do much damage unless they hit the fuselage or the rotor blades at just the right angle, but an SA-7 could have caused a big problem. No matter how quiet the pilots tried to be, the thunderous sound of six helicopters flying in the dead of night could definitely be heard if anyone was out there. The trick was to get in and do the deed before anyone caught on.

Approximately ten miles south of the target sites, the Pave Lows peeled off and headed for their rendezvous points to wait.

Each team headed for its target, flying those last miles unescorted. At 0237 hours, both the Red and White Teams were in place, each waiting for the "ten seconds" radio call from their team leader. This was to ensure that their missiles hit each target site, simultaneously, at precisely 0238 hours. LT Drew, of the White Team, made the first radio call of the night: "Party in ten!" Sixty miles away, CPT Shufflebarger made the same radio call to the Red Team.

Simultaneously, both teams counted down and then unleashed their fury. The next four minutes were a barrage of missiles and rockets that lit up the sky. As they moved in closer to the targets, they fired every weapons system they had. It was obvious from the beginning that the enemy never saw them coming. Even if they had heard the Apaches at the very last second, they would have looked skyward, expecting fast movers (jets). They never anticipated that helicopters would take them out.

When it was over, the Apaches made sweeping passes over the sites just to make sure nothing had survived. Dick had promised 100 percent, and anything less than that was unacceptable. The two teams radioed ahead to the Pave Lows: "California Alpha, Alpha," and "Nebraska Alpha, Alpha," the code words for "mission complete."

Back at Fort Campbell, I woke up on January 16 and, as with the previous days, couldn't wait to turn on the TV, but I waited until the boys got on the school bus. Again, nothing had happened overnight, so I went about my day, all the while with a feeling of dread that never left me.

That evening, I was in the middle of making chicken-and-broccoli casserole when the phone rang. It was Denise Davis, Mike's wife. "Vicki, it's started! Turn on the TV. The war has started!"

The boys and I went into the den and just stared at the TV, watching CNN's Peter Arnett hiding under a table in his room in Baghdad as bombs from Air Force jets exploded all around his hotel. All hell was breaking loose. I had never seen anything like it.

Clint turned to me and asked, "Mom, is this the war?"

"I don't know. Maybe it's just the Air Force doing some raids."

I really didn't know what it meant. After months of waiting and trying to imagine how a war would actually begin, somehow, I was surprised. I had not expected it to actually unfold on live TV during dinnertime.

The phone rang again. It was Gail.

"Vicki, do you have the TV on? I think it's started."

"We've been watching, and I don't know if this is really it. Gail, do you think it's just the Air Force?"

"This is not what I expected."

"I know. Me neither."

I couldn't tear myself away from the images on the TV. Usually, you watch things after the fact; I had never seen something like that in real time. The commentators, when they could catch their breath from their excitement of being in the middle of it all, referred to it as an "air campaign." That led me to believe it was just that and that the Army was not yet involved.

I turned to Clint and Tyler and said, "Boys, we need to eat dinner and get your homework finished. Then we'll put a movie on before bed."

I knew that it wasn't healthy for them to go to bed with those images in their heads. If it was unsettling for me, I could only imagine what was going through their minds.

The phone rang nonstop from that moment on. I talked to Dick's and my parents and some of our siblings, but it was getting late and I wanted to spend some time with the boys. I graciously told callers I needed to get my kids to bed and that we could talk more tomorrow. I know the calls were well intended, but Clint and Tyler needed me, too.

Later, when I tucked them in, each one had questions. Clint asked, "Mom, do you think Dad is involved in this? Will the war come here?"

"I don't think Dad is involved in this. It seems to be just the Air Force right now, not the Army. So try not to worry about him."

Then Tyler asked, "What about basketball? We start practice tomorrow. What about school?"

"Of course you'll have school and basketball! The war will not change our lives here at Fort Campbell. It's something that's happening far away."

I received a few more late-evening phone calls before I tried to settle down and get to sleep. I prayed that Dick and his guys were safe. I prayed that whatever he was up to, he would be okay and be able to come home soon. These were the same prayers I had been saying for months, but they had more urgency that particular night. And thinking about Dick meant worrying about him.

Then I remembered something from my college days. I had a sociology professor who started each class with a meditation exercise. He would dim the lights while we students closed our eyes, and then, in a soothing voice, he would talk us through five minutes of calm, instructing us go someplace beautiful and peaceful in our minds. Back then, we did not use the term "happy place," but that was exactly what we were doing.

I remember peeking out of one eye, checking to see whether everyone else was going along with it, because initially, I didn't get it. I was a twenty-year-old college student at the University of Vermont, was in a great sorority, had the boyfriend of my dreams and lots of friends, and did plenty of partying; in my mind, I was *living* my happy place! But I did learn something valuable as I thought of somewhere I liked to go: sitting on a beach, with the warm sun on me. I imagined the smell of the Coppertone that glistened on my body, and waves lapping at my feet. At the same time, we practiced deep stomach breathing, and, sure enough, I could get into it.

All those years later, lying in my bed, tossing and turning, I thought of that. I revisited my happy place and concentrated so hard on my breathing and on capturing the perfect beach scene that I eventually fell asleep. I would use that technique again and again in the coming weeks and months.

Journal Entry

Parenting is tricky. There's no written manual to guide you through the unexpected, often challenging times in life. When something big going on involves the world around you, whether a war, a terrorist attack, or any crisis, it's hard to know just how much to shield your kids and how much to involve them. So often we just rely on our gut instincts. Really, no one knows our own kids better than we do. They take their cues from us, and the way we handle difficult times sets the tone for how well they do.

Clint and Tyler are at good ages right now and can understand most of what is going on and what their dad is doing. Without worrying them needlessly, I find that being forthright, calm, and positive works best for us. I can't shield them from too much, as they are surrounded by Army brats who are living the same life they are. They're all discussing these world events amongst themselves. But I want to be the one who puts things in perspective for them and provides the context they need.

23

As the White Team and the Red Team flew away from their respective target sites, the pilots had a hard time containing their excitement. But any celebrating would have to wait. Things were still happening at a frantic pace in each cockpit as they made sweeping turns over the target area, each helicopter on a different heading. They were lighter now, having unloaded their weapons and used up some of their fuel, so they were flying at faster speeds. The most critical time after a mission is the link-up to get back in formation, and those first minutes were surely chaotic.

What they had done had been the adrenaline rush of a lifetime. They had kept their promise and destroyed everything at both radar sites. Within minutes they began to hear the roar of jets overhead, flying in the direction opposite them, toward Baghdad. The coalition air strikes had begun.

Just hours before, as Dick was leaving the Air Force briefing in Al Jouf, he had asked the commander one more time, "Do the fast movers know we will be below them, one hundred feet off the deck? I don't need friendlies mistaking us for the enemy!"

"Roger that; they know you will be below them."

Now, as they flew just four hundred feet below the jets, Dick couldn't help feeling nervous; mistakes happen. And it would be another fifteen minutes before he could make radio contact with his Red Team. CPT Shufflebarger and the Red Team were just as anxious to contact Dick and the White Team. The teams were converging on and would link up at a preselected rendezvous point (RP) just over the Saudi border. Dick would feel no relief until all were accounted for and out of Iraq.

The Pave Low crews had already radioed the good news back to CENTCOM. General Schwarzkopf breathed a sigh of relief and said, "Thank God!" Later, in a news conference, he said, "Army AH-64 Apaches plucked out the eyes of the Iraqis' air defenses."

Dick would not know the general's reaction until later because he was still in radio silence. He finally made contact with the Red Team and heard that everyone was okay: total destruction of their targets, with no damage and no loss of life. He could breathe again. A few minutes later, they all reached the RP (rendezvous point) where the extra Apache and the Blackhawk, *Goodwrench*, were hovering, waiting to fly back to Al Jouf with them. But trying to line up the teams was like a reining in a gaggle of geese, made all the more difficult in the pitch-black night, with no lights to see tail numbers, and flying at 140 knots. It takes only one wrong move, one helicopter out of sequence, and, in an instant, you have a midair collision. It was ten long minutes before both teams were back in formation and on their way.

En route, they saw flashes of small-arms fire coming at them. Looking through night-vision goggles, it looked like glow-in-the-dark tennis balls were flying toward them. They heard *pings* as bullets hit their aircraft, but because Apaches can withstand small-arms fire, there would be no stopping or putting down the aircraft in the desert that night, short of an engine failure.

With less weight in the helicopters, they made good time and landed back at Al Jouf at about 0430 hours. The once quiet little air-strip had become a hub of activity in a matter of hours. This time, the Apaches had to request permission to land, as C-130s were landing and taking off. As the Normandy pilots emerged from their cockpits, Dick went up and down the flight line, giving everyone a thumbs-up, but not much was said. It was dark and cold; if congratulations or handshakes were exchanged, they were drowned out by the roar of the cargo planes taking off. The energy the teams had expended to fly and complete their mission had pretty much zapped any desire to make small talk.

They stretched and relieved themselves. They had worn absorbent pads in their flight suits to take care of that during the mission, since there was no stopping before, during, or after. The maintenance-crew chiefs worked quickly, refueling the aircraft and assessing damage, making sure the helicopters were ready for the long flight home. Most of the aircraft had some dings and dents, but nothing significant, except for Tom Drew's aircraft, which had notable damage to one of the rotor blades: a gaping two-inch hole causing a vibration that had become increasingly violent by the time he and Zeke landed. During that brief pit stop, Dick was able to make arrangements to have a new blade flown up to Al Jouf the next day, courtesy of an Air Force C-130 plane. But that meant Drew and Zeke were forced to stay on at Al Jouf for another day or two to wait for the new blade. *Goodwrench* would stay as well, along with the mechanics who would install the blade. Dick hated to split up the group, but there was no point in having everyone stay; they needed to get back to King Fahd that same day.

Dick had planned for various contingencies, since no one knew how Saddam would react to the initial strikes by Task Force Normandy and now the coalition air strikes on Baghdad. He did not rule out the possibility that Saddam could launch a Scud missile attack at KKMC, since it was close to the border, and/or at KFIA and the huge base that was home to the 101st Airborne Division.

The sun was coming up as Dick and the task force took off from Al Jouf. He felt vulnerable with no rockets or missiles, just some guns, on their aircraft. He couldn't wait to get to KKMC, where he had prepositioned a stash of Hellfire rockets and missiles. He wanted the Apaches fully armed for the flight from KKMC to KFIA; they needed to be ready for anything.

The fuel stop at KKMC was as brief as the previous one at Al Jouf. Dick and the others noticed that most of the airmen there were wearing their gas masks, as a precaution against a possible chemical attack. Again, the pilots had just enough time to stretch and grab a cup of coffee while their aircraft were refueled and rearmed, and then it was back in the air for the final leg. It was a monotonous flight even on a good day, but after being up for more than eighteen hours, strapped into their tiny cockpit seats, every pilot had to fight off the overwhelming fatigue that was creeping in. They did whatever it took to stay awake. They took turns on the controls; Dick sang Elvis songs to his copilot, Brian; and they did a lot of chattering about anything and everything. The minutes crept by, as if in slow motion, as they checked their watches to see how close to their ETA of 1600 hours (4:00 p.m.) they were. They scanned the horizon for that first glimpse of KFIA. They made their approach call long before they saw the tower and the white tops of the "tent city." It had been four days since they had departed, but it seemed like forever.

As they taxied in and parked at their ramp, they saw nearly all of the Expect No Mercy soldiers, officers, pilots, and crew chiefs waiting to greet them with back slapping, high fives, and all the other things excited guys do. They all must have felt relief mixed with excitement about what had just transpired. Even though sixteen individuals had fired those first shots, the entire unit, the whole team, had played a role in the mission's success. It was a defining moment for every member of 1-101st, the Expect No Mercy battalion.

The day would not be over for Dick for another four hours. He had debriefings to conduct and a million loose ends to tie up. LT Stinger collected all of the video gun tapes from each aircraft, and they hooked up the VCRs in their headquarters, anxious to see what it all looked like on tape. A combat video crew arrived immediately, having flown in from General Schwarzkopf's headquarters at CENTCOM, to get the tapes, which would be shown from Riyadh to the White House briefing room. Dick spent hours with that crew, briefing them as they watched the tapes. He drank cup after cup of coffee to stay alert.

It was while he was describing the attack, with his pointer and maps, listening to his and his pilots' voices on the recordings, that what they had accomplished began to seep into his consciousness. The mission itself had been so fast and furious, and then he'd been responsible for getting everyone back home. Between those factors and the long flight, he had had no time for reflection. Suddenly, while explaining the events of the past twelve hours to someone other than his crews for the first time, everything came into clear focus for him and he realized just how significant a role he and his fellow pilots had played. The first reports of the air campaign were astounding: no aircraft shot down, and no loss of life within US and coalition forces. Task Force Normandy had literally blinded Saddam's military.

Dick wanted nothing more than to get to his small cubicle of a room and lie down on his cot. But he had one more thing to do that night before he could sleep.

I woke up the morning of January 17 when my eyes popped open like someone had flipped a light switch. Nothing felt fuzzy or foggy, and I hadn't even had my coffee. I was wide awake and anxious to see what had happened overnight. Images of the night before and the bombing in Baghdad were front and center in my mind. I wanted nothing more than to sit and watch the news, but, as usual, I would wait until my sons left for school. I did not want them to see something on TV and then have to sit in school for the next eight hours with that on their minds. *No, I thought, I can wait just a little longer.*

I jumped out of bed and got the boys up. I busied myself packing lunches and eating breakfast with them, but the usual knot in my stomach had already formed.

Tyler asked, "Do you think Dad is okay?"

"I think so, Ty. I really think this is just the Air Force doing stuff."

"What do you think Dad is doing now?" Clint asked.

"They're probably packing up to move somewhere else. The whole division will move pretty soon. Everybody's dads will be going together."

As they were walking out the door, I said, "While you're in school, I'll watch the news, make some phone calls, and see what I can find out. I'll fill you in when you get home. Try not to worry."

As I watched them get on the bus together, I thought, not for the first time, *How lucky they are to have each other and to be in the same school. And when they get there, they will be surrounded by their friends, who are going through exactly what they are.*

I was already in the den, with the TV remote in my hand, as I heard the hiss of the bus door closing. General Powell was in the middle of his daily briefing. I was just settling in on the couch when I heard him say something like, "And Apache helicopters from the 101st went into Iraq."

What? I thought I heard the word "Apache," but what else did he say? My heart was beating out of my chest. I had no way of rewinding and wasn't sure if I had heard him right.

The phone rang. It was Dick's dad. "Vicki, we just heard Colin Powell say that Apaches were involved last night. Do you think it was Dick?"

"Bob, I just turned on the TV and heard that, too. But I didn't hear the whole thing. I have no clue what he meant. As soon as I find out anything, I'll call you guys."

"Good, because we're worried sick. Jan and I didn't sleep at all last night."

I hung up, and then my mom called. My dad was at work, and she had seen General Powell on TV and, of course, had heard about the Apaches. I told her I would call back when I knew more.

I was on the phone for most of the morning. I talked to some of the wives in the unit (Denise Davis, Carolyn Killian), but none of us understood what was going on. I talked to Gail. The consensus among we wives was that the Air Force was conducting the air campaign, and it sounded like that would go on for days and weeks. But we had all heard something about Apaches from the 101st.

Mahaffey Middle School (the boys' school) called to tell me they were having an emergency meeting that afternoon for the parent advisory council. I told them I would be there.

The phone rang again, and, expecting it would be another call from our family, I almost dropped it when I heard Dick's voice. "Vicki, I'm okay. We're all okay! I didn't want you to worry about me. I'm back at King Fahd."

"Oh my God, Dick, I didn't think I would hear from you!" And then, all in one breath, I added, "General Powell said something about Apaches from the 101st but I wasn't sure if I heard him right but then everyone was calling and asking me and I think maybe you did something big but I don't know what it is but I am so glad you are okay!" Big exhale.

"Vicki, I cannot confirm or deny anything."

"Jeez, you sound so official!"

"The mission is still classified, so I can't talk about it. When the time is right, I will tell you everything. What I *can* tell you is that we flew almost twelve hours, and it was great! My guys did great. I'm so proud of them. In the coming days, you might see something in the news."

I couldn't see him, and yet I knew he was beaming. I could hear it in his voice. I didn't want to let him go, but I could tell he was exhausted. "Dick, I'm not sure what you did, but whatever it was, I am so proud of you! I have a feeling it was something extraordinary, because I *know* you."

"Vick, I need to get some sleep. I just didn't want you to worry about me. I will try to call again soon. I love you!"

"I love you, too!"

I hung up the phone and felt like screaming with relief. *He's okay, his guys are okay, and that's all that matters. I'll get the details at some point, but I can relax now.*

The next call was from my good friend Lynn Carden. Her husband, Mike, commanded the aviation maintenance battalion.

"Vicki, Mike just called and told me to call you and to tell you that Dick made history last night. Those were his exact words!"

"Oh my gosh. What do you think he means?"

"I don't know, but he wanted to make sure I told you. He said something about how Dick and his guys flew into Iraq and took out radar sites so the Air Force could get through to Baghdad."

"Holy shit, Lynn! I've been trying to figure this out for the past six months!"

I didn't care why or how Lynn's husband was able to share such details with her, because I finally had the information I had been searching for. But I needed to be careful, since Dick had said their mission was still classified.

After I hung up the phone, my mind wandered back to all the hints that Dick had dropped and it began to make sense. I finally realized what his reference to his previous, 1981 mission meant. Thinking back ten years, I remembered that he *had* told me something about a mission to take out the radar sites leading into Tehran, Iran, so the rescue planes could go in and get the hostages. But over the years I had forgotten that detail and always thought of it as having to do specifically with hostage rescue, which was why I had never connected that mission to this one.

I called Dick's parents back. His dad picked up on the first ring, and I could hear his mom pick up another phone. I got right to it: "Hi! Dick called me, and he's fine! Everything is okay, and they're back at King Fahd Airport. He didn't give me many details, but he was pretty excited and he said everything went great."

"Oh, thank God!" they both said.

I relayed what Lynn had told me and said we would probably get more details in the coming days. I ended by saying, "For now, he's safe. I think we can all breathe a little easier. Try not to worry."

I had spent so much time on the phone that I had to rush to get ready for the meeting at the school. I was curious and thinking maybe it had something to do with the war. How strange to say those words, "the war," even to myself. When I pulled up to the school, I was surprised to see trucks moving the big trash dumpsters from the back of the building, far off to the side. *Hmm*, I thought, *I wonder what that's about.*

As I walked inside, my mind was a million miles away. I couldn't get past my conversation with Dick and everything I had learned since then. I thought my heart would burst wide open with the pride that I was feeling for him. I put my feelings on hold for the time being so I could focus on the meeting. But deep down, in a place where only I could go, I was falling in love with Dick Cody all over again.

After the meeting, I got home just before the boys did, anxious to hear how their day had gone.

Clint said, "All my teachers talked about the war, and they said we shouldn't worry because it's just the Air Force that is involved."

Tyler added, "My teachers said the same thing. They're nice, and they still give us time every day if we want to write letters to our dads or moms. You know our friend Ben—both his mom and dad are deployed."

"I know. That must be really hard for him. His grandparents are living with him. But guess what? Your dad called today, and he's safe and sound! He didn't tell me too much, but he sounded good. He said that he and his guys had been flying all night; everybody was fine, and they were back at King Fahd. I also heard on the news something about how Apaches from the 101st went into Iraq, so that was probably your dad."

Clint and Tyler said in unison, "Really?"

"Until we get more details, I'm not sure we should talk about it with anyone else. It was a secret mission."

"Wow, that is so cool!" Clint said.

"Awesome!" Tyler echoed.

Then Clint asked, "Can we tell our friends?"

"I guess we can talk about what's already been on TV." I didn't see any harm in their discussing the subject with their friends. It wasn't as if they had classified information to divulge; none of us did.

While the boys did homework, I finally had time to call my parents and repeat what I had told Dick's parents. They worried about Dick like his own parents did. And I knew that because I was their daughter, they worried about me. None of our parents had been through anything like this before. In my most reassuring voice, I said, "Just talking to Dick today has put my mind at ease. The boys and I are fine. Honestly, we will be fine."

And then it was time for basketball practice, dinner, and a movie. It was important for us that some things remain the same, regardless of what was happening on the other side of the world.

Journal Entry

When things are changing all around you, it's important to grab onto whatever you can to keep you grounded. We need familiarity, and, no matter what our age, we need to feel safe. And when a particularly frightening event happens, we need to know we are not alone.

During this time at Fort Campbell, the boys and I have found our comfort zone in being with others who are going through exactly what we are. The boys have their fellow Army brats and amazing teachers who understand them. They have coaches, who are their dad's soldiers. And I am surrounded by my fellow Army wives. Together, as an Army community, we have carved out a little piece of the world where we are supported and safe during a very scary time.

24

The next day, the *Nashville Tennessean* newspaper published an article about troops from the 101st Airborne Division's being "possibly" involved behind enemy lines. "Senator Jim Sasser hints at secret force. Apache helicopters from the 101st aviation battalion at Fort Campbell engaged Iraqi ground forces firing Hellfire missiles." The article went on to describe the Apache and its weapons systems. I felt like I was on a scavenger hunt, searching for clues, and that article gave me another piece of the puzzle.

I was starved for details of the mission, but I had to rely on news reports. Even then, I wasn't sure how much to believe. Many of the articles focused on the Air Force's bombing of Baghdad, and when they listed the types of aircraft participating in the air campaign, the AH-64 Apaches were always at the bottom of the list, almost as an afterthought. Initially, the media did not receive any specific details about Dick's classified mission, as the enemy could have used that information for a retaliatory strike against the 101st. Dick's name was never mentioned, but we all knew his was the only Apache unit in the 101st. I had yet to hear the words "first shots of the war" in conjunction with Dick or his unit, so I vacillated between believing he had done something big and thinking he was but one part of the overall picture.

We entered the next stage in the deployment, creating another new norm for us at Fort Campbell, Kentucky. We had all gotten used to being on our own and living on a post made up of mostly moms and kids. When Desert Shield became Desert Storm, our post went to a higher alert/threat level, meaning higher security. The meeting at Clint and Tyler's school was all about new security measures and how to keep the students safe during the war. I had always felt so protected and safe living on a large Army post with military police at every gate, I hadn't stopped to think that the post could also be a potential target. The school administrators brought up some great points and some new changes: All doors would be locked during the day, no one could enter the school without checking in at the office with their military ID, the dumpsters were being moved away from the school so no one could plant a bomb or device in them, and all school buses would be checked for devices before and after pickups. You have to remember, this was years before the school shootings, mass shootings, and terms like "shelter in place" and "lockdown" that have become so much a part of our lives today. It was before schoolkids had to do emergency drills for active shooters, and it was ten years before terrorists attacked the United States.

As I sat there listening, for a brief moment, I tried to get my head around the idea of someone coming onto our post and targeting a school. I had just come through three of the scariest days of my life, not knowing where my husband was, if he was in harm's way, and if something had happened to him. When he called to say he was okay, in my mind my life was good again and nothing was going to burst that bubble. Also, having lived on an Army post for so many years, Dick and I and the boys were used to the rules and regulations, all of them designed to keep us safe. So, that day, I was just glad that the school and the Army were being proactive about protecting the post.

Like everyone back then, I was learning about war, as seen on live TV. We watched it unfold right before our eyes, starting with the opening scenes of the air strikes. I read everything I could get my hands on, two or three newspapers per day; I read both *Newsweek* and *TIME* every week because someone told me each magazine had a different political slant and I wanted to get all perspectives. I watched enough news to stay informed but tried not to overdo it. And anytime I heard the words "101st Airborne Division," my ears perked up and I hit the record button on our VCR, which always had a tape in it. I scanned articles looking for anything about Apaches. I had already filled one scrapbook by January and started a new one. I wanted to keep a good record of everything so that when Dick returned, he would have an idea of how it had all played out for us back in the United States. I also wanted to record history in the making, for my sons and for myself. I never dreamed that one day I would write books about it.

Two days after the start of the war, I had a particularly interesting call from a friend of Dick's, Tom Rains, a senior executive at McDonnell Douglas Helicopters (MDH). Tom was in charge of the Apache program, and, though I had never met him, I knew his name from Dick. I was surprised when I answered the phone and he identified himself and said, "Vicki, I am so proud of what your husband and 1-101st Aviation battalion have done! Everyone here at MDH has been cheering since we got the news. Dick just proved to the world how great the Apache is, and he used it for exactly what it was designed for."

How thoughtful that this person, whom I don't even really know, took the time to call me, I thought. I also recalled an *Army Times* issue that I had read recently. In huge bold type, the cover said, "Apache: Weak Link or Key to Desert Victory?" The brand-new Apache had yet to prove itself and had been maligned in the press, which claimed it was too expensive and too hard to maintain, that it could not perform in the desert and could not compete with the Air Force, and a number of other issues. But in one blazing mission, Dick proved them all wrong.

At the monthly aviation brigade meeting for all of the commanders' wives, the brigade commander's wife, Betsy, opened the meeting by saying, "In case you don't know, Dick Cody fired the first shots of the war."

Bingo! This is the missing clue I haven't heard before! Not wanting to draw attention to myself, I busied myself by doodling on my notepad, but I could feel the flush creeping into my face. I had been around the Army long enough to understand an unwritten code among wives: No one's husband was any more special than another. Every person in the Army—soldier, NCO, officer, no matter the branch or the job—works for the good of the team. And whether the team is a squad, platoon, company, troop, battalion, regiment, brigade, or division, the very essence of the Army is built on teamwork. No one individual takes the credit. We wives worked the same way, so I knew that I would not be bragging about Dick to my peers—not even to my fellow aviation commanders' wives, who were sitting next to me. I wouldn't even call my best friend, Gail, and say, "Hey, guess what? Dick fired the first shots of the war!" Everybody's husband was over there doing his job; everyone was sacrificing. It just so happened that on January 17, Dick's job was more dangerous than usual.

But I figured hearing those words "first shots" gave me license to talk about it with my boys and our parents. With my family, I would not have to hide my feelings and we could share our pride. That was really all I needed.

Nevertheless, I knew that a ground war was on the horizon and would involve Dick and everyone in the division, and with that, my fear would return. The ground war was more of the unknown, just as we were all getting used to this thing called an air war.

I went to a lot of meetings that January, most of them routine FSG meetings but some generated by the start of the war. When I met with my battalion wives, I wasn't sure how much they knew about our unit's exploits, and since I didn't know the names of the pilots who had gone on the mission, I was careful not to discuss the details. But in talking with individual wives, I realized many of them knew more than I did. I'm sure there were phone calls to wives back home, but at least there had been no leaks *before* the mission. I realized that Dick was actually protecting me from scrutiny among the wives by not giving me too much information.

When talking to the group, I was reassuring, like Dick was with me, and never missed an opportunity to share what Dick said about the women's husbands and the unit. I wanted them to feel the same pride that Dick had for every member. I talked about the team effort and never singled out individuals. The wives seemed more upbeat; I could see it in the way they interacted with one another, and they asked fewer questions and did less complaining.

I anxiously awaited the mail every day, hoping for a letter from Dick that was dated *after* January 17 and that would surely contain more details. I was tired of second- and third-hand bits and pieces. I just wanted him to tell me the story from start to finish, and then I would leave him alone. Maybe.

The following week, two letters came on the same day. One was addressed to Clint, Tyler, and me, and the other one was just to me. I opened mine first. It had been written on the eighteenth. Good!

King Fahd Airport

Dear Vicki,

It was so good to talk to you last night after I returned here. Sorry to be so evasive, but any discussion on the role of the Apache is still classified. Suffice it to say, we did great! The mission went off without a hitch. At the appropriate time, the story will be released to the press.

It was a very emotional "welcoming" when I returned with Task Force Normandy. We had flown over 1,450 nm in two and a half days! It sure was good to see the rest of the battalion waiting for us. All my guys are doing well.

Right now, I am in the middle of pulling the entire battalion task force together to begin moving up north to our tactical assembly area (TAA). Hopefully, the Air Force will continue to bomb and "soften up" the enemy so we can go in and mop up.

Tom Greco and his battalion moved out today, and most of the division will be in place at the TAA in the next four days. Every night we listen to BBC and CNN to get news on the air raids by the Air Force. Last night it was quite a sight as we watched F-16s and B-52 bombers fly overhead—literally hundreds of them! We have gas attack drills two or three times a day. Yesterday morning at 0500, we had an alert and I had to sleep with my mask on for an hour!

I know this particular time is tough on you and the boys. Say some prayers, have faith, and know that I only take "prudent" risks. My commanders get better every day at handling the stress of combat, so I have a strong team with me. I really am fine, maybe not totally relaxed, but very alert and focused. I feel strong mentally and physically.

Take care of yourself. Love you more than anything. I will be home!

Always,
Dick [smiley face]

I then opened the letter addressed to my sons and me. It too was dated the eighteenth.

King Fahd Airport

Vicki, Clint, and Tyler,
Hi! I am doing fine. The war officially started at 0300 hours on the 17th, and the Apache was the first aircraft in Iraq and fired the first shots! My guys did great, and 1-101st is combat ready! I wish I could give you more details, but more to follow on that when the time is right.

We, the entire division, will be moving forward pretty soon. Please remember that we are a great division and the forces all around us are very strong. The Air Force owns the skies now! I cannot predict if this will be a long or short war. Much of that depends on the psychological effects the bombing has on the Iraqi military. We really caught them off guard, giving ourselves the upper hand, for now, at least. Hopefully by the time our ground forces go up against them, they will be ready to retreat. We have a lot of tanks and attack helicopters over here, so I am confident that we will continue to be on the offensive.

This will be short, as I still haven't been to bed. I've been up for forty-eight hours! But I wanted you to know I am being careful and that I love and miss you all. Say some prayers, be strong for each other, and we will get through this.
Love,
Dick/Dad [smiley face]

After I read both letters, a couple of things struck me. First, Dick had to have been exhausted when he wrote them. He probably wanted to get a quick note off to the three of us so we wouldn't worry. He didn't have time to write three separate letters, but then he decided to write one to me alone. The tone and intent of both letters was the same: He was trying to reassure us. My eyes had been dry for days, but now, tears started rolling down my face. I thought, *I love this man who loves us so much and is trying to prepare us, as best he can, for what is surely coming.*

Journal Entry

Waiting, worrying, fretting—whatever you want to call it—uses up a lot of energy. It is time-consuming and exhausting. Sometimes you have to settle for what is right there within your reach, even if you don't have all the facts, even if you don't know the whole story. And sometimes you have to move on because you will drive yourself crazy if you continue your quest for all the answers. Things are often revealed when they are supposed to be revealed.

Dick's letters give us the reassurance we need to go about our daily routines. His confidence is infectious, giving us strength and courage; his honesty keeps it real, so we are not fooled or lulled into a false sense of security. I understand that there are no guarantees, no promises of a perfect ending, but I know how much he loves us, and that counts for something. It actually counts for a lot.

25

I was naive to think that just because Dick had made it back from his secret mission, my dread would leave me. I remembered what he had told me at the very beginning of the deployment: "They don't send most of the US military and all these coalition forces to the other side of the world just to sit and watch. There will be a war." Armed with knowledge from my very own crash course on war, my readings and research, I knew there was more to come. I figured that at some point in the near future, when the bombers had taken care of the biggest targets in and around Baghdad, the next phase would begin: boots on the ground. The tanks and helicopters and ground troops would move in to fight on the ground and then secure the area. Until then, the waiting game continued, and with that, the feeling of something looming never left me.

And then Dick called on a Saturday morning, about a week after his mission.

"Hi, Vick! Everything is good here. I just wanted to talk to you and the boys. I don't have long, because we're moving out today, so can you put Clint and Tyler on the phone? And then you and I can talk."

Clint and Tyler each got on and had a typical father-son conversation about school and sports. Each one asked when he was coming home. I remember watching them and thinking how brave they were for their ages, thirteen and eleven, respectively. Just as I had, they had matured over the past six months and had come to accept what was.

I got back on the phone and steeled myself for another goodbye. The headlines in the paper that morning read, "Air War Escalates" and "101st Moving to Border."

Dick started by saying, "You've probably figured out that I'll be leaving soon. We're all packed up and ready. Have you gotten my letters? I told you as much as I could about TF Normandy and what's ahead."

"Yes, we got the two letters you wrote on January eighteenth. And, Dick, this morning's headlines said it all. I understand what you guys have to do; just promise me for the hundredth time that you'll be extra careful."

"You know I always am. We need to get this done so we can think about coming home. This puts us one step closer to that happening. But listen, this is going to be even tougher for everyone now, and especially for you families back home. We won't have phones for a while, and the mail will get backed up again as we move forward. You and the boys keep writing, and I will write you every day. Eventually, the mail will get through; it always does. Try not to worry about me. I will take good care of myself and all my soldiers."

While he was talking, I thought, *We just ran this scene about eight days ago. I don't want to say goodbye again. What if our luck runs out this time?*

But of course I didn't let on to what was in my head. Instead, I said, "Remember how proud we all are of you. I love you, Dick! Fly safe!"

"I love you too, Vick."

I hung up the phone and tried not to think ahead. It was a long weekend; Monday was a school holiday. There was no basketball that day, and Gail and her kids were busy, so I knew my sons and I needed to get out of the house. We went to the movies to see *Flight of the Intruder*, and it was the perfect distraction. On Monday, we went to the local mall for cheap thrills: The boys played in the video arcade while I browsed at Dillard's; then we had lunch and went to Champs Sports for new basketball shoes. The mall had a kiosk selling metal Desert Storm wristbands that you could get engraved with a soldier's name. The boys and I each got one, inscribed with LTC DICK CODY—APACHE PILOT. We would wear those bracelets for the rest of the deployment to show our support.

As I had done so many times in the past, despite all the talk on the news about Scud missiles and a possible chemical attack on our forces, I forced myself not to think about where Dick was living and what he was heading into. Just days after he fired the first shots and the bombing commenced, Iraq began firing Scud missiles at Israel. They also tried to launch against some of our bases, but US Patriot missile systems preempted those strikes.

The air campaign became routine, in that we heard about numbers of sorties flown and targets hit each day. There were some visible reminders that we were living in a different time: more force protection at every gate, random vehicle checks, bomb-sniffing dogs, and even some concertina wire at a few of the gates that were permanently closed. But for the boys and me and the rest of the families, life at Fort Campbell continued.

And then one day in late January, the doorbell rang and I opened the door to see our mailman standing there with two big boxes. *Oh no—I know what those are.*

"Mrs. Cody, these are pretty heavy, so I would be glad to put them inside for you."

"That would be great! Thank you!"

He slid them along the floor in our small foyer. I barely got the door closed before the tears came. Dick had told me he was sending all of his belongings back; he called it "sanitizing," getting rid of the things he could not take with him when they moved forward. I knew that nothing had happened to him—it wasn't like the Army was returning his personal effects—but in that very moment, I couldn't reason that. I slid down onto the cold, hard linoleum floor. That particular day in January, those boxes were my demon.

I looked at them and decided I was not going to avoid them by shoving them into a closet to go through later. Nope, no way—not that day. I was going to get into those boxes, and I didn't care how much it messed with me or upset me—it was time to face the demon. Part of me wanted to kick the shit out of those boxes, but the other part of me needed something that would connect me to Dick.

I sobbed as I looked through his possessions, his few comforts of home: the things we had sent him for Christmas; the framed pictures of the boys and me, and one of me alone. Also, there were his tennis rackets and some cans of tennis balls, crossword puzzle books, some small games, extra sunglasses, newspaper clippings, magazines with tabs on articles that he wanted me to read, a stack of *Doonesbury* cartoons that he had cut from newspapers, books, decks of cards, rolls of film, and other incidentals. I noticed that his Bible was not in either box; at least he had that with him. But all mixed up with *his* possessions were *my* emotions. *The poor guy—he's already living such a sparse existence, and now he can't even keep the things I sent him? I miss him so much; I don't know how much longer I can do this. If I could quit right now, I would!*

I was tired of the whole damn "Army wife" game: being separated from the person I loved, having no control over what was happening, grappling with the fear that never left me, and always trying to be strong. There was a very fine, powdery sand, almost like dust, in and on everything in the boxes, and it was making a mess all over the floor. *And while I'm at it,* I thought, *I'm sick of living in crappy Army quarters with these ugly linoleum floors!*

Then I noticed some things for the boys with little notes on them. I felt a smile beginning and then just a little warmth creeping into my heart. I realized I was stiff from sitting on the floor, so I got up, went into the kitchen, and called my mom.

"Hi, Mom."

I barely got the words out before she jumped right in. "Vicki, are you okay?"

"I'm okay. Everything is fine. I'm just having a rough day and needed to talk to you."

"I could tell by your voice. What's wrong?"

"I just got the boxes that Dick sent home with all of his stuff. They have moved forward and can take only the bare necessities with them. He warned me, but still, it hit me like a ton of bricks. Something about going through his stuff . . . Mom, I just miss him so much."

"Oh, Vicki, I wish there was something I could say or do for you. I feel so helpless. But you've come this far; I know you can get through the rest. You have more courage than anyone I know."

"I know, but I feel like my whole adult life I've been saying good-bye to Dick. I'm tired of having to let him go. I want him with me."

"Maybe this will all be over soon. Just hang in there and know how much we love you."

"Thanks, Mom. I guess I just needed to hear that. I love you, too."

I hung up the phone and organized the mess I had made but left the boxes there, knowing the boys would want to look at everything.

When they came home from school, they ran right to the boxes. They oohed and aahed as they rummaged through the contents. You would have thought it was Christmas morning.

"Mom, look at these incentive coins! They're from an Air Force special-operations unit!"

"And Desert Storm collectors' cards for both of us!"

"Mom, what's this powder stuff all over everything?"

"That's sand from the desert. Weird, huh? It's so different from the sand at our beaches."

There was some Saudi money, coins and bills, and some little trinkets Dick must have picked up somewhere. The boys enjoyed rifling through everything, looking at some of the magazines and pictures, and didn't seem the least bit traumatized, like I had been. I thought, *How completely different from my reaction. Thank goodness for these boys, who keep me grounded and at times give me perspective.*

King Fahd

Dear Vicki,

I wanted to get one last letter off to you before we leave. I promise to write every day, even if it's a short note.

We've had a rash of Red Cross messages come through, wives wanting to get their husbands home, and for the most stupid reasons! Red Cross messages are for dire emergencies, like illness or the death of an immediate family member—not because a wife is lonely or can't handle her kids. Nine times out of ten, it's a bogus request, and they don't realize how time-consuming it is for the division, the brigade, and the battalion to track down and verify the information. It pisses me off; we have so much to focus on right now. I've told my guys from day one, "There is no easy way out of Saudi Arabia. We are going to see this thing through!" But it seems to be the wife that gets the soldier all spun up. I feel like telling them that you can't just quit when the going gets tough. I hope everybody calms down, because we've still got a war to fight! Sorry—I needed to vent.

It was great talking to you and the boys. They sound so grown-up! I probably won't recognize them when I get home. I really miss you guys. This has not been an easy separation for

me, now that the boys are at the age where I can play ball with
them, coach them, etc. I hate missing out on things with them.
   Remember to be patient with the mail!
   Love you,
   Dick

Journal Entry

We don't get to write the screenplay for our life. Sure, there are times
when we think we're writing it: We come to a fork in the road and
make a choice, which gives us a feeling that we're in charge. When you
start to believe that you get to script your life, you set yourself up for
disappointment. Let's be honest—if we got to write it, our lives would
be perfect, filled with happiness, joy, nothing but the best of times. But
life doesn't always play out the way we want it to.

   My screenplay was written the day I fell in love with Dick. I can no
more change the course of events and my destiny than anyone else. But
the challenges, the fears, the looking into boxes when you don't want to,
and the many "not so perfect" moments are what make everything else
so sweet, creating a rich and meaningful life.

26

Dick's letter reminded me of something. We had approximately two hundred wives in the battalion, and maybe half of them participated in FSG meetings and activities. There were various reasons for that number: We still had some soldiers who didn't want their spouses to participate, telling them that we were nothing more than a group of gossipy officers' wives. We also had many wives who worked full-time and went to school, or who did not have childcare and couldn't come to meetings. There were some who felt comfortable going only to the small group gatherings within their company, and I got that. Everyone's needs are different; not everyone wants to be part of a group. That was why we had phone trees and monthly newsletters, hoping to keep everyone informed. As time went on, though, we did have more participation at the battalion FSG meetings, run by the rear detachment, because the wives knew that was where the most current information was and perhaps were hoping for a connection.

At the meetings, I continued to remind everyone to check on their friends and neighbors who couldn't come. I figured if I had a rough day here and there, some might be having a rough week or month. It was a challenge to keep everyone connected. We each did our best, but some people were unreachable, no matter how hard we tried.

I was fortunate in so many ways that, except for being lonely at times, I couldn't complain. Gail and her three kids were just a block away or a quick walk through the field behind our houses. We usually got together on the weekends, either going out for dinner or taking turns hosting at our houses. Once in a while, I had an evening function or get-together with wives—usually a potluck, but sometimes we met at a restaurant. The boys were almost past the babysitter stage but not quite old enough to stay by themselves. Luckily, Brownie (SGT Brown) and his wife, Charlotte, enjoyed having them over to their apartment, and sometimes they spent the night. I was so thankful to have people I trusted to look after them, and Clint and Tyler needed a break from me sometimes.

Mixed in with the doom and gloom of war and daily updates on the air campaign were the usual hype and excitement surrounding the upcoming Super Bowl. We all needed a distraction, but it felt strange to be thinking about something so frivolous while a war was going on.

On January 27, just ten days after Dick fired the first shots and the Gulf War began, Super Bowl XXV was set to play in Tampa, Florida. The New York Giants and the Buffalo Bills would play before seventy-three thousand fans in Tampa Stadium. Behind the scenes, the game was almost canceled because of the onset of the war, out of respect for our military and also because of security risks. But the NFL commissioner made a last-minute decision, and President Bush issued a statement saying, "Life goes on"—and so did the game.

Gail and her kids came over to watch with us, as we did every year with our husbands. She and I had carefully planned our party foods, which were the most important part of the game for us. We were munching on nachos and chicken wings when the game came on and we heard the familiar voice of Frank Gifford announcing the national anthem. Something in the way he said the following words got all of our attention: "To honor America and especially the brave men and women serving our nation in the Persian Gulf and around the world, please join in singing the national anthem, sung by Grammy award winner Whitney Houston, to be followed by a flyover of F-16s."

Whitney proceeded to sing the most beautiful and stirring rendition of "The Star-Spangled Banner" that I have ever heard. As the cameras showed the crowd in the packed stadium, tears welled up in my eyes. For a song that we sometimes take for granted, especially before a big sports event, when people are anxious for the start of the game, we don't always stop to think about the words. But that night, something was different and everyone was singing.

I turned to Gail. "Wow, what did we just witness?"

"That was really amazing!"

That night was all about the red, white, and blue and the US military. People were waving flags, rather than team banners, and signs that said Go USA and Support Our Troops. I had never seen patriotism on such a grand scale at a sporting event or so much recognition for our military, unless it was Veterans Day or the Fourth of July.

As we sat in my den, watching the F-16s fly over the stadium and feeling the patriotism and the American spirit bursting out of that arena, the main thing that kept going through my mind was, *This is bigger than I am.* Dick, Tom Greco, and all of their fellow soldiers were part of something undeniably important. Whether right or wrong, regardless of the politics of war, they had raised their right hands and taken the oath "to protect and defend the United States of America against all enemies, foreign and domestic."

Many said that Super Bowl XXV was defined as much by the launch of Desert Storm and Whitney Houston's performance as by the game itself. For me, the event came at the right time, because just two days before that, I had questioned everything about being married to a soldier.

Back on January 18, the entire 18th Airborne Corps began its massive movement out of the Dhahran vicinity and headed northwest,
toward the Iraq border. It was an approximately 350-mile trek, and
the units left in staggered increments. At that time, 18th Airborne
Corps included the 101st Airborne Division, the 82nd Airborne
Division, the 24th Mechanized Division, the 3rd Armored Cavalry
Regiment, all of the supporting specialized groups and brigades,
and a French division. All of them together exceeded one hundred
thousand soldiers. There were also more than 25,000 vehicles, 980
helicopters, and nearly 1,400 Air Force transport sorties to deploy an
additional 2,700 vehicles and 15,000 personnel, and tons of supplies,
food, and ammunition. It was even larger than the mobilization of
General Patton's Third Army in World War II. Imagine all of that
and only two available routes through the desert. The huge convoy
would take four to five days to get everyone to their TAAs.

Task Force 1-101st formed up in their trucks and vehicles to join
the convoy on January 20. Their luxurious living conditions—i.e., the
parking spaces at KFIA—were now but a memory in their rearview
mirrors. The Expect No Mercy soldiers were ready for whatever was
ahead; they had been waiting for almost six months to do something,
anything, and it was finally showtime. But it would be a long and
arduous drive to get there.

Dick and the flight of helicopters waited to leave, timing their
departure so they would arrive at their destination when the truck
convoy did. Their flight would take just two days, including an overnight stop near KKMC.

So, while the boys and I were enjoying the Super Bowl, Dick and
his guys were settling into their new home in the middle of the desert.
TAA Eddie was just east of the town of Rafha, less than ten miles
from the Iraq border and about twenty miles from TAA Campbell,

where the division had set up a large tent city as its headquarters. All of the other brigades and battalions were dispersed but within driving distance of each other. Dick's battalion had nothing but tents and camouflage netting and some folding chairs; that was it for his 350 men. Don't get me started on the lack of basic necessities, like showers, toilets, and running water!

By then, we were almost six months into the deployment. With each passing month, I told myself we were another month closer to the 101st coming home. My life had a definite pattern to it: adjust, get a little comfortable, say goodbye to Dick on the phone, and then get another dose of the unknown for a while.

As February began, I knew that we were approaching another hurdle. I sensed that we wives needed to stay connected even more. I had my company commanders' wives and first sergeants' wives over to my house for dinner. No potluck that night—I cooked for them to show my appreciation for all their hard work. We all needed a break from routine meetings and briefings, so I told them no business either. We talked and laughed and enjoyed each other's company, and it was the most relaxed we had been as a group in a long time.

As we sat there in my living room, balancing our bamboo trays on our laps and eating the dinner I had prepared—Swiss chicken casserole, wild rice, and salad—I looked around the room and felt such kinship with these women who were sharing the journey with me. I did not know what the coming weeks would bring, but that night I took a break from thinking about it.

Someone brought up the fact that many wives still did not participate in our meetings. I thought about Dick's recent letter to me about the Red Cross messages and said, "Ladies, I'm sure your husbands have told you that things are about to get busy again as they move forward. We need to be even more diligent about checking on wives who might be at risk. Are you hearing anything from within your company support groups?"

One wife spoke up: "It seems to be the ones who don't come to anything who have a hard time, but I don't know how else to get them to participate."

"Just keep the phone tree going and keep inviting them," I said, "and let's hope more people start to come. I worry about what could happen in the coming weeks, with little communication from our husbands."

I had also invited the brigade commander's wife over. Betsy chimed in, "We have to prepare for the guys being gone well into the summer and possibly the fall."

At that, there was some moaning and groaning. I was preparing myself for a couple more months—any more than that was too overwhelming to consider at that point. Whatever the timeline, though, we needed to keep watch over our wives and families and plan frequent get-togethers to stay connected.

To change the subject, I got up and refreshed wineglasses and beverages. Over dessert, we compared notes from our husbands' letters. Kay Drew shared some details of a recent note from Tom that gave us some insight into Task Force Normandy, and Chris Shufflebarger actually knew the names of the pilots. All of that was news to me, and I mentally added the new information to my existing account of what I thought had gone down. The conversation was lighthearted. In the safety of my home, and maybe because it was two weeks after the fact, we bonded over the events that we had been afraid to discuss anywhere else.

I was exhausted when the evening was over. I had gotten used to gatherings where everyone brought something; doing an entire dinner for about fifteen women had tired me out. But it was a good kind of tired. As I fell asleep, my last thought was *How nice to be surrounded by such brave women who give me strength, as I hope I give them.*

Journal Entry

We get the support we need from various sources and in many different ways, whether physical, emotional, or spiritual. But first you have to be open, aware, and receptive. If your heart is closed, it's hard to let love and support come into you. You have to watch for it and wait for it; sometimes you don't see that it's staring you in the face, and sometimes you don't realize it until after the fact, when you feel better and realize someone or something just gave you what you needed to go on.

I am luckier than most. Among my blessings, I have various sources of support, especially right now, during this very scary time in my life. I have my parents, especially my mom, whom I can call day or night; Dick's parents, who are always in my corner; my sister and brother; and Dick's siblings, who give me huge amounts of love and reassurance with their calls and notes.

I have Clint and Tyler, two pretty amazing and squared-away kids, I have my faith, and feeling the support of our nation is a new and unexpected blessing. But being among other Army wives is the greatest source of strength I will ever know.

27

The first weeks in February were more of the same for me, meetings and phone calls, and for the boys, school and basketball. Except for the alarming headlines, our day-to-day life was routine and mundane.

One Sunday after leaving church, we just kept driving, right past our neighborhood, out the main gate, toward Interstate 24. I couldn't take one more Sunday with nothing to do and no hope of even a call from Dick.

The boys erupted in cheers. "Yay, we're going to Nashville and the big mall!"

An hour later, we pulled into Hickory Hollow Mall on the south side of Nashville, and it felt like we had gone on a road trip to a place with new sights and surroundings and way more choices. I dropped the boys off at the big video arcade with some chump change, and off I went to shop for myself. I got a cute outfit at the Limited, with no occasion in mind—I just wanted something new. I met the boys for lunch at the big food court, and then we did some clothes shopping for them, which was brief, given their short attention spans.

On the way home, Clint said, "Thanks, Mom. That was the best day!"

Tyler said the same thing and added, "It feels good to get away!"

"I feel the same way, and I'm so glad you guys like to go to the mall with me!"

As we pulled into our driveway, they each thanked me again. *It sure doesn't take much to please them, or me, for that matter,* I thought.

Soon after that, our division commander's wife, Pamela Peay, invited the command group (the battalion and brigade commanders' wives) over to her house for a potluck dinner. The commanding general's quarters at Fort Campbell were situated down a long, tree-lined driveway. Quarters 1, aptly nicknamed the Farmhouse, was a large, two-story, white clapboard house with green shutters and a large front porch.

It was the first time I had been there. As Gail and I drove down the long driveway, I said, "Wow, look at this house! Can you imagine living here?" Most of us lived in small brick duplexes that were adequate but not what you could call beautiful. The Farmhouse was "Southern grand."

Like the recent dinner I had hosted at my house, this too was meant to be a relaxing, no-business gathering. A large group had already assembled when we arrived—at least fifty women, the same ones who met every month for the information exchange. At the monthly meeting, we sat with our brigade group and it was more formal, with guest speakers and an endless flow of information. Oftentimes we were all in a hurry to leave after the two-hour meeting, so we didn't have the time to chat with friends in other units.

Gail and I immediately noticed the difference in the atmosphere on this night: It was livelier and full of laughter. Unlike some generals' wives, who could be imposing just because of their husbands' rank, Pamela Peay was unassuming and approachable, qualities that made it easy to look up to her. The other general's wife, Carolyn Shelton, whose husband, Brigadier General (BG) Hugh Shelton, was the assistant division commander, had the same easy-to-be-around demeanor.

Because our husbands were gone, there were none of the big division functions or events that would normally have put us all together in a social setting, and we had all missed that. We were busier that year, but in a different way—we were busy within our own battalions and brigades—and that night we all agreed that we would make more time for each other.

Sitting among my fellow Army wives, feeling special because I was a commander's wife, I thought what I had thought many times before: *Dick and I are the luckiest couple in the world. With each new rank that he rises to, we feel like we have made it to the pinnacle and we don't think beyond that. Whatever moment we're in, we just enjoy it for what it is.* What I could never have imagined back then was that within nine years, Dick would be the commanding general of the 101st Airborne Division, we would live in that beautiful farmhouse, and *I* would be the general's wife hosting large gatherings of spouses. That night in 1991, I was just honored to be a battalion commander's wife.

On the way home, I told Gail, "That was really fun, and so relaxing."

"I agree," she said. "It was nice to see everyone in a different setting."

In mid-February, after twenty days with no letters from Dick, hallelujah! I hit the jackpot. His letters started coming, sometimes more than one a day. The boys got letters, too. Sometimes the postmark was the same for multiple ones. As the structured person that I am, I would open each letter without reading it just to determine on what date he had written it, then put it in chronological order, as I did not want to read something out of sequence. It was a process, but I had time on my hands.

TAA Eddie

Dear Vicki,

We made it to the new tactical assembly area okay. All my trucks made it in the convoy, which is a miracle in and of itself. We (the flight of nineteen helicopters) got weathered in partway and ended up staying with the 11th Aviation Brigade from Germany. An old friend of mine is the XO there, and they put all of us up, all nineteen aircraft and crews! He and the other battalion commanders from Germany had heard about "the mission" and wanted a briefing on TF Normandy. I of course obliged [smiley face]. They were pretty pumped up, since they all fly Apaches, too.

It was a long drive for the vehicles and a long flight for the aircraft, but nothing broke down and no one got stranded, which was my biggest fear. All of our training and maintaining paid off. Also, my pilots flew great! I can't tell you the relief I feel.

We call this TAA Eddie, named after our mascot, Ugly Eddie. All of the TAAs are separated by a mile or so; in case of an attack, they don't want us clustered together. The division headquarters is farther away. It is pretty stark living out here in the middle of the desert. We have huge, tan-colored camouflage nets that look like Thunderdome that keep us hidden pretty well. We also have built underground bunkers for artillery attacks, just like the forts we used to build when we were kids!

It is rainy and cold here, so we wear our cold-weather gear day and night. My food trucks are getting set up, so pretty soon we'll get one hot meal a day. The rest of the time, it's MREs. Morale seems to be good so far. Everyone is busy getting things set up. I have my flight crews flying border patrols at night to get them used to the terrain and the area.

I haven't seen a newspaper in four days. Like everyone else out here in the desert, I crave any kind of news about how the air war is going. I mean, I know how I think it's going, but we play such a small part in this huge conflict. Hopefully the Air Force jets I hear buzzing overhead will continue to blast Saddam's army, making our jobs easier when the time comes.

I am keeping my promise to write to you every day. I hope the mail is getting through.

Have to run; it's getting late. At least out here we're away from Scud Alley, and maybe I can finally get some sleep!

Love you and miss you,

Dick

So, while I was going to meetings and potlucks, Dick was doing patrols and reconnaissance along the Iraq border. Talk about a contrast in living conditions! And if I thought February started out boring, it sure ended with a bang, and not just because of the commencement of the ground war but because I had a chance-of-a-life-time meeting.

The headlines on February 20 got my attention and my adrenaline going: "Desert Storm 'Ready to Go.'" There were two separate articles about Apache helicopters: "Guns Thunder Along Desert Front" and "Apaches Launch Night Raid into Iraq."

It felt like January 15 and 16 all over again. The difference was, before Task Force Normandy, there was no reporting about it, so I didn't know it was happening. But now that the media were covering this phase of the war, it was around the clock. In addition, seven other Apache battalions, from other divisions, were in the same region, so I was never sure if it was Dick's unit that was being reported on.

That same day, we got word that, in just two days, First Lady Barbara Bush was coming to visit Fort Campbell. There would be a big rally out at the airfield for all the wives and families, and there would be no school that day.

We activated our phone trees that night, calling all the wives. It was nice, for a change, to have good news to report. Everyone I talked to was excited, and more than one wife said how special it felt that the First Lady was coming to *our* post. It was perfect timing, and, looking back now, I realize that was exactly the point of Barbara Bush's visit: to show support and rally the families the day before the actual ground war kicked off.

Early the next morning, Carolyn Shelton called me to say, "Vicki, you have been selected, along with a small group, to have a private meeting with Mrs. Bush before the rally."

"Wow, how did that happen? Why me?"

"We did a random selection of wives of different ranks, from different units, and your name came up."

"I would be honored! Thank you so much!"

She went on to explain the security measures and logistics. She also told me that Pam Mathias, the brand-new wife from our unit, had been selected as well.

I hung up the phone and immediately called my mom. "Mom, you'll never guess who's coming here. Barbara Bush! But the biggest news is that I get to meet her!"

By then, we were both shrieking as my mom said, "Oh my goodness, Vicki, how did that happen?"

I explained the details, and her next question was "What are you going to wear?"

"It just so happens that I got this cute outfit at the Limited a few weeks ago, so I'll wear that."

"Vicki, that's wonderful. I am so excited for you! Can you believe you get to meet the First Lady?"

"It's pretty amazing. I never imagined this would happen. I just wish I could tell Dick."

My next call was to Pam Mathias, and we made our plans for the next day. Pam was just as excited as I was. She was probably the only wife whose husband *and* father were deployed together, so I figured that was why she was included. If I could have picked a wife, I would have picked Pam for that reason. But the why and how of it all didn't really matter—we were going to meet Barbara Bush!

I couldn't sleep the night before. The next day, I met Pam at the Eagle Conference Center, along with the other family members, and we boarded a mini-bus for the ten-minute ride out to the airfield. I said to Pam more than once, "Can you believe we're doing this?"

I don't remember anything about the drive to the airfield, the same drive I had made with my mom all those months ago after the helicopter accident, and one that I had made many times before to either say goodbye to or welcome Dick home. Nothing felt the same that day.

"Pam, I wonder if we'll actually get to meet her and talk with her, or if we're just part of a larger group."

"I've been wondering the same thing."

"Well, either way, it's the chance of a lifetime, and even if we're just in the same room with her, I'll be thrilled. She is such a wonderful First Lady."

At the airfield, we were ushered into the base operations building, after our IDs were checked not once, not twice, but three times. Each door we went through required another check of our IDs and purses.

About fifteen of us were present, including one male spouse and a couple of kids. It was a cross-section from throughout the division, so, except for Pam, I did not know anyone in the group. Pamela Peay and Carolyn Shelton were greeting *Air Force One* and would come in with Mrs. Bush. We were in the VIP waiting room, which had chairs set up in a circle, a couple of couches, and a table with some finger foods on it. Any other time, I would have been all over the hors d'oeuvres table, but I didn't want to eat and mess up my lipstick or, worse yet, get something caught in my teeth. *No,* I thought, *meeting Barbara Bush is far more important than eating a finger sandwich and some chips.*

I struck up a conversation with a few of the other wives, but it was a distracted kind of talking, as we were all watching the door for any movement, any sign, that *she* was entering. I was so glad for Pam's company in those minutes, because I could be myself and not feel embarrassed to be so nervous; Pam was as well.

Finally, after about forty-five minutes, the door opened and a small entourage of personal assistants and Secret Service came in, with Barbara Bush right behind them. I was grinning from ear to ear, and, through no volition of my own, my eyes filled with tears. I had never been in the presence of someone like her, and I had to remind myself, *She's just a woman—a wife, a mother, a grandmother.*

We all sat down; she was directly across from me, and we went around the circle, introducing ourselves. Heart pounding, mouth dry, I said, "My name is Vicki Cody. My husband commands 1-101st Aviation Regiment, the Apache helicopter battalion." *Is that my voice? It doesn't sound like me.*

Once we had finished these introductions, Barbara broke the ice by saying, "I am so glad to meet you all. My husband wanted to be here today, but he's a little busy right now." We all chuckled, as it was such a normal thing to say. She went on to ask how we were doing and coping with the deployment. A few people spoke up, but I don't remember what they asked her or told her. I was having my own happy moment just sitting there in her presence.

Barbara asked the group, "Is there anything you want me to tell George when I get back home?" She said it with such sincerity.

Someone spoke up and asked, "When is the ground war going to start?"

Deep inside, I cringed. Even though that was the critical question on all of our minds, I would never have put the President's wife in a position to have to answer it. *Like she's actually going to spill the beans on something top-secret?*

But Barbara took it like a pro, chuckled, and said, "Hmm . . . I'm not sure." With that, the circle of wives laughed right along with her.

Then we each had our picture taken with her, and as she put her arm around my waist, I thought, *I will never forget this moment.* The official party left, and then our group headed over to the hangar where the rally was taking place. Large hanging banners read UNITED IN PRIDE, and the huge hangar was filled to capacity. Pam and I stood in the back. There was no way to get any closer, but that was okay. I couldn't see everything that was going on, but I could hear it. Barbara Bush mounted the stage to cheers of "We love you!" and chants of "U-S-A, U-S-A!" Her remarks were brief but heartfelt, and she ended by saying, "The President and I want you to know that you are in our hearts. The entire country supports all of you." Then Lee Greenwood sang, "God Bless the USA," and the crowd went wild.

I realized I had not thought about the war all day—I had not worried about one thing—and it sure felt good.

Journal Entry

Life is a series of highs and lows. If you are lucky, there are times in between that are like a plateau. While they may seem boring in the moment, they actually represent an opportunity to catch your breath. Or maybe that plateau you're on is there so you can stop and smell the roses.

Barbara Bush's visit to Fort Campbell came at a time when many of us are on a plateau—tired of waiting, wondering, and worrying. Standing in the back of the hangar today, I absorbed the beautiful scene before me: thousands of families, and some soldiers, too, reveling in the spirit and patriotism, and all of us singing along with Lee Greenwood. I just met the First Lady of our country, who came to show her and her husband's support for all of us. It was the sweetest rose I had smelled in a long time.

28

By the time I got home from the rally, it was 5:00 p.m. The boys needed dinner, and I had an FSG meeting that night with the whole battalion. I was back to my real life as mom, cook, chauffeur, and FSG leader. Calling my mother would have to wait until later.

I had not read the newspaper that morning because of my frenzied state of getting ready to meet Barbara Bush. I glanced at the paper before my meeting and almost wished I hadn't. I saw the headlines: "Four Killed from 160th SOAR"; "Two Copter Crashes in Saudi Desert Claim Nine Lives." *Oh no! Not what I wanted to see!*

While not part of the 101st Airborne Division, the 160th Special Operations Aviation Regiment and the 5th Special Forces Group were based at Fort Campbell and part of our community and Army family. I read the article as fast as I could because I knew that there would be questions at the meeting that I was on my way to. An OH-58 scout helicopter had crashed and a Blackhawk had crashed in separate incidents. I was thankful that the rear detachment commander, Mike Dousette, would be at the meeting so he could handle the questions about the accidents. It had been such a wonderful day, and I wanted to hold on to that feeling a little bit longer. Still, I knew

I had to stay grounded in reality, so I gave myself a little pep talk: *Okay, Vicki, time to shift gears back to your real life—one that's about war and helicopter crashes, not mixing and mingling with the First Lady.*

When I arrived, most of the wives already knew about the accidents and that the aircraft involved were not part of our unit, so they asked very few questions about what had happened, much to my relief. When it was my turn to speak, I told them about my experience with Barbara Bush. Many of them had gone to the rally, but they enjoyed my firsthand account of having actually met the First Lady. I was glad I had something positive to talk about that night.

I was exhausted by the time I got home. It had been quite a day. After the boys were in bed, I finally had time to write to Dick. As tired as I was, I stayed up late composing one of my lengthy, spare-no-detail letters. My letters to him and my journal were the two places I could go into such depth on whatever subjects I chose. He told me he loved reading my letters, which gave him a glimpse into our everyday lives back home. More than once he said I should be a writer, but I sometimes wondered if my attention to detail was a bit too much. I didn't just write about a topic; I shared everything about the First Lady's visit: what I wore, what I ate, if my hair was or wasn't perfect that day, what I said, what others said or did.

I pictured Dick sitting on his cot, in his tent, in the middle of the desert, reading my letter, maybe getting only halfway through it before something urgent came up and he took a break to go fight a war or something. Then he came back and finished reading it. But isn't that what love is: reading each other's letters, regardless of the length and subject matter, savoring each word, and feeling as if you're with the other person? I wondered how long it would take for my letter to get to him and if somehow he already knew that I had met Barbara Bush.

The next day, Saturday, President Bush gave the final ultimatum to Saddam Hussein to get out of Kuwait, by noon EST. The boys had basketball games in the morning and afternoon, but I snuck home in between to check the news and see if anything had happened. (What I would've given for an iPhone back then!) The United States had reportedly begun "jamming" the Iraq radar system, or what was left of it. I knew that meant that something was about to happen. I went back to the basketball games and tried not to think about Dick. The day before had been an ideal reprieve from the stress, but then reality and the demon had crept back in. I was staring it down again and determined not to flinch.

That evening, as Tyler watched a movie on one TV, Clint watched a show on the other TV, and I folded laundry, the ground war began. All of a sudden, Clint yelled, "Mom, I think the war started again! Come look at the TV!"

Tyler and I raced into the den, and there it was. "Breaking news: US and coalition forces are moving toward Baghdad as Air Force jets continue to bomb!" And just as we had when the air war started, we sat there and watched it unfold on live TV. The difference that night was that I knew without a doubt that Dick was out in front with his Apaches, leading the air assault for the 101st Airborne Division. You would think I would have been prepared, and maybe I was, but I still felt panic rising as I tried to anticipate the boys' questions.

In a split second, Tyler asked, "What do you think Dad is doing right now?"

"Boys, I think your dad and his pilots are flying their Apaches, making sure everything is ready as the ground troops move forward, protecting them from above."

That wasn't enough of an answer, because Clint came back with "But is he shooting at the enemy? Will they shoot at him?"

Oh, man, how do I answer this stuff? "Your dad and his pilots are lucky to be flying Apaches, because not much can hurt that aircraft. You guys know everything there is to know about Apaches; they're the most powerful helicopters, with all those guns! And your dad is the best pilot, right?"

"Yeah, and he has Hellfire missiles!"

"You are absolutely right, Clint. He does have missiles. So I believe he will be okay. We are going to pray extra hard when we go to Mass tomorrow. And every time we pray, we will pray for your dad and *all* his soldiers."

The phone rang and I ran into the kitchen to answer it. It was my father.

"Vicki, are you watching the TV?"

"Yes, Dad, we've got it on. I'm worried all over again. But we all knew this was coming."

"What do you think Dick is doing? Vicki, your mom and I are so worried about him and for you and Clint and Tyler. Are the boys doing okay?"

"They're doing amazingly well, I think because we've had so much time to get ready for this. And maybe because Dick already did something dangerous, I have to trust that he'll be okay again."

"Call us anytime. We're here thinking of you, and we love you."

"I love you too, Dad."

The boys and I watched some of the coverage and then put a movie on. When they went to bed, I reaffirmed to them that the war was not coming to the United States and that this part wasn't much different from the beginning of the air war. "Try not to worry about your dad. He'll be okay." I think my approach worked, because they didn't ask any more questions.

I, on the other hand, had trouble getting to sleep. I prayed as intensely as possible, even out loud, to make sure God heard me. I made some bargains, too, hoping that would give me an edge. Finally, I tried to get into my beach chair in my happy place, but no amount of imaginary ocean breeze and sunshine was going to work that night. While tossing and turning, I realized that Barbara Bush's visit was not just a random thing, like, *I think I'll go visit the wives and families at Fort Campbell, Kentucky, this week, just for the heck of it.* For her to take time out of her busy schedule to visit us and show her love and support just hours before the ground war began gave me a whole new respect for her and her husband, our president.

For months I had known that it would inevitably come to this. I knew that I would have to face it and I was pretty sure I could get through it, but in the middle of the night, none of that reasoning gave me comfort.

The next morning, the headlines in the Sunday paper read, "'Final Phase' Begins, Gulf War in Deadly End Game." The boys and I went to Mass that morning, as usual, and it took every bit of my resolve not to start crying. I was tired from my restless night, and my heart was pounding. For the hundredth time, I thought, *How in the world am I going to do this? How can I keep moving forward, taking care of Clint and Tyler, watching out for my "flock" of wives, and not fold like a cheap suit because of the pressure? I have never experienced anything like this.*

That afternoon, I talked to my parents, Dick's parents, my sister, my brother, and some of Dick's siblings. As nighttime approached, I dreaded going to bed, afraid that I wouldn't be able to sleep. I had never had insomnia issues before and certainly did not want to add that to my list of worries. But I was okay that night; talking with family during the day had somehow eased the burden. Just being able to share my feelings and knowing they were in it with me did the trick.

However, the next day, I got frustrated all over again when I got two letters from Dick and realized he'd written them at the end of January. At that rate, I would be lucky if he got my letter about Barbara Bush before he returned from the war! But as I read the letters, I realized I had to stop focusing on when he'd written them. Dates didn't matter; only his words and his love for me were important. That was what would sustain me during the dark days of February.

TAA Eddie

Hi Vicki,

I'm doing fine. Another day has gone by—amazing how fast they go. I went to Mass this morning with some of my guys: Tim DeVito, Howard Killian, and Jorge Garcia. Father D. said the Mass, and Mark Curran and Jim Mullins were there as well. It felt like a typical Sunday at Soldiers Chapel back home, except our families weren't with us. It was weird—such a normal thing in such an unusual setting.

Then we scrambled to provide gunship support to some 3rd Brigade elements who had stumbled into some Iraqi ground positions. We spent a couple of hours covering them and "targeting" the enemy. We did not do any shooting, as the higher-ups aren't ready for us to do that, and based on our ROE [rules of engagement] orders. That was fine by me, but it was good training, especially for my guys who haven't had any action yet. It was like a practice scrimmage. Right now, we do a lot of border patrolling and monitoring the air campaign so we will be ready when we get the call to move forward.

Tonight I walked our perimeter, which is huge, to check on all my troops and guard posts. They are all doing super. So many other units are having all kinds of discipline and morale issues, which also mean safety issues. There have been lots of accidents and mishaps, like guys shooting themselves while cleaning their weapons, truck rollovers, hard landings and crash landings in aircraft . . . I could go on and on. And the ground war hasn't even started yet! My unit has had none of that. My guys are so focused and ready for the mission.

For instance, today when we launched to go out, the troops literally jumped into action, no questions asked. Each one knows exactly what to do. My refuel guys sped over to the aircraft and topped me off in less than three minutes. Just like an Indy race car team! They make me so proud!

I am learning to fly another helicopter, the OH-58 AHIP (the newest version of the 58). It flies just like the OH-58 but has more power and night/day systems similar to the Apache. We have seven of them attached to us, and I like to fly whatever my pilots are flying. I should need only about three hours in it with an IP [instructor pilot] to get it all checked out.

It's so cold here, I can see my breath while I'm writing this! Luckily, CSM Ehrke got us a nice kerosene heater for our tent, so we have some heat when we get up in the morning. Sometimes I think about how simple life is over here—so different from what we are all used to back in the States.

I haven't gotten a letter from you in over two weeks. I know you are writing, and I know you must be experiencing the same thing on your end, but I really miss hearing from you!

I better go; it's almost midnight and the last of my OH-58 scouts just landed, so I can sleep now.

Take care, and don't worry about me.

Always remember I love you more than anything.

Dick [smiley face]

Journal Entry

Have you ever reached a point where you've been praying and asking God for something like the safety of your loved one but then you think, Who am I to ask this? Why should my prayers be answered? What makes one person's request any more important than another's? Why are some people spared tragedy when others have to suffer?

Even when I feel bogged down by an endless stream of unanswered questions, I somehow know in my heart that Dick will be okay. I will hang on to any small glimmer of hope I have, because it does no good to give up, and that makes all the difference when you're facing a challenge.

29

Even after he moved to his new TAA, I was surprised that Dick still had time to write almost daily. And even though it took almost two weeks for a letter to arrive, once the mail started flowing again, I got one about every other day. His letters gave me a good sense of his new surroundings and even a little bit more clarity about Task Force Normandy.

However, I never quite got past my disorientation when he said, "If this thing [the ground war] kicks off," when it had most definitely kicked off! With no way to know how he was in the moment and whether he was safe, I vacillated between feeling like nothing would ever happen to him and feeling like our luck was going to run out.

To compound my inner conflict, it was midwinter and the weeks stretched on and on. All of the major holidays were over; we had nothing to look forward to, no trips to plan, and no idea when Dick would get home. I had to work even harder to get the three of us through it. But somehow, we made it.

TAA Eddie

Hi Vick,

I hope all is well with you and the boys. I think about you guys all the time! I am doing fine. I just got your letter dated January 18, so you already knew a little bit about my mission. You asked me just how dangerous it was and if there was a moment when I was scared. Now that I have had time to think about it, I suppose the most dangerous part was flying so low (fifty feet above the desert floor) at night, with no lights and no radios. Many things could have gone wrong, not to mention someone getting a fix on our positions and taking us out. I was praying the entire time.

Every time I brief the mission, I am amazed at how it went down. The attack went just as we practiced it. I have viewed the unedited gun tapes, and it was a chaotic and ferocious four and a half minutes, but very precise and surgical. Those radar sites never knew what hit them. I take no pleasure in the fact that Iraqi soldiers were killed; my only pleasure or pride is that my guys executed my plan flawlessly and with true professionalism. At the end of the day, we carried out our orders to destroy military targets, and that is how I look at it. Bottom line: It was us or them!

Now it's on to the ground war, if they ever get this thing started. I went over to see Tommy Greco and get some info on his war plans. I'll be covering him and 3rd Brigade during the crucial part of the ground campaign. So glad to be supporting my West Point buddy!

We've been having these tremendous sand/dust storms called shamals. Out here in the middle of the desert, there is nothing to break the wind, so these are worse than the occasional ones we had back at King Fahd. They are unlike anything I have ever experienced. They wreak havoc not only on our sparse living conditions (tents) but on our aircraft. The dust and sand get everywhere, and if we don't stay on top of things, it could be devastating to our helicopters. I went out in the last storm and walked the area to check on my guys and inspected the aircraft for proper tie-down and covers. It was like a hurricane with sand. I couldn't see five feet in front of me. But I'm glad I went out, because I found some things screwed up. My people were hunkered down in their tents and sheltered from the storm, and I told them, "I refuse to let this desert beat us! I refuse to give in to this and say this is too tough!" I know they think I'm relentless, but I got my point across. They can't let the elements get the best of them, especially when we're on the brink of war. The war does not stop for weather. I reminded everyone that things are about to get even tougher.

I tell you, Vick, I was beat when I got back to my tent. It was exhausting being out there in those conditions. Even with goggles on and a scarf around my neck, my face got sandblasted. Actually, it feels pretty smooth right now [smiley face].

Our food trucks are up and running, and we get one hot meal a day. My mess hall guys are so creative, and Staff Sergeant Longstaff was able to score cases of Dinty Moore-brand dinners. (I didn't ask how or where he got them—some things are better left unsaid!) They heat them up in these big chafing-type dishes, and you would think we were at a buffet! Such a welcome change after months of MREs!

I wrote to both boys yesterday. I hope they are being good for you. I know how it is in the winter when they don't get outside as much. Glad they have basketball a couple of days a week, and especially for you! I know this isn't easy. If we can just get this thing finished, we can think about getting back home.

Gotta run; it's late and I've got to be up early for briefings
tomorrow. I am being careful, so try not to worry about me.
   I love you!
   Dick

Every night after getting the boys settled in bed, I usually had
a phone call to make or take, but the last thing I did was write in
my journal. After Dick's recent letter with details about his mission, which was more of his perspective than I'd had, I found myself
thinking about what it must have been like to fly through the desert
at night, low-level, with no lights. As hard as it was to imagine, my
thoughts drifted back to when I went through flight training to get
my private pilot's license. I realized I *could* relate, just a little bit, to
what Dick's flight was like that night.

About seven years before, we were stationed at Fort Leavenworth,
Kansas, and we had recently bought a small airplane. Flying was
Dick's life, but it also became mine and eventually the boys' as well.
That year, I decided to get my private pilot's license. During the training, among the many requirements, I had to fly a few hours at night
with my instructor. The thought of doing so was scary to me until
I actually did it. I was surprised that I liked it. In the evening, the
winds were usually minimal, compared with the air thermals and
gusts that I typically dealt with in the heat of a Kansas afternoon.
For my debut night flight, my instructor and I took off and flew to
a small airfield about thirty miles north of Leavenworth. The first
thing I noticed was how quiet and smooth and peaceful it was. There
was little to no traffic in that area, and at that time of night, I was the
only one making radio calls. Also, in that part of the country there
were huge expanses of land with just a farm here and there, so, with
no cities or towns, it was pitch black.

I was apprehensive about landing that first time, but as I turned
on final approach, I keyed the mic five times, per my instructions,

and, hallelujah, it turned on the runway lights! I was so excited to see those blue lights to guide me in.

Another requirement was to log some instrument time with my instructor. That meant flying with a blackout hood over my head that allowed me to see only the instrument panel, nothing outside the cockpit. I had to rely completely on the instruments. That was difficult for me, and at first I felt disoriented and a little claustrophobic. I had to keep breathing and talk myself out of getting vertigo. I was so glad to have my instructor with me, walking me through everything.

All of that was going through my mind that night in 1991 as I lay awake, thinking about Dick and his guys in the middle of the desert, with nothing to light their way, nothing but their instruments to guide them. I had a whole new appreciation not just for their flight but for the fact that they did it amid the danger of being detected and shot down. That took some serious balls!

Thinking about all of that made it hard to sleep, as my mind naturally wandered toward the what-ifs and the gray areas of life. I had to devise a new happy place to go to, as my beach chair just hadn't been cutting it lately. My new destination was skiing in the Colorado Rockies at Keystone and A-Basin, our two favorite places. I visualized the whole scene—skiing (fast) down a pristine groomed trail, nothing but corduroy; making amazing, giant slalom–type turns; bright blue sky; warm sun on my face; and an endless run skied to perfection—and thought, *I'm happy.*

For the next few days, February 23–27—one hundred hours, to be exact—the ground war raged and I fought hard to keep the demon at bay. But it seemed like every time I turned around, there it was again. The news was on twenty-four-seven on every channel. The local stations reported every move by the 101st Airborne Division. Even CNN announced that the 101st had made the largest air assault in history, with Apaches leading the way. See what I mean about the demon? How could I have gotten away from it? At the same time, reports of low numbers of US casualties and of Iraqi soldiers surrendering by the thousands made me think, *Maybe Dick will be okay after all.*

But then, on February 26, it was a different story. A Scud missile attack hit a barracks, killing twenty-seven US servicemen. The Marines were in Kuwait City and *almost* had control of it. Simultaneously, the 101st was involved in heavy fighting in Iraq as they pushed toward Baghdad to surround Saddam's Republican Guard. How could I not be scared for Dick when so much was going on all around him?

On February 27, General Schwarzkopf was supposed to give a big briefing on the progress of the ground campaign. I'll be damned if I didn't have to go to lunch with our brigade commander's wife and my fellow aviation commanders' wives the same day. And then we had our monthly information exchange right after that! All I wanted to do was sit in front of the TV and wait for the press conference.

At lunch with my peers (nine of us), Betsy Garrett talked about brigade news that we needed to disseminate to our battalion groups. Our conversations naturally turned toward the war, as we speculated about when it would end, when the guys would come home, how horny we all were, and things of that nature.

Later, during the information exchange with the entire commanders' wives' group, the garrison commander, LTC Lynn, came in to give us an update on the division and the war. I had never heard the room so quiet as he addressed the group of about seventy, and I'm sure every one of us was thinking, *Oh, good—maybe we'll find out something like when this will be over!*

It was as if the whole room held its collective breath as LTC Lynn said, "The war is almost over. The Iraqi army is surrendering and is literally crippled."

I sat there thinking, *Can this really be? Is it over? They predicted it would be quick, but this is unbelievable!*

Just when I began to very slowly let out my breath, LTC Lynn added, in an *oh, by the way* tone, "Two helicopters from the 101st went on a rescue mission, and one of the helicopters was shot down."

His words nearly knocked the wind out of me. I looked around the room; no one else was reacting, not even my fellow aviator wives. Everyone was staring straight ahead. *Am I the only one who just heard that? Doesn't he realize that at this point, any mention of a helicopter of any kind can freak us out? Why is he being so blasé? Jeez, Vicki, get it together! You know the deal—he would've have said if it was from our brigade.*

In those few moments, as the meeting came to a close and we gathered our things, I took my cues from everyone else in the room and gave one of my best command performances. I surmised that the crash most likely had not involved any of our guys, since LTC Lynn had not specified the unit and aircraft type. If the crew involved in the accident had not been identified, then the Army couldn't release any information. Maybe it was from a unit attached to the 101st. If it was of no concern to everyone else, then I could play that game, too. But deep down I was getting just a little bit sick and tired of keeping my game face on. I couldn't wait to get home to see what I could find out.

Gail came over to my house later that afternoon. As we drank our afternoon coffee and discussed the day's events, I remarked, "I don't want to get my hopes up just yet. After all this buildup to the war, I can't believe it would end so quickly."

"I know; it seems too good to be true."

"But if it *is* over, I wonder how long it will take for our guys to get back home."

The phone rang, and I rushed to get it. It was my friend Denise Davis, the S-3's wife.

"Vicki, put the news on! They're talking about an Apache that got shot down!"

Gail and I ran into the den and saw the report. Tyler came in just as we heard, "Two helicopters from the 101st went on a rescue mission, and an AH-64 Apache was shot down behind enemy lines."

I thought I was going to be sick. I went into the bathroom because I didn't want to overreact in front of Tyler and Gail. For the first time in months, my panic was physical. I was having trouble catching my breath. And, right on my heels, that demon followed me into the bathroom, trying to get the best of me.

I barely had time to get myself together before Tyler opened the door. "Don't worry, Mom. It's not Dad. He would never get himself into a situation like that."

Gail was standing there, too. "Vicki, it's probably not even Dick's unit."

"It just hit me like a ton of bricks, and for a minute, I began to think the worst. I know the media gets things wrong. I just wish someone could let us know. The wondering is the hardest part."

"I know it's hard, but you'll be okay," Gail said.

I didn't want to concern them, so, to deflect, I said, "You're right—it *will* be okay. Let's get dinner started." I had to keep moving.

During dinner that night, I could sense Clint and Tyler watching me for cues.

"Mom, there's no way that was Dad," Tyler said in a reassuring voice.

Clint chimed in, "Yeah, Mom, no way. Dad wouldn't be involved in something like that. I just know it."

"You're right. Thank you for being so sensible right now. I need that, because I just got a little scared today."

I said that to ease their minds, but I had trouble believing it and was not able to shake those feelings for a few more days.

Journal Entry

As hard as you try to maintain composure and control in a difficult situation, sometimes it's impossible. Maybe, for a second, you just kind of lose it and think, I'm done; I've reached my limit. That's okay if it doesn't affect those around you. But when it begins to creep in on the mood and the safe world you have worked so hard to create for your kids and your family, then it's time for a restart.

Like what I felt on Christmas morning when I had to take a knee, the same feeling washed over me again today. For a brief moment I gave in to it, but then seeing Clint and Tyler's looks of concern watching my every move, I realized I can't take a knee right now. We have come so far and are in the home stretch. I can't have them worrying about me. This feeling of wanting to shield them is all the motivation I need.

30

A four-and-a-half-day ground war may seem totally insignificant to the average person in today's world. It *was* brief in terms of its length, but for the families back home, there was nothing short about it. In fact, it was excruciatingly long, because the clock really began ticking and our stress started back in August. Anything could have happened then to change the outcome. We had lived with that stress for the past six months, so by the time the war started, we were already worn out.

In 1990–'91, we were in a whole new world of technology, war fighting, mobility, and capability. So when Saddam Hussein invaded Kuwait and the first US troops were sent to Saudi Arabia, the eyes of the world were on every movement over there.

I knew there were reporters embedded with units during the combat; Dick had told me that. They reported back to their news bureaus, and, because of the transmission capabilities in 1991, we got those reports way too quickly, before things had been sorted out. Mistakes are not intentional, but in the chaos of battle, a journalist, in the attempt to get a story out, sometimes misrepresents a situation or makes a mistake, or something gets lost in translation. I know all of that now, as I look back on those days. But at the time, we depended on, we expected, and we craved news that was just minutes and hours old, and we wanted that news to be perfectly accurate. That was unrealistic—after all, how could we have expected things to go smoothly during a war? Still, our lives felt miserable when things did not go as planned, as was the case with the vague reporting on the downed aircraft.

After the initial news reports, our local newspaper was cautious in its coverage. It stated that it was "in the dark about the helicopter rescue mission." It quoted General Schwarzkopf as saying, "Two helicopters from the 101st volunteered for a search-and-rescue mission for the downed F-16 crew. One of the helicopters was shot down, and we are still in the process of sorting it out."

At the same time, President Bush announced the cease fire and official end to the war. But how in the world could we celebrate when our soldiers were still in harm's way?

In the meantime, I spent hours on the phone, as usual; my parents, Dick's parents, our sisters and brothers, the wives in our unit, and our friends all called with concerns and questions about the helicopter crash.

Each time I answered the phone, I steeled myself for the inevitable:

"Mrs. Cody, I just don't understand why you can't tell us if the accident involves our husbands or not."

Or: "But the newspaper said the aircraft are from the 101st."

Or: "I heard it was two Blackhawks and an Apache. That must be our unit. Why won't you tell us who it is?"

I tried to keep my responses to a minimum and not speculate, but that was hard to do when I was feeling just as frustrated. "I know this is difficult," I kept saying. "I'm concerned and scared, too. But until someone gives me information, I can't put anything out."

"But why is it taking so long? How can they not know who was involved?"

"Sometimes it's not easy to locate the site and identify who was involved. Department of the Army has to be one hundred percent accurate before they make notifications, and that takes time."

I did not want to bother our rear detachment during such a critical time, but I had nowhere else to turn. After two days of endless phone calls, I called Mike Dousette.

"Mike, I'm spending all day on the phone with wives asking for information about the accident over there. I need help. Is there anything you can tell me about what's going on?"

"Ma'am, you know I would tell you if I had anything official to report, but it's been pretty much radio silence from your husband and the command center over there since the ground war kicked off. I'm sure the incident doesn't involve our unit, though."

"But you can't imagine the phone calls I'm getting; the wives act like I know something that I'm not sharing with them. Even my own family wonders how and why no one knows the details."

"Something significant happened, and either they can't identify the downed crew or they can't find them. And I think there was more than one incident. These things can take a few days to sort out, and they have to get it right before they make any notifications. It probably should not have been reported in the first place, since they didn't have all the facts."

"Well, it's making our lives a living hell."

"I know, ma'am. There's nothing I can do right now about the lack of information, but refer all the calls to me. Let me handle this. And remember, we just have to be patient."

"Okay, I will. Just be prepared to be on the phone twenty-four-seven!"

I was beginning to dislike myself for giving in to unsubstantiated reports. I had always been an optimist, but I was seeing signs of a side of me that I didn't like: a pessimist. I stayed as busy as I could, but I needed to keep away from the TV during the day. If I had had more of a life, maybe that would have been realistic. *You* try staying away from the news and the rumors when your husband is in a combat zone and you've had no direct communication with him in weeks!

By the beginning of March, I was hanging on by a thread. It didn't help that I kept seeing headlines like "When Will 101st Return?" I even saw an article talking about plans for welcome-home ceremonies and flag-waving rallies. I thought it was a bit premature, but that was just me being cautious, and maybe a little of that new, pessimistic side of me. Still, how can you not get caught up in the excitement when you see such a bold, front-page headline?

The next day, the details of the downed aircraft finally emerged. The confusion was that two separate incidents involving Blackhawk helicopters had occurred. One was a Blackhawk on a combat mission that crashed in Iraq, killing all six members onboard; it would take days to identify the crew and then notify next of kin. The other incident involved two Blackhawks assigned to the 101st that went in to rescue the downed F-16 pilot. One of those Blackhawks got shot down in the process, so the mission was aborted and the other Blackhawk returned to its base. The F-16 pilot and the four crew members on the Blackhawk were listed as missing in action. In a separate incident, an Apache got shot at but was able to return to its base.

All of that tempered any excitement I had begun to feel. As long as so many things were up in the air, I knew the war was far from over. But once I had some closure on the accidents, I gradually let go of the fear and the knot in my stomach began to unwind. I had expended way too much energy on that story, and for too long. It was time to move forward again, as difficult as it was to do so when I knew that other families in our community had just lost loved ones.

Dick's letters were still taking a week to ten days to get to me. Given how quickly things were happening and changing, and how rapidly the war advanced, the slowness of the mail just added to everyone's stress levels. But every time I saw one of his letters in the mailbox, my heart did a little happy dance, giving me a momentary fix.

His letters from mid-February told me he still hadn't gotten any letters from us, and that broke my heart. His letters ran the gamut from his perspective on world news to talk of war plans, mission briefings, what-if scenarios, all the mishaps and screw-ups of other aviation units, and the pressures of command. Sometimes he talked about the future, speculating about what and where our next duty assignment would be, since he was due to change command that summer. That gave me hope that there would be life after all of this. He talked about all the buddies he continued to run into from his days at West Point and other duty assignments. He told me what was going on with his siblings back home in Vermont; they each wrote to him faithfully. I loved that he shared all of his musings with me. He needed a sounding board, and I was it, even if it happened two weeks after the fact.

TAA Eddie

Hi Vicki,

I hope you and the boys are doing okay. I am fine. I got the letter that you sent over with SFC Anderson; otherwise, I haven't gotten any letters since we moved to our TAA. I know you are writing; I just hope mine are getting to you and the boys.

We continue to be poised and ready. The waiting and wondering are the biggest challenges for everyone here. I'm just glad to stay so busy, I don't have time to think about being bored!

We have been flying missions inside Iraq (unofficially), trying to get a sense of the battlefield. It gives my pilots an opportunity to rehearse and keeps them focused. There is always that outside chance that a deal will be brokered and that this will end before we send in our ground forces. I really don't see that happening, but you never know. We have crippled some of Saddam's army, and the bombing continues, but he still has more than five hundred thousand men and five thousand tanks that could launch a "suicide attack." We can't let up. My hope is that by the time we launch our ground attack, it will go precisely and quickly.

Here is my Air Medal for the Normandy mission in Iraq on January 17. It is supposed to have a "v" device (for "valor") on the ribbon, but they ran out. I will get that later. All of my guys got Air Medals, too. Colonel Garrett came to our area and presented them to us yesterday. He put me in for a Distinguished Flying Cross as well. Don't know if that will happen, but I appreciate being nominated.

The pressures of commanding in combat are tremendous! There are so many decisions to make that have huge consequences. Sometimes we get spotty intelligence, and I have to make a split-second decision while answering to the higher-ups. And sometimes the people at the top want to do risky things. I am lucky to have Garrett and Peay as my direct chain of command. They have enough respect for me that they allow me to make decisions, and if I don't like something, they don't pressure or second-guess me. I have to do what is right, and my goal is to lessen the risk for my guys while still completing the mission.

I hope you are doing okay. I got a note from Mike Dousette, and he said you continue to do a great job with the wives and families back there. I am sorry for putting you and the boys through this. I know being an Army wife and family is not easy. I just want you to know I appreciate all that you do to make our family better and to keep it in good shape while I

am deployed. And, of course, you know I love you very much
[smiley face]!

   Take care of yourself!
   Love,
   Dick

PS: Tell your dad thanks for the subscription to the Burlington
Free Press. Even though the issues are backed up, I don't care.
I love reading about home, and, of course, the crossword puz-
zles, too! I'll write him when I get a chance.

I was touched that Dick sent his Air Medal to the boys and me. I
knew it meant a lot to him, but I also knew he couldn't keep it with
him—not where he was going. He obviously did not want to lose it,
so we would keep it safe until he returned.

I had never realized how much Dick appreciated what I did for
him and our family, because he was not one to say it on a daily basis
in the middle of our busy lives. When I read his words, in all their
simplistic sincerity and totally unprompted by me, I felt his devo-
tion to me and our sons. I told myself to remember his letters in the
coming years when life got busy again and maybe we didn't take the
time to profess our love in quite the same way or as often.

Journal Entry

Maybe we don't say it enough; maybe we don't share our feelings as
often as we should. We think we have endless tomorrows, so we tend
to put things on the back burner as we go about our daily lives. How
often have you heard someone say after a tragedy that they wish they
had said "I love you" more often? It is not enough to think it or feel it;
we need to show it, say it, and demonstrate it. The opportunity may be
gone in the next instant.

What gives me comfort in these days of war are the words Dick writes to me. His letters give him a way and more opportunities to convey his feelings to me and the boys. I am a verbal person, so I leave nothing unsaid. Maybe I talk too much, write too much, but Dick will never doubt my feelings for him. And neither will our sons.

31

TAA Eddie

Hi Vicki,

By the time you get this letter, we will be in Iraq. Hopefully things will be going as rehearsed and we will be kicking ass! I really think this will go quickly, based on all the intelligence we've been gathering, but you never know.

Time is passing quickly, as we are in continuous operations, day and night. All of my guys are doing great. All of the infantry brigades want us for air support, as they know they can count on our Apaches to keep them safe. It's great for my pilots and our entire unit because we are the talk of the division. The Expect No Mercy legend lives on!

I banged up an Apache the other night while landing on a dusty, blacked-out pad back here at the TAA. Brian and I were returning from a combat mission around 0200. I got into total brownout at ten feet off the ground and landed it using instruments off the eyepiece. We didn't hit too hard, but the rotor blades flexed down and knocked out the pilot's night vision system, so then I was totally blind! It didn't scare me, but I was a little embarrassed that I dinged it up. In retrospect, I'm glad it happened to me. I had eight other aircraft in the air at that time, so we diverted them to an oil-soaked landing area about twenty miles away. We have now rain-soaked our area and put in more tactical lights. That same night, two other aircraft from other units had the same thing happen, but they rolled over and totally destroyed their aircraft! So, we were lucky, and a lot of lessons learned.

With all of the combat flying and the hits we've been taking, it's amazing how indestructible the Apache is. Plus, my pilots and gunners are doing such a great job. Still, I never take anything for granted; tomorrow is another day and another set of circumstances with all new variables. I've learned that nothing remains the same when you are in combat and the battlefield is ever-changing. Long story short, DO NOT worry about me. I'm being safe, and I know which risks to take and when [smiley face]!

When I'm not flying my Apache, I have an OH-8 scout helicopter at my disposal. I use it to get around the battlefield quickly and with a lower profile. When something comes up, I hop in the "58" and off I go. I love the freedom and flexibility it gives me; it's like having my own car!

I better get going. I hope you and the boys are doing good. It is so hard not to be able to talk to you. I hope you're getting all of my letters. I've been getting some of yours and also from my family and yours.

I hope this will all be over soon so I can get home to you and the boys.

Remember how much I love you,
Dick

The roller coaster ride that was pretty much my life continued through mid-March, with no letup in sight. President Bush had declared a cease-fire on February 28, with "all military objectives met." The coalition forces were able to push Saddam's army back to Baghdad, liberating the tiny, oil-rich country of Kuwait. Iraq accepted all of the UN resolutions, so the war was officially over, but pockets of resistance remained throughout Iraq, and those made it difficult for our soldiers and the aircraft to know who was really surrendering. Some Iraqi soldiers waved white flags, luring the helicopters toward them, only to fire on them as they got closer. Troops on the ground and pilots in the air had to make tough judgment calls as they made their way in those days after the cease-fire.

US and coalition POWs were being held in Iraq. More helicopter crashes occurred. I had not talked to Dick in more than a month, and his letters from February that arrived in March were so out of context that I felt anything but excited. To all of the families back home, it didn't *feel* like the war had ended.

Some Special Forces units were returning home to Fort Campbell, as their mission was done and they had been the first ones to deploy. Everywhere I went, I could feel the excitement as people talked about and planned welcome-home parties and ceremonies. Speculation about who was coming home and when dominated every conversation, but at the same time, the memorial services on post for the fallen created a somber mood and a tangible reminder of the cost of war.

On March 7, I watched in fascination as Major Rhonda Cornum, one of the American POWs, was released from captivity. With both arms bandaged, she walked down the steps of the plane to be greeted by General Schwarzkopf. I thought, *Oh my gosh, I know her!* She was a friend of Dick's and not only a Blackhawk pilot but also a flight surgeon. Rhonda was in charge of aviation medicine at Fort Rucker, which is home to all army aviation schools and courses. I had met her the year before when Dick was going through the Apache transition course there. And then I remembered that Dick had told me Rhonda had been assigned as the flight surgeon to the Apache unit from Fort Rucker that was attached to the 101st Aviation Brigade. I was now learning that she had been on the medevac Blackhawk that was shot down while attempting to rescue the fallen F-16 pilot. The images of Rhonda's release kept running through my mind, since I knew her and because she was the first female POW that I was aware of. I wanted so much to talk to Dick and find out what he knew about the whole situation.

Although the release of the POWs did a lot to enhance our sense that maybe things were winding down, my cautionary side knew we were still a long way from a homecoming. It had taken six weeks for the 101st to deploy to Saudi Arabia, so why did any of us think that the redeployment back home would go any faster?

The images on TV were hard to look at: miles and miles of bombed-out, burned-out vehicles along the major highways in Iraq and shells of what had once been buildings in Baghdad. The weeks of bombing by the Air Force had taken their toll, and the ground forces and helicopters had finished the ground war quickly. The Iraqi army was surrendering by the hundreds. They waved white flags and knelt as American and coalition soldiers took them in. They were not the well-equipped, well-clothed, well-fed army I was expecting to see; rather, they looked like an ad hoc, ragtag team of citizen soldiers who had probably been forced to fight for their dictator. Saddam's Republican Guard was the opposite, but they stayed close to their dictator and were not part of the surrender.

Juxtaposed with all of the war talk was a feel-good story from Hollywood about a group of celebrities, entertainers, and sports figures who got together and created a music video to show their support of the US troops in Operation Desert Storm and to raise money for the Red Cross. "Voices That Care" was the name of the song, as well as the name of the group that came together to make it. The charity single and follow-on documentary music video were a presentation for the troops, which aired on TV on February 28—coincidentally, the same day the war ended.

Dick knew nothing about the music video, as he was still in the middle of the desert, conducting combat operations, but all of us back home felt the impact of it. Clint, Tyler, and I watched it on TV that night, naming the celebrities we recognized: Celine Dion, Michael Bolton, Kenny G, Will Smith, Kevin Costner, Chevy Chase, Richard Gere, Meryl Streep, Sally Field, Dominique Wilkins, Mike Tyson, and Wayne Gretzky, to name just a handful of the more than one hundred who took part in the video. And, just as we had the other times that year when anyone paid tribute to Dick, his soldiers, and the entire US military, Clint, Tyler, and I felt special. The timing was perfect, as we were worn out, stressed out, and wondering when our loved ones would come home and what they would come home to. But that song, in all of its simplicity—a song that was neither pro-war nor antiwar, a song that crossed political lines—was a unifier, not a divider. Like Whitney Houston's rendition of "The Star-Spangled Banner" at the Super Bowl, it gave Americans an outlet to feel proud of their country and their military. I doubt something like that could be replicated in today's world, where so much seems to be about what side people are on, who or what they support. I'm sure that social media would get ahold of the song, the performance, and the performers and analyze it to the point of missing its whole purpose, which was to say, *We are in this together, and we support one another.*

To this day, when the boys and I talk about that song or one of us Googles the video on YouTube, the feelings from all those years ago come flooding back. We are instantly transported to 1991 and the days right after the war.

Every time I began to feel some excitement about Dick's return, the news would jolt me back to reality. A headline on March 16 read, "101st Back in Iraq; More 5th Special Forces Come Home," was somewhat of an oxymoron. *How can we be going back in to fight when units are being welcomed home?* I wondered. *It ain't over till the fat lady sings!*

Without any official word on a return, we wives decided to start making plans for a homecoming. We got together and created banners and posters and tied hundreds of yellow ribbons to put up around our houses and the barracks. We had a great turnout. It didn't matter that we didn't have an exact date, because we knew at some point, whether in a week or a month, our loved ones would be returning. Working together as a team and doing something positive and tangible made it start to feel real that they were coming home.

Journal Entry

Anytime you move forward or even take a step in a positive direction, it beats sitting on the sidelines like a bystander. It's a purely psychological tactic, but it usually works to help you feel better. And whether the outcome is what you wanted or a different version of that, at least you feel like you took some control, like you were in charge, even for a brief moment. You have to create your happiness any way you can.

This winter has been too much waiting for the phone to ring, waiting for a letter, waiting to hear something on the news. None of that is helping me be the person I want to be. Something as simple as gathering to make things for our soldiers' and husbands' return is a turning point for all of us.

32

When the phone rang at four in the morning on March 20, it did not scare me. In that split second between sleep and eyes wide open, I just knew it was Dick.

"Hi, Vick. I'm okay! Everyone is okay! This is the first chance I've had to get to a phone. We had to drive forty-five minutes through the desert, but I just had to call you."

"Oh, Dick, it's so good to hear your voice! I've missed you so much and worried about you every minute of every day! You can't imagine what this has been like. I'm so relieved that you and your guys are all okay."

"I know it's late, but I want to talk to the boys. Can you get them up?"

I put down the phone and ran to Clint's room. "Clint, Dad is on the phone and he wants to talk to you."

He jumped out of bed and made his way to my room while I went to get Tyler from the adjoining room.

"Tyler, can you wake up? Dad is on the phone."

I watched the boys, in their pajamas, rubbing their eyes and yawning but smiling as they each talked to their father.

"We're okay, Dad," Clint said. "How are you? Is the war really over? When will you come home?" A pause and then "We miss you, too!"

Tyler pretty much asked the same questions, ending with, "We can't wait for you to come home." They handed the phone back to me, and I told them, "Try to go back to sleep. We have to get up in a few hours for school."

I got back on with Dick, and we talked for the next thirty minutes. It was such a normal thing to be doing, like we were just chatting. He could have been anywhere, but the significance was not lost on either of us. Anything could have happened in the past six weeks since we had last spoken, and that certainly put things into perspective. As I lay there in my bed, I savored every word he said.

"I know this has been really hard on you and the boys, but you all sound so good. I don't think it will be too much longer."

"Do you have a date in mind? Anything, Dick—I will take any tidbit, any hint of a date. Some people from division say it will be this summer. How can that be? The war has been over for days now."

"Vicki, you know how it is. There are so many variables. But we are starting to move back to TAA Eddie, and from there we will go back to King Fahd Airport. Then we have to pack up, load up, and do all the things we did to prepare to come over here. I don't think that will take more than a couple of weeks. But I will warn you, nothing happens quickly and we're still mopping up the mess over here from the war. The biggest variable is waiting for Air Force or charter flights to take us back to the States. That's where there could be unpredictable delays. Remember OPSEC, so I can't say a specific date on the phone, but, unofficially, think about Clint's birthday."

"*Yay!* I can do that, Dick! I could even do May if I had to, but if you told me June or July, I would lose it! We're having a big FSG meeting next week. I want so much to give the wives some information so we can start making plans. What can I tell them? I need something."

"Here's the thing: Don't quote me directly. Tell them what I just hinted at, *but* tell them it is *my* opinion—not the brigade's, not the division's. And remind them about OPSEC and not to talk specifics on the phone. You never know who's listening."

"Okay, I got it. I just can't wait to see you!"

"I know. Me, too. I better get going; there are always guys waiting for a phone. I will call you again when we get back to King Fahd and have more information. I love you!"

"I love you, too! Hurry home!"

As we hung up, my mind swirled with all kinds of thoughts and ruminations. *Clint's birthday is April 9.* That gave me a window. I tried to temper my excitement and the buzz that was coursing through my body, because that date was still weeks away and anything could change the timeline. But if I did fall back to sleep that night, I'm pretty sure I had a smile on my face. I had talked to Dick, I had heard his voice, he was fine, and I had a tentative date for his return. Now, what to do with this information?

Two days later, I went to the meeting for the battalion commanders' wives in our aviation brigade. An officer from the division rear detachment was there to brief us on the particulars of the welcome-home ceremonies. Each battalion would have its own ceremony at the airfield when the time came; flights would come in a few at a time, so the entire battalion wouldn't necessarily arrive at the same time. For a typical battalion to be fully accounted for, it would take at least two Air Force transport planes or two charter flights. The officer did not have a specific timeline and told us not to get our hopes up for anytime soon, that it could take weeks, possibly a month or more. For a moment, I sat there thinking, *What the heck? Dick told me one thing, and now I'm hearing something very different.* But I figured Dick knew more because he was actually over there and not in the rear detachment at Fort Campbell.

I raised my hand and said, "My husband has an idea when they might be coming back—"The officer cut me off before I could say another word, and I immediately regretted having opened my mouth.

"Your husbands do not have a timeline! All of that will come from division, and not from a battalion commander!"

I cringed as I realized what a touchy subject it was and thought, *From now on, I'll keep my thoughts to myself!* The problem was, we were having our battalion meeting in a few days and I really needed to give my wives something.

I was already getting calls from soldiers' parents and relatives from out of town who wanted to make plans. Having to help people decide when to come to Fort Campbell put me in a tricky position. Just as Dick had warned me, all kinds of variables could change the date, so I wasn't sure what to tell them.

The day of our battalion FSG meeting, I went to see Mike Dousette to talk about what information we were going to put out. We both knew that attendance numbers that night would be high; people who had not come to anything all year would be at the meeting just to see if we could tell them when the guys were coming home.

When I told Mike about the hint that Dick had given me, he said, "Ma'am, I don't have any official word on a return date. I have to get it from division, and they're not saying anything just yet. I'm not sure we should say anything about what your husband said."

"But do you agree we need to give the wives something to go on? Today is March twenty-third, and if the unit is coming back in April, that's less than three weeks away. Can't we just give them a heads-up, with the caveat that the date can and probably will change—that it could be plus or minus some days on either side?"

"I guess you can tell them that, since your husband said you could. Just make sure you say it's your husband's opinion, not an official statement."

"Good, because I trust my husband's instincts. He was right about when they were leaving back in August, when no one else was talking about it, and I believe he has a good idea now about their return. He wouldn't have said that, he wouldn't have gotten my hopes up, if he didn't think it was a possibility."

Mike and I were prepared for the meeting that night, and then Mother Nature took over. By 5:00 p.m., we were under a tornado warning, with torrential rain, wind, and flooding. Mike made the decision to cancel the meeting. It was too dangerous for people to be out driving.

We activated our phone trees, and I could hear the disappointment in the wives' voices as the news spread. I empathized, wanting to give out any information I could. I absorbed all that stress until I just wanted to crawl into bed and go to sleep until Dick returned.

Luckily, the boys had basketball games that weekend, so we stayed busy. When alone with my thoughts, I found myself doing mental calculations about how many more weekends we might have to get through without Dick. I felt like we were down to single digits, and that was a huge psychological milestone for the three of us. *I can do this!*

I had been in touch with Dick's brothers about the Corvette that I had seen at the family dealership back in December. Armed with my new information of a possible return date, I decided it was time to act on it. I had saved some money while Dick was gone, and the combination of that and the trade-in value of his current car made my plan feasible. I called his brother Bill to see what I needed to do and if we could make it happen in time for Dick's homecoming. Again, like making posters and signs, taking steps to buy Dick a car made me feel like we were getting that much closer to a homecoming. Clint and Tyler agreed that it was the perfect gift for their dad.

The following week, on March 26, we had the rescheduled battalion FSG meeting, and, as we had anticipated, there was a big turnout. Mike ran the meeting; then I spoke and told the attendees what

Dick had told me, as well as all the cautionary caveats that the actual return date could be plus or minus days around April 9. I told them we would know more when the unit got back to King Fahd and was actually packed and loading up. I warned them that it would be hard to pin down the date and a specific time until the soldiers were actually on their way.

"I know the challenges in getting family here for a homecoming, especially if they're traveling long distances," I added. "I have family in Vermont who want to be here, and I just keep telling them they'll have to be flexible; their trip may be spur-of-the-moment. And not everyone will be able to come."

I think back to air travel in 1991, when there was no such thing as going online to book flights. You had to call and talk to the airline, and once you booked your tickets, there was no changing them without incurring huge fees. That sure made things difficult for the average person in the situation we were in. I could tell by the questions that night that the wives had one thing, and one thing only, on their minds: *When will they leave Saudi Arabia, and when will they arrive at Fort Campbell?*

The other big question I heard was, "Can I tell our families back home?" I knew that most of the wives had probably already talked to their husbands and probably knew as much as I did. It's hard to keep some things contained, but I reminded them again about OPSEC and told them to be very careful making and talking about plans on the phone. *I hope they have code words like Dick and I do*, I thought.

"The rear detachment and I will keep you informed as best we can in the coming days. We will use our phone trees to disseminate information and any updates. We will do the best we can, but keeping everyone informed will have to be a group effort. We need to be patient, and I understand that gets harder to do the closer we get."

Our other guest speaker that night was a counselor from Behavioral Health Services who had been assigned to our battalion.

She came that night to talk about what to expect from our husbands' return and to answer questions. She told us that a counselor was also talking with our husbands in the combat zone.

She advised us, "In the first few days, you will be so glad your husband is home. Everything will seem perfect; we call it the honeymoon phase. But soon after that, reality will set in and you can expect issues, whether big or small, to creep back into your lives. If you had problems before the deployment, they will resurface. Those problems did not vanish; they were merely put on hold. So be cautious; don't make any big decisions the first week or two, and I would hold off on going on leave for a week or so. You need some time to settle in with each other; your husband needs some time to acclimate after what he has been through. It is going to take patience, compromise, and resilience, but you can get through it. Here at Fort Campbell, there are plenty of facilities and programs if you, your spouse, or your kids need help."

Since most of us had not been through a combat deployment before, I knew that it would be different from other deployments and separations. But I had such confidence in Dick and me, our relationship, the family that we had created, I was sure we could weather any storm ahead. We all appreciated what the counselor had to say that night, but mostly we just wanted to get the show on the road and not think about anything negative.

While I was planning Dick's homecoming, his letters still talked of war. By then, I had gotten quite good at shifting back in time to his world, but I never forgot that I was reading about something that had happened weeks before.

TAA Viper

Hi Vicki,
I finally have some time to put my thoughts on paper, as it has been a crazy week. The 101st launched the huge air assault

into Iraq early on February 24. In fact, we had to delay the start of the war because the fog was so thick. I, along with some of my Apaches and OH-58s, flew into Iraq a few hours before the official start time to clear the routes and check the zones. We couldn't see ten feet in front of us; aircraft were getting lost, and we were flying as low as we possibly could. I made the weather decision for MG Peay, and we changed H-hour by a couple of hours. It was a tough call on my part, because everyone, and I mean the entire division, was locked and loaded and ready to strike, but it would have been a disaster to launch such a massive air assault in those conditions. I had to do the right thing with so much at stake. The weather has continued to be a problem, and we've actually had more mishaps and accidents due to that than actual combat.

Speaking of accidents, one of my OH-58s from E Company (the company from Fort Lewis that's attached to us) crashed just inside the Iraq border on the first day of the ground war, trying to land in fog and dust. Everyone was okay. In fact, when I got there and saw the aircraft engulfed in flames, I was amazed to see all crew members standing next to the wreckage. That was a close call! You can't imagine the relief we all felt.

On Day 1, the 24th, we encountered medium resistance initially. I took some mortar fire and machine gun fire, but all were poor shots [smiley face]. We finished the first day and got our battalion to the objective area, some ninety miles inside Iraq, before nightfall. But then we launched again that night to secure and protect the area.

Day 2, we airlifted Tom Greco's battalion and most of 3rd Brigade into the Euphrates river valley for the assault and then covered them through the night.

Day 3, the 26th, a huge shamal came in and wreaked havoc on all the plans and aircraft flying. I had my C Company trapped in the valley; Howard Killian and the HEMTT [heavy expanded mobility tactical truck] convoy were trapped between our first objective area and the river valley, and they all had to wait it out. It took most of the day to recover everyone, just before nightfall. More of the same that night, covering units.

Day 4, the 27th: We launched early and flew 110 miles east toward Basrah to provide security for 2nd Brigade. The terrain was puckered from bombs and artillery; everywhere we look it is total devastation. We landed at objective area Viper and then started guiding over 150 Blackhawk and Chinook helicopters as 2nd Brigade came in. I had my companies spread out, taking out enemy vehicles and artillery as they were trying to get out of Kuwait. It is evident that the Iraqi army is collapsing.

It is now the 28th, and we have a CEASE-FIRE! Whew! We expected far more resistance, and it was pretty intense there for a few days, but overall it has been easier than we anticipated. The past five days seemed like weeks. I don't even remember sleeping; I lay down on my cot once or twice but never slept. It has been all-out and nonstop.

Now that the worst is over (I think), I am catching up on paperwork, writing up all the awards for my guys. I don't want to leave that for when we get back; I like to stay on top of it. I have been going around to each company, talking to the troops and personally praising them for their superhuman efforts and answering their questions about what is in the immediate future.

I really miss you and the boys. Even surrounded by all my guys and all the chaos, I get lonely here. I wish I could talk to

you in person about everything that's happened and what I've
experienced. Hopefully we will get home soon.
  Love you all so much,
  Dick

Journal Entry

When much in your life is out of your control, you control what you
can; oftentimes, that means your emotions. It takes a lot of energy to
control them, especially for long periods of time, and then it is difficult
to shift gears when the situation changes. You might be apprehensive
to let down your guard, something you've worked so hard on. It might
feel weird because you have been suppressing emotions in order to get
through the days, and then suddenly you're allowed to feel excitement
because the worst might be over. But maybe your emotions need time
to catch up with reality. Or maybe you feel like if you give in, something
might change again and then you will be caught off guard.

Why am I so afraid to give in to the excitement that Dick is coming
home? Is it because there are still so many unknowns? Is it because
every time I think the worst is over, something else happens or someone
rains on my parade, telling me a different story? I've been waiting for
eight months to hear him tell me he's coming home, and yet I'm still
expending way too much energy trying to temper my excitement. It's
like I'm eating a hot fudge sundae but allowing myself only one bite of
ice cream a day, never getting to the hot fudge, the whipped cream, the
nuts—and forget about the cherry on top! But a hot fudge sundae is not
as delicious one bite at a time—it is meant to be eaten all at once, in all
its calorie-laden glory, just for the sheer pleasure of it all.

Deep inside me, and probably because of all the things Dick and I
have been through, I carry a fear that something will happen to him
before he can get out of there, or that someone will change the rules
and the timeline. Maybe in a week or two, when he calls to say they're

boarding the flight to come home, maybe then I will feel like I deserve to eat the entire hot fudge sundae in one sitting. Until then, I will guard my excitement.

33

I appreciated Dick's sanitized version of the ground war, but I continued to read everything I could get my hands on. I saw the horrible images of war, the toll it takes on both sides. I knew that it wasn't as easy as he depicted, but that was okay, too. *There are some details the boys and I just don't need to know,* I reminded myself.

A few days after Dick's phone call, the 1-101st made the long journey back to King Fahd, their old home in the parking garage. During the ground war, the vehicles had traveled more than 5,000 miles and the aircraft had flown more than 5,700 miles. All vehicles and aircraft made it back safely, which was a tremendous feat unto itself.

It was going to take a herculean effort to get everything ready to be shipped from the port or flown back to the States. The 1-101st was just one of thousands of units that made up the coalition forces wanting to get back home. Dick was counting on his chain of command to keep the promise "the first ones in are the first ones out." He knew it was unrealistic to expect the pecking order to remain intact, but he had more important things to focus on those first days back at King Fahd. Every single piece of equipment had to be pressure-washed because of the months it had spent in the desert sand.

The aircraft were going by boat, so they would have to be flown to the port, washed, broken down like before, and then shrink-wrapped to protect them from the salt spray.

I cannot imagine the exhaustion of having just fought a war and had little to no sleep, no good food, and no clean clothes, only to arrive back at King Fahd and have all that work to do. I would need a break—some quiet time, a hot shower, a nice nap, some coffee, and a decent meal. But I guess when you've been through what these soldiers had been through and leaving for home is on the horizon, you do whatever it takes to get you to that point.

Back at Fort Campbell, I had my own hurdles to clear. The phone was becoming my demon; it rang all day long, sometimes before I had even gotten out of bed and had my coffee. I empathized with every mom, dad, spouse, and grandparent who called me. I understood their dilemma—if they lived far away, not everyone had the money to hop on a plane at a moment's notice—but there was only so much information and predictability. It was a game of risk—get there in time, but don't get there too early, because if delays occur, you might be sitting in a hotel room for days.

One call was from the mother of Dick's copilot. "Mrs. Cody, my husband and I want to be there when Brian arrives, but we're driving up from Alabama. My husband is a crop duster and I'm a waitress, and we can't miss work for days. Can you tell me when you think we should come?"

"Mrs. Stewmon, depending on the length of the drive, I think you should wait to leave until we get word that they have taken off. It will take at least twenty-four hours, with stops, for them to get here, so that should give you enough time to drive here. If you can leave on the spur of the moment, that's what I would do. I or someone else will call you the minute we get word they have left Saudi Arabia."

I shared everyone's concerns and their overwhelming need to be there, but the closer we got to a homecoming, the more difficult my job as the commander's wife seemed to be.

And then I would get a note from Dick, peppered with his hand-drawn smiley faces, describing his situation, and it didn't matter how many phone calls I'd gotten that day or how much I believed I couldn't stand another day without him; after reading one of his letters, I knew that I could make it until he got home.

TAA Viper

Dear Vicki,

We are still in the middle of Iraq, southwest of Basrah, living in a tent, taking dumps in folding chairs that have a hole cut out, and showering under a five-gallon bucket! I'm not complaining, though—we have it better than Tommy Greco and his infantry guys. Speaking of Tom, I flew up the Euphrates river valley today to see him. Bob Van Antwerp came by to see me and wanted to check on some of his engineer guys up there, so I said, "I'll fly you up there in my OH-58, and we'll go see Tommy while we're at it." Van just laughed and said, "Cody, you are the only one I know who has his own aircraft to fly around in. I knew you could get me up there." We loaded up some cases of MREs, and I still have a big stash of M&M's and some Coca-Colas (real ones) that my uncle Fred sent me from his movie theaters. I like to take treats with me for Tom and his guys; they are living in harsh conditions. We had a great visit; he was so glad to see us. We sat there eating our MREs, and you would've thought we were just some West Point classmates getting together for lunch somewhere, but we were in the middle of a combat zone in Iraq! We had someone take some pictures of us. It was the highlight of our week.

Hey, someone just told me you met Barbara Bush! That is awesome! How was it? I bet she was down to earth and nice. I can't wait to get your letter giving me all the details, which I'm sure is on its way [smiley face].

In your last letter, you asked me for my personal thoughts on what this has been like. I think as pilots we have a slightly different view, as we see things from up above and most often through the lens of our eyepiece, which gives us almost a video game perspective. But when I fly around in my OH-58, low-level and with no eyepiece, I see everything that happened on the ground. It is so hard to capture and put into words. Sometimes when I finally lie down at night, I have images that are hard to get out of my head. We saw a lot of death and destruction, and that is tough to erase. But don't worry, I won't come home with a bunch of hang-ups after seeing such carnage; if anything, I will have a deeper appreciation for life in general [smiley face].

I really enjoyed the last letters from Clint and Tyler. They are so expressive; I'm amazed at their maturity in these past months. Great boys! The mail is still slow, but when you think about how it makes it all the way to my tent here in Iraq, two to three weeks is not that bad.

Last night I finally had time to sew my Screaming Eagle patch on the right shoulder of my uniform. From now on, I will always be a combat veteran of the 101st Airborne Division. All my soldiers were doing the same thing. We used the crappy little sewing kit from our mess kits, but it worked, for now, at least. Luckily, I learned how to sew back at West Point!

I hope you are doing good and more at ease now that this part of it is over. I hope it's not too much longer. There's talk that we might be moving back to TAA Campbell pretty soon, which puts us one step closer to King Fahd and eventually home. I will call as soon as we get out of Iraq and back to Saudi Arabia.

I miss you so much and can't wait to see you . . . and other things, too!

Love you always,

Dick

In a letter to Dick, I asked him what he wanted to do when he got back, as far as a vacation went. I narrowed it down to two choices for him (oddly enough, they were *my* happy places). I had learned that Dick liked me to plan things and that he would usually go along with anything. When he called again the week before he came home, I said, "You haven't told me which one you choose: the beach in Florida or spring skiing in Colorado."

He was kind of clueless about the choices, because that was the one letter he never got, but he quickly said, "Vicki, I've had enough sand and heat in this desert to last a lifetime. Let's go skiing! Will there still be snow in April?"

"I've been researching, and yes, there's still plenty of snow. A-Basin has so much, it will be open for months. We can drive so we can take our time and not worry about dates. It will be so much fun, just like old times."

And just like that, I was ready to enjoy the whole hot fudge sundae. *He's coming home, and we're making plans. It's really happening.*

The last week felt like an eternity, and yet it was a blur. Phone calls continued to take up most of my time if I was at home. I was helping other people make plans while making our own. My parents couldn't swing the spur-of-the-moment trip, but Dick's parents were flying down and a few of his siblings were trying to make arrangements. One of his brothers would drive the Corvette down as soon as we had an arrival time. It was a twenty-two-hour drive from Vermont, no easy feat.

Chuck Noble, the pilot who had been injured in California the year before, had been in touch with me throughout the deployment. He had been in a rehabilitation center all that time and had made tremendous progress, though he'd had to relearn everything, including how to walk. He had made a promise to Dick and his fellow pilots that he would be there to greet them when they returned. When I talked to him the week before, he already had his plans to fly from California to Fort Campbell.

I went shopping for a new outfit and other girlie things. The boys were on spring break the last week of March, and Easter was on March 31 that year. After Mass, we went to the officers' club for brunch, and all we talked about was their dad coming home. Dick had called again; it was looking like he would arrive on or around April 6.

"Boys, do you realize this could be our last weekend without Dad and hopefully will be the last holiday without him?"

"Will Dad be home for my birthday?" Clint asked.

"I think so, but there's always a chance of a delay. We'll hope he gets here, but if not, we could wait to celebrate, if you want to."

"Do you think he'll want to play tennis when he gets home?"

"He might be a little tired, but I'm sure he'll want to play tennis with you boys. He has missed that as much as you have."

Tyler chimed in, "I can't wait to go skiing with Dad. We've never been to Keystone and A-Basin. And we have new skis!"

We talked about the fact that they were on spring break and could miss school if we went on vacation.

"The schools have already told us they will make exceptions for families who want to go on vacation. They understand that you haven't been with your dad for a long time, so you can miss a week. I will get your work before we leave, and you can do your assignments while we're gone."

"Oh, good!"

The next day was April 1, and everything seemed different. We were down to just days, not weeks, until the homecoming. It was springtime, and life seemed so beautiful. *I want to savor this feeling,* I thought. *It's like coming out of a dark tunnel into bright sunshine.*

Dick's parents, Bob and Jan, arrived. Even though I continued to spend time on the phone and had a stiff neck to prove it, just having them there with us was a wonderful distraction. It helped us get through the last days. Dick's dad played tennis with the boys; his mom and I cleaned and cooked and got everything ready so we wouldn't have much to do when the call came. There were a few more hiccups with arrival times, but in the end, Dick's battalion left Saudi Arabia on April 4. He called me from Shannon, Ireland, early on April 5 when they stopped to refuel. They were having a beer, their first in eight months. Things were on schedule, and they would arrive on Saturday morning, April 6. A flight containing his command sergeant major and half the battalion would arrive the night before.

"Vicki, would you go out to the airfield and greet the flight coming in? I would appreciate it, and I know my soldiers will, too."

"Of course, I will! I just can't believe you're halfway home!"

"I know, Vick; it seems like it's been forever."

I went out to the airfield Friday night to greet the first arriving flight from our battalion. Even though I wished it were Dick I was greeting, I told myself, *At this time tomorrow, he will be home.* It was dark and hard to see who was who, but I found CSM Ehrke, Dick's right arm, and gave him a big hug. We talked briefly about the deployment before he was pulled in another direction. It was somewhat chaotic, with soldiers and their families milling around, but I loved watching the scene. It was the first time I felt like it was really happening and not just a dream or a wish.

It was hard to settle down that night when I got home. The anticipation felt like the night before my wedding. Dick called again early Saturday morning, from Bangor, Maine, on their last refuel stop.

"Vicki, you can't imagine how we were greeted here. It was, like, four in the morning, and the airport was filled with people who lined up, forming a gauntlet that we walked through as we got off the plane. There were so many people cheering us, shaking our hands, and thanking us. And, Vicki, there were Vietnam veterans there as well! It was the most heartwarming thing I have ever experienced. It was wonderful for my soldiers."

"Oh, Dick, that is amazing. You all deserve it for what you've done. I'm so glad the people of Bangor feel that way, too."

"And, Vicki, I realized the Vietnam vets were giving us the welcome they never got. I will never forget this."

We talked for a few more minutes, neither one of us wanting to hang up, but there wasn't much more to say. Anything else could wait for our reunion in person. Dick assumed that his parents were with me, but I didn't tell him that some of his siblings would be at his homecoming or that a Corvette was on its way. I wanted to have some surprises for him.

Journal Entry

Maybe this is the time to remember, in the quiet hours before life gets crazy again, before you settle back into your normal schedule, before everything becomes routine again. In those hours leading up to your getting what you have been waiting for, you realize it really was worth the sacrifices, the hard work and effort, the sleepless nights, and the waiting patiently. Soon you will have the tangible reward that makes it all worthwhile—that person or thing that is part of a happy ending that is so hard won. He's almost home!

34

I couldn't fall back to sleep after Dick's phone call from Bangor. Excitement, adrenaline, and some insecurities crept into my thoughts. Lying there at four o'clock in the morning with nothing to occupy my mind except Dick's return was quickly chipping away at my self-confidence. My thoughts included *Will he still think I'm pretty? Do I look fat? What if it rains and my permed hair gets frizzy? Have I aged from all the stress? Did I choose the right look for my outfit?* It was totally unlike me, but I had had far too much time on my own with no feedback from the most important person in my life. While I knew my thoughts were frivolous and had no bearing on Dick's and my love for each other, they still chipped away at my usually high self-esteem, making me feel like that sixteen-year-old schoolgirl who was falling for Dick Cody and just hoping he felt the same way.

I drifted off to sleep for an hour or so but then awoke and was out of bed in seconds. "Boys, it's time to get up! Today's the day!" I peeked quickly out my window to find the sun shining. *No rain—a good hair day!* "Your dad called a few hours ago. He was in Bangor, Maine. He really is on his way! He should be here by noon!"

In unison, they said, "Yay!"

Dick's parents; his older sister, Diane, who had flown down at the last minute; and his brother Bill and Bill's wife, Paula, who had arrived in the middle of the night with the Corvette, were all staying at a nearby hotel and showed up bright and early. The welcoming party was all in place. We spent the morning making banners for the house while the boys and Uncle Bill washed the Corvette. Then we decorated that as well. We tied a huge yellow ribbon around it and backed it into the driveway, facing out, so Dick couldn't miss it. We hung a large banner, made from a white sheet, from the top of the carport. The yellow ribbon that we had tied around the tree next to the driveway was weathered and faded but remained in place.

The phone rang a lot, with updates from the rear detachment; the time continued to change, but only by hours, not days. We had to link everyone up, so we finally told people to go over to the battalion headquarters and wait; that way, we could get updates as a group and we would be together when the time came to ride buses to the airfield.

Our drive to the headquarters that morning, the same place I had been going on a regular basis to meet with the rear detachment, to write newsletters, to get phone calls from Dick, and the very place where the boys and I had said goodbye to him eight months earlier, suddenly had a different feel to it. The day I had thought would never come was finally here, and it was as if an electric current was flowing through me. I could barely make small talk with Diane, who was riding with us.

We gathered outside in the quad area between the barracks. It wasn't long before Mike Dousette announced that the plane was about an hour out. We boarded no-frills, troop-carrying buses for the short ride to the airfield. It was noisy as people found seats. There were families that I recognized and some complete strangers, but everyone was chatting as if we had known each other for years. I looked at Dick's mom and dad sitting together in their seats, his dad wearing a neon pink Cody Chevrolet hat, and they looked so cute to me—like two kids on a school bus waiting for someone to tell them what was next. Their anxiety, mixed with anticipation, was noticeable: Dick's dad held an unlit cigarette, which he was not supposed to have, for health reasons, but I knew he was hoping to sneak away and light it. Dick's mother, rosary beads in hand, was quietly saying Hail Marys. I thanked God that they were there to welcome their son home.

The area outside the huge hangar had been roped off for the families. There were bleachers set up and some people were sitting, but most were congregating near the ropes meant to keep us off the tarmac. The division band was playing. Everyone was waving flags, kids were running around, and some mothers were holding brand-new babies who had not yet met their fathers. In one of Dick's last letters to me, he had named all the babies who had been born during the deployment: thirteen in all, including a set of twins.

As I looked at the crowd of spouses, parents, grandparents, family members, and friends, I was struck by the fact that we were one and the same. We were not defined by rank or race, riches or poverty, ethnicity or religious preference, or where we came from; we were all patriots who had one thing in common: a loved one who had raised their right hand to defend and protect our constitution and our nation. We shared a bond, an experience, that few others would ever know. We had lived through a stressful yet incredible time; our loved ones had made it through a combat deployment. Standing there that day, in that crowd of Army families, I never dreamed that there would be more welcome-home ceremonies in my future—far more than I could have imagined.

Somehow the minutes ticked by, and then we heard that the plane was on its final approach. Campbell Army Airfield has one of the longest runways on the East Coast and is an alternate landing site for the space shuttle, which means when a plane is descending, it is so far in the distance that even on a bright, sunny day, you really can't see it until just before it touches down.

We were all on tiptoe, scanning the sky for that first glimpse. Clint and Tyler were running around but staying near me. Bill was filming with his video camera, Dick's dad was pacing (his cigarette lit), and Jan and Diane were next to me with tears running down their faces as we finally saw the plane land. The crowd erupted, and everywhere I looked, people of all ages were crying and cheering at the same time.

As the plane taxied down the runway and made the turn toward us, we could see on top of it a soldier standing up in an opening in the cockpit, holding a flag. I later learned that it was Spec 4 Mike Fanning, who was given the honor of carrying the B Company guidon. The scene is forever etched in my mind.

The plane seemed to be taxiing in slow motion. It took forever to come to a stop a few hundred yards away from us. We watched the "official" party walk up the steps of the ramp that had been wheeled over to the aircraft. The door opened, and the party boarded. *Jeez*, I thought, *can you move any slower? Let's get this show on the road! I've been waiting for eight months to see my husband!*

And then there he was, emerging from the airplane door, in his desert camouflage, carrying a satchel-type briefcase. In those seconds when I first saw him, I felt like the wind had been knocked out of me. If someone had spoken to me then, I could not have responded. Down the steps, coming toward us, Dick and his soldiers filed past, but they were still about twenty yards away and there were people in front of me. I waved frantically. I had no clue where Clint and Tyler were, but all I wanted to do was get close enough for Dick to see me. The soldiers were headed for the back entrance of the hangar, so I quickly realized that I had better get around the crowd and head for the other entrance. Back then, there was no official ceremony, no guidance on where we were to meet the soldiers. Nowadays it's all carefully orchestrated; the families sit on bleachers inside the hangar as the unit makes a grand entrance through the doors. This time, we were on our own—and it was chaos.

Somehow, Clint and Tyler knew exactly what to do and where to go. At one point, out of the corner of my eye, I saw them moving like greased lightning in the opposite direction of the crowd. Those skinny boys traveled at warp speed, jumping over people, bleachers, whatever was in their way, and made it into the hangar just as their dad was coming in. By the time I got through the crowd and to Dick, the boys had already greeted him. I hugged him with all my might and started crying.

Dick looked at me and said, "Why are you crying?"

"What do you mean? Why wouldn't I be crying?"

"It's over. I'm home."

"I was afraid I might never see you again!"

He just smiled at me and said, "Why would you think that? I told you I would bring everyone home."

And then everyone was clamoring to get to him: his parents, siblings, friends, the public affairs officer. I stepped back, watching him, and thought, *He just doesn't get it. In his mind, he went, he did his job, he's back home, what's the big deal? That is so Dick Cody, and one of the reasons why I love him so much.*

Periodically, Dick's eyes met mine, and it was like we were each checking to see where the other one was. But he didn't need to worry—even in that throng of people, I was not letting him out of my sight.

I had goose bumps as I observed families reuniting—in particular, the soldiers who were seeing their newborn babies for the first time, and the newlyweds; I could spot them from a mile away as they kissed and made out like no one else was around.

There was a lot of hand shaking among Dick and his men, soldiers bringing their wives and family over to meet him, cameras clicking nonstop. I overheard so many people say to him, "You kept your promise—you brought everyone home safe."

Even though Dick and I were not supposed to have favorites in the unit, we did. There were some guys I was closer to than others, like Brownie, who was there that day to greet his fellow soldiers. And there were others I had grown close to, guys who had coached the boys in sports, single guys we'd invited to our house for holidays, guys who had written to me during the deployment, guys who were like sons to me. I found one of them, Jody Bridgforth, and gave him a big hug.

Also in the crowd was Chuck Noble. He had indeed made the long flight from California to welcome home his fellow Expect No Mercy brothers. I saw him standing with his cane, in a group of C Company Paladins, and overheard more than one person say, "Wow, Chuck, you're doing great!" and, "Look how far you've come!" As I watched that scene unfold, I realized it represented closure for Chuck and his "brothers," who had not seen each other since the crash almost one year earlier.

Soldiers brought their parents to meet me, and they expressed their appreciation for my efforts.

"Mrs. Cody, we can't thank you enough for including us in the family support group, even though our son is not married and we don't live here."

"Thank you for the continual updates, especially these past few days."

"Thank you, Mrs. Cody, for sending us the monthly newsletters. They meant so much to us and made us feel connected to our son's unit."

Early in the deployment, I had followed my instincts to include parents of soldiers, fiancées, and, in some cases, grandparents (some of whom had raised our soldiers) in my communications. It was the first time we thought beyond spouses and widened the circle to extend our FSGs to any family member. Meeting these people whom I had been corresponding with and hearing their words of appreciation made me realize I had done the right thing and that maybe I had made a difference. I never imagined that one day I would be one of those parents myself, waiting for an update, a phone call, or a news-letter from my son's unit.

The local media were there to interview Dick, so the boys and Dick's family and I went outside to watch him answer questions. The boys and I were literally pacing behind the scenes, anxious to get that finished so we could head home. Listening to Dick, observing him from the sidelines, I couldn't help thinking he was like something out of a movie: slim, tan, and in his desert uniform—such a turn-on. And how he had the energy to handle all of the reporters' questions when he was clearly exhausted was beyond me. *What a rock star*, I thought. *I can't wait to get my hands on him!*

Finally, that was over and the organizers announced that it was time to get back on our buses and go back to the battalion headquar-ters, where we would link up with our soldiers. It felt weird to sepa-rate so soon after reuniting, but I understood that they had to ride on separate buses, as they still had their weapons with them. I figured I could make it another fifteen minutes.

At the headquarters was a huge crowd of soldiers and their families, plus kit bags, duffel bags, and equipment. It was more of the same: meet-ing people, reuniting with others we had not seen, making small talk, but really just wanting to get home. Dick had a few loose ends to tie up, so he told us to head to the house and that he would meet us there shortly. We had dropped off his regular car the day before so he could drive home with all his gear. The Corvette was waiting for him in our driveway.

On the drive, Clint and Tyler talked nonstop.

"Dad looks good; he looks the same."

"Yeah, and he's going to be so surprised to see the Corvette."

"I can't wait to see his face! Mom, do you think he'll be surprised?"

While I was driving, my mind was going in a million directions. I was still a bundle of nerves, but they stemmed from happy anticipa-tion of Dick's reaction to the gift waiting for him.

Dick arrived home shortly after we did, and when he pulled into the driveway and came face-to-face with the Corvette with the huge yellow ribbon tied around it, I could see him grinning before he even came to a stop and got out of his car. Maybe he had figured it out, I don't know, but seeing him smile was all I needed.

"Vicki, how did you do this?"

"Are you surprised? I was so afraid someone would tell you. Your dad and brothers gave me a good deal, so it wasn't that expensive." I knew what he was thinking: How could we afford a Corvette on a lieutenant colonel's pay?

"I love it! Thank you! I thought something was up a while back when Bobby mentioned you looking at a 'Vette during your Christmas visit. But I didn't think you would actually have it here for me now."

We eventually made it into the house, his brother carrying some of Dick's bags and everyone talking at once. Dick's dad asked if he was hungry but didn't even wait for a reply before he announced, "Dick needs a good meal tonight. I'll go get some steaks for the grill."

Bob left on a quick run to the grocery store, and the women started putting together some side dishes while Dick and the boys lingered over the Corvette. I heard the engine revving (as I'm sure everyone in the entire neighborhood did), and then they took turns going for rides. I looked out my kitchen window and thought, *How quickly we return to normal.*

After a long, hot shower and a good meal for Dick, we sat around our picnic table in the backyard, talking about random things that had happened in the past months. Neighbors stopped by, some who had recently returned, and Gail Greco, who was still waiting for Tom to come home. We took pictures; we all wanted to record and preserve those magical hours. The sun was setting, it had been a long day for everyone, and Dick and I had yet to have any time alone. So I could have kissed Dick's mom when she turned to Dick's dad and said, "Bob, let's take Clint and Tyler out for ice cream." I looked at Jan, and she winked.

My eyes met Dick's, and in that moment, without saying a word and not wanting to react in front of the others, but with my heart beating out of my chest, I felt the undeniably strong connection between us. For months I had envisioned, dreamed up, and choreographed our first "rendezvous with destiny" after his return. In my mind, it would be like a scene from a romantic movie: We would run to each other in slow motion, fall into each other's arms with a kiss that went on for hours, and then slowly make our way to the bedroom.

The reality that day was, the second everyone was out of the house, we were running to our room, nearly tripping over each other and the clothes that were coming off. There was no long, slow kiss; there were kisses, but everything happened fast. It was frantic, it was urgent, it was like a hunger. Maybe it wasn't a romantic scene from a movie, but it was *our* scene from the screenplay of *our* life. It was pure pleasure, and I'm not sure the car with the grandparents and the boys had even left our driveway when the fireworks started going off. We were satisfying a deep desire and need in each other that few can understand unless they have been in that situation—separated for months, living with the overriding fear that something could happen to your loved one.

Afterward, as we lay there, I turned to Dick and said, "Holy crap! What was that?"

"I know—that was explosive!"

I started giggling. "Yeah, it was like one of your Hellfire rockets going off!"

We both burst out laughing. It was as if a valve that had been shut off had opened up and the pressure of eight months had been released. What an amazing feeling.

Later that night, when everyone was gone, the boys in bed, the house silent, and Dick snoring quietly next to me, I opened my journal to write one last entry.

Journal Entry

April 6, 1991

I am in my happy place. I have made it through eight months. I don't know what lies ahead, but I do know that I am capable and can handle whatever comes my way. I have faced the demon and come out on top. And my best friend in the world is home safe! I can put this journal away, for now.

Epilogue

The weeks and months after Dick's return were a time of transition. Initially, like most couples, we experienced a honeymoon phase. Then reality set in, and we moved into a phase of working through disconnections, power struggles, and day-to-day issues. There was never anything that we couldn't handle, but it took communication, understanding, patience, and teamwork. After the fact, I realized it was good to air out the laundry, tackle things that had been swept under the carpet, and then start fresh with a clean slate.

All the angst, stress, and loneliness of deployment faded away. In the coming years, I would encounter reminders from time to time, such as when someone would come to interview Dick for a book or a magazine article. We would see Dick and his Task Force Normandy mission on the History Channel or the National Geographic Channel. I would listen to him speak at events, about his exploits in the Gulf War, and for those moments, I was back in 1990–'91. But not until I started writing about our Army life would Dick and I spend time reflecting in-depth on some of the events of that year.

We got busy living, and it was a good life. Dick rose in rank; I continued my role as an Army wife and commander's wife. My days were full and gratifying, but then I began to feel the stirrings of wanting to write something. I didn't know what or how, just that I wanted to try telling stories about our way of life. It would be years before I would have the time to act on that impulse.

In the meantime, our boys grew into fine young men. There were many more moves for us, plus a few more separations, and yet Army life did not have a negative impact on any of us. As a family, we were stronger than ever.

From the time they were young boys playing soldiers with their buddies in the backyard, Clint and Tyler had talked about wanting to be in the Army. Dick and I did not take that as a given, since they were young, impressionable, and surrounded by their dad's helicopter pilots. In many ways, it seemed a glamorous life to children. But there was a specific moment when Dick and I realized that they really were serious about the military. It was 1997, just six years after Desert Storm. Clint was twenty, had just finished two years at New Mexico Military Institute (NMMI), and was on his way to the Corps of Cadets at Texas A&M. Tyler, eighteen, had just graduated from Fort Campbell High School and was following his brother to NMMI and then to Texas A&M. On this particular occasion, they were being interviewed by an old friend who was making a documentary film about elite helicopter pilots and their families. When he asked the boys what they wanted to do when they finished college, they answered the question in unison, with almost the exact same words: "I want to fly Apaches like my dad and hopefully serve with him in the Army someday." It was the first time they sounded so sure and voiced their desires in such a public forum.

As I watched them that day, I thought, *It's funny how over the years, the scary and stressful times, the uncertainties, the separations, the dozens of moves, the three high schools that each one attended, all of that recedes to the back of the mind. The four of us have mastered the art of living in the moment. We don't dwell on the past; we don't take the future for granted; we are so very present in this moment, and it feels right. I am fine with this. I really am.*

Dick and I were beaming as we watched them being interviewed that day, not just because they wanted to follow in their dad's footsteps but because they knew what they wanted to do with their lives; they had a clear sense of purpose and a focus. As parents, what more could we want for our kids?

And then, on a beautiful September day in 2001, the rules of the game changed. That day was a game changer not just for Americans, our country, and our way of life, but especially for those in the military. Within six months of the terrorist attacks, Clint was in combat in Afghanistan, on what would be the first of many combat deployments. By early 2003, he would be in Iraq. If I thought that I had been through the worst, I was wrong. I realized that all of the challenges, the hurdles, and the fears from the past had definitely made me stronger and maybe more prepared, but those tests were mere pop quizzes compared with the final exams I would face with our sons in the coming years. And Dick's hopes that his sons would not have to fight the same fight he had were dashed.

Sure enough, that demon showed up again, *and* it had doubled in size!

May 2003
Q West, Iraq
B Co., 3-101st Aviation Battalion

Hi Mom,
Sorry I haven't been able to call or email; the phones suck and the server is down half the time, so we can't even email. I'll just write letters for now. We are settling in at our FOB in northern Iraq, just south of Mosul, at a former Iraqi air force

base called Qayyarah West (Q West). I guess this will be our new home now.

I'm doing good, so don't worry about me. The past two months have been pretty unreal, but I think things are going to settle down now. Did you see on the news that US forces reached Baghdad and toppled the statue of Saddam Hussein on April 9, my birthday? Pretty funny, huh?

I got your package; thanks for all the goodies and snacks. The pretzels and chips taste so good, since all we have to eat are MREs! I'm amazed how the mail gets through, all the way to northern Iraq. I've been getting your letters and Dad's. Mail is the highlight of the day!

It was pretty exciting, our move up through the desert back in March and April. The sandstorms were unbelievable, and there were times when we were completely shut down for days at a time. We had nothing but our Apaches and a pup tent for protection. We couldn't see a thing, and we worried that the enemy would sneak up on us and we would never see them coming. Mike Wells (my copilot) and I just hunkered down and waited for it to pass, but I have to tell you, it was pretty stressful. Mike and I get along really well. It helps that we flew in combat together in Afghanistan. We make a great crew. So don't worry about me. I always fly safe!

On our way to Baghdad, we had quite a fight in Al Hillah. Some crazy shit went down, and many of our aircraft got shot up and took a real beating, but no one got hurt or killed, thankfully. I got to shoot seven Hellfire rockets and 350 rounds of 30 mm. I've been put in for an Air Medal with valor for that battle. I was just doing my job, protecting the troops on the ground and taking out some stuff at the same time [smiley face]. Our unit is doing good, but the other aviation units have crashed aircraft and done some stupid shit. LTC Richardson is the best, and I feel lucky to have him as my commander.

It's starting to get pretty hot, temperatures around 100 degrees during the day. I'm sure the worst is yet to come later in the summer. Speaking of which, we just heard we're being extended another nine months. I can't say I'm happy, but there's nothing I can do about it. We hear lots of rumors, and I'm anxious to talk to Dad to see if there is any truth to them.

So, if we are staying here that long, that means Tyler will be coming over when he gets out of flight school and signs in to the 101st. That sucks for him, since he and Brooke are just getting married. But at least I will have something to look forward to and I can show him around when he arrives. Don't worry, Mom, we will look after each other over here.

I have been getting lots of letters and packages from your side of the family: Grandma, Dicky and Patti, Chris, Ashley, your cousins Terry and Toby. I hear from Dad's family, too, most recently Nana, Lauri, Diane, Robin, Cathi, and Bobby. Tell them thank you when you talk to them, but I am going to start typing a newsletter to keep up with everyone. Then I can just personalize it, like a Christmas letter, and I think that will work better.

I ran into Scott Greco the other day. He flies Apaches with the 3rd ACR [armored cavalry regiment] from Fort Carson, Colorado. Haven't seen him in a few years, so that was great. We were saying how crazy it is that we're both flying Apaches over here and our dads were together here back in the day. Who would've thought?

I hate to miss Tyler and Brooke's wedding in June. I will ask Dad to stand in for me as best man, and I will send a letter for him to read at the reception.

I better get going; we are flying some missions for the next *few days. I will call as soon as I can get a phone line. Keep the letters coming. Don't worry about me, and I promise to fly safe!*

Miss you and love you both,
Clint
Blue Max 26

October 2003
Q West, Iraq
1-101st Aviation Regiment

Hi Mom,

How's it going? I am fine. Sorry I haven't been able to call; the phones are always down, and when I can get a line, I call Brooke. I know you understand. The internet is still spotty, so I'll try to write letters, but no promises there!

I'm sure you heard that I ran into Dad on my way here. I was in Kuwait, waiting for the C-17 to take us into Iraq, and I heard some soldiers saying, "General Cody is coming! His plane just landed here!" Sure enough, a few minutes later, there was Dad, with his entourage and personal security detail, getting off a C-17. They were just coming out of Iraq. I got to spend a few minutes with him before I boarded my plane. He said he saw Clint and got to promote him to captain. Pretty amazing, huh?

Clint was here to greet me when I landed. It was great to see him, and I know we're lucky to have each other. He has been showing me around. He has been here so long; he knows everyone and where everything is!

In some ways, this is not as bad as I expected, but I also know that this base has come a long way since Clint arrived. There are small PXs and mess tents with hot meals and decent facilities. But trust me, this is no picnic! You never forget you're in a combat zone. In fact, my first week here, we got mortared. The enemy is just outside the wire, so we have to always be prepared for anything.

I am settling in to my unit and fitting in pretty well. I am working on my RL [readiness level] progression, and all my flights have gone well. And guess who my copilot is? CW3 Tim (Vinny) Vincent, the very same Vinny who was on Task Force Normandy with Dad! He is great, and I really like flying with him. He has so much experience that you don't have to worry about me.

Morale is good in my company and the battalion overall. I am really glad to be in the Expect No Mercy battalion with LTC Gabram as my commander. It's weird to think that LTC Gabram was a captain and one of Dad's company commanders back in Desert Storm. And there are still some of the original guys that served with Dad. But what's really surreal is, Vinny and I are flying Ol' Rigormortis, Dad's old aircraft from Desert Storm! I knew the aircraft was still in the unit, but I never thought I would get to fly it. Every time I strap myself in, I look at the brass plate on the cockpit that reads AT 0238 ON JAN. 17, 1991, LTC DICK CODY FIRED THE FIRST SHOTS OF THE GULF WAR, *and it really hits me what Dad did all those years ago.*

Most nights I get to eat dinner with Clint, and then we play ping-pong. We get quite an audience—the soldiers like watching two brothers really go at it. We're pretty competitive when it comes to ping-pong. LTC Gabram said he used to play with Dad when they were at King Fahd Airport during Desert Storm. I guess even in a combat zone, guys can figure out how to make a ping-pong table. It's a great stress reliever.

My company is moving to Kirkuk this weekend. We will

be there for about a month to support the 173rd Aviation
Battalion. It's too bad that I'm moving, because I will miss
seeing Clint every day. He is doing really good over here and
has a great reputation.

Thanks for all the support you have given me and Brooke.
We really appreciate everything. And thanks for the letters
and packages; they really help. I will try to write again soon,
but sometimes it gets busy here. Don't worry about me. I will
be fine. Clint and I will look out for each other. And I promise
to fly safe!

Love you and miss you both,
Tyler
Paladin 16

I often tell people that the tragic events of September 11 actually
led me to where I was supposed to be and where I am today: writing.
Because of my sons' deployments, I wrote a book for other parents of
soldiers coping with the stresses of deployment. When Dick retired
from his thirty-six-year military career, after rising to the rank of
four-star general and vice chief of staff of the Army, I finally had
the time to write. Writing opened up in me a need to explore, relive,
come to terms with, and ultimately put in perspective our way of
life. The result was my first memoir, *Army Wife: A Story of Love and
Family in the Heart of the Army.*

In the twelve years following Dick's retirement and our transition into the civilian world, he had a second career, in the corporate
world. Although he has since retired from that, he continues to have
a number of "gigs," as he just can't sit still for any length of time.
Living in the Washington, DC, area gives both of us opportunities to
continue to serve our army. He is chairman of the board of the non-
profit Homes for Our Troops, which builds specially adapted homes
for severely wounded warriors; he is on the board of the Intrepid

Fallen Heroes Fund; and, most recently, you might see him in the halls of the Pentagon as a senior mentor. Dick also bought a helicopter, an OH-6 (Little Bird), and, among the many pleasures it gives us, we use it to give rides and bring smiles to wounded warriors and their families during a day away from the hospital. We are always looking for ways to give back to and lighten the load in the rucksacks of this generation of Army families.

Dick's retirement also means we *finally* have the time and the means to enjoy our many blessings. Both Clint and Tyler are married and have kids. Clint and Kimberly have two sons, Connor and Dillon, and Tyler and Brooke have two sons, Austin and Zachary. Although our sons are grown, I sometimes look at them and can still see them as young boys "playing" soldiers, making videos, and dreaming of flying Apache helicopters. They are living their dreams doing just that, and doing it well. Clint recently commanded an Apache squadron, 1/6 CAV, out of Fort Riley, Kansas, and will soon be promoted to colonel. Tyler, a lieutenant colonel, is currently commanding an Apache squadron, 2/6 CAV, at Wheeler Air Base on Oahu, Hawaii.

However, Dick and I also know firsthand the burden that this generation of soldiers has had to bear through frequent deployments, and the stress that puts on their families. In the past nineteen years, our sons have had many deployments to Iraq and Afghanistan. While going back through their letters from earlier deployments, I couldn't help but notice the similarities between their words and what their dad wrote to me years ago. During more recent deployments, there were fewer written letters and more emails and phone calls. While I love the technology of today, I sure miss those handwritten letters, and I'm glad that I saved every one of them, from Dick *and* the boys. Who knew that they would inspire me to write this book?

One of the things that struck me while I was working on this book, certainly while finishing it, was that back in 1990–'91, I expressed in my journals feelings and sentiments that are timely for and pertinent to what we are going through during the COVID-19 pandemic. Entries about fear of the unknown, navigating a new normal, facing challenges, acceptance, moving forward and clearing that next hurdle—all of that suddenly feels familiar all over again, so much so that it's as if I could be writing a book about this year, 2020. I hope that through the lens of my perspective, my experiences, and my candor, readers will find inspiration to handle the challenges of today's world and to know that they are not alone in their feelings.

There's one other thing that hasn't changed over the years. Whenever Clint and Tyler go out to fly, whether in a combat zone or at their duty station, I say to them what I've been telling their dad for all these years: "Fly safe." Saying that has become a ritual—one that gives me comfort that they will be okay.

Acknowledgments

When I began writing this memoir, I had no idea where it was going or if it was even a story worth telling. My mother's passing in 2018 was a catalyst for self-reflection, and, as with the other times in my life when I felt untethered, I had feelings of longing for what *was* and a desire to put things in order. When you lose someone so dear to you, you can't help feeling as if time is passing all too quickly. All of that led me back to my writing. I sensed that there was a wide-open road in front of me, just waiting for me to drive down it. The road led me to Dick's letters from Desert Storm and the journals I kept from that time. I felt sure there was a story in them; why else had I kept them for all those years?

Armed with ninety-four letters, two journals, scrapbooks, and photo albums, I reached out to my editor, Annie Tucker, to see if she would guide me again. At first I was overwhelmed, but once I got started, I never stopped and I never looked back. The story unfolded so easily that many times I had a feeling that it had been there all along, just waiting for me to tell it.

What a pleasure it has been to work with Annie Tucker, for the second time! You have taught me so much about writing and editing. I have such respect for you and what you do. Thank you for helping me to navigate the creation of this type of memoir and bring this story to life. A big thank-you as well to the teams at She Writes Press and SparkPoint Studio, led by Brooke Warner and Crystal Patriarche, who make it easy for we authors and give so many female writers a voice and a platform. I appreciate all of your efforts on my behalf. Thank you to my project manager, Lauren Wise, for guiding me through this process.

My mom was one of my biggest fans, and I missed being able to call her on the phone and read her my chapters. However, many times while I was writing this book, I felt her presence and believe she was looking over my shoulder, reading it as I went along.

Now that all of our parents are gone, Dick and I are so lucky to have our siblings, their spouses, and many nieces and nephews to enrich our lives. On my side of the family, Chris and Tom, Dick and Patti, my cousins Toby and Terry, and on Dick's side, Diane and Bill, Bill and Paula, Cathi and Peter, Robin and Mark, Bob and Dena, and Lauri and Carl. You all supported me during the most challenging times when Dick was deployed, and you continue to do so now in my writing endeavors. Thank you for your love and support and for cheering me on.

To Clint and Tyler, I am so proud of your service to our nation and for stepping up time and time again, answering your call to duty. You and your wives, Kimberly and Brooke, who represent this generation of Army families so well, are raising amazing Army brats—our grandsons, Austin, Zachary, Connor, and Dillon. Thank you all for believing in me and encouraging me to tell *our* story.

To the man who is the inspiration for all that I write about, Dick, aka Commander Cody, thank you for being not only the love of my life but my proofreader, my sounding board, my biggest fan, my teacher, and my true north. Thank you for letting me share intimate details of our amazing life with the rest of the world. And if the ninety-four letters you wrote to me during Desert Storm were a testament to your love for me, then this book is *my* love letter to you.

About the Author

Vicki Cody grew up in Burlington, Vermont, and graduated from the University of Vermont in 1975 with a bachelor's degree in education. For the next thirty-three years, she was an Army wife, supporting her husband, Dick, in his career. Her first memoir, *Army Wife: A Story of Love and Family in the Heart of the Army*, published in 2016 by She Writes Press, won the 2016 USA Best Book Award for narrative nonfiction, was a finalist for the 2016 Foreword INDIES Book of the Year in the military category, and was named one of Kirkus Reviews' top 100 books of 2016. Cody is also the author of *Your Soldier, Your Army: A Parents' Guide* and, most recently, the revised edition, *Your Soldier, Your Army: A Family Guide*, both of which were published by the Association of the United States Army. Her articles have appeared in numerous military magazines and publications. She and her husband of forty-five years live in the Washington, DC, area.

SELECTED TITLES FROM SHE WRITES PRESS

She Writes Press is an independent publishing company founded to
serve women writers everywhere. Visit us at www.shewritespress.com.

Army Wife: A Story of Love and Family in the Heart of the Army by Vicki Cody
$16.95, 978-1-63152-127-0
A rare glimpse into the heart of the Army, as seen through the eyes of
Vicki Cody, an Army wife of thirty-three years who fell in love with a
lieutenant and stayed by his side as he rose up through the ranks, all the
way to four-star general and Vice Chief of Staff of the Army.

Motherlines: Letters of Love, Longing, and Liberation by Patricia Reis
$16.95, 978-1-63152-121-8
In her midlife search for meaning, and longing for maternal connection, Patricia Reis encounters uncommon women who inspire her journey and discovers an unlikely confidante in her aunt, a free-spirited
Franciscan nun.

Naked Mountain: A Memoir by Marcia Mabee
$16.95, 978-1-63152-097-6
A compelling memoir of one woman's journey of natural world discov-
ery, tragedy, and the enduring bonds of marriage, set against the backdrop of a stunning mountaintop in rural Virginia.

How Sweet the Bitter Soup: A Memoir by Lori Qian
$16.95, 978-1-63152-614-5
After accepting an exciting job offer—teaching at a prestigious school in
China—Lori found herself in Guangzhou, China, where she fell in love
with the culture and with a man from a tiny town in Hubei province.
What followed was a transformative adventure—one that will inspire
readers to use the bitter to make life even sweeter.

Gap Year Girl by Marianne Bohr $16.95, 978-1-63152-820-0
Thirty-plus years after first backpacking through Europe, Marianne
Bohr and her husband leave their lives behind and take off on a yearlong
quest for adventure.

Green Nails and Other Acts of Rebellion: Life After Loss by Elaine Soloway
$16.95, 978-1-63152-919-1
An honest, often humorous account of the joys and pains of caregiving
for a loved one with a debilitating illness.